LISTENER'S G

Tuning In the U.S.A.

RADIO PLAYS BY
Stuart Leigh and Rebecca Kalin

CHARACTERS CREATED BY
Alvin Cooperman and George Lefferts

PROGRAMS 27–52

Maxwell Macmillan International Publishing Group
New York   Oxford   Singapore   Sydney

Collier Macmillan Canada
Toronto

Copyright © 1991 by Maxwell Macmillan International Publishing Group

All rights reserved. No part of this book or related audiocassette may be reproduced or transmitted in any form or by any means, electronic or mechanical, including photocopying, recording, or any information storage and retrieval system, without permission in writing from the Publisher.

Collier Macmillan Canada, Inc.
1200 Eglinton Avenue E.
Don Mills, Ontario M3C 3N1

Illustrations: *Shelley Matheis*
Cover Design: *BB&K*
Interior Design and Production
Superervision: *Publication Services*

Acknowledgments: Pronunciation Key reprinted with permission of Macmillan Publishing Company, a Division of Macmillan, Inc., from the *Macmillan School Dictionary 2*. Copyright ©1990 Macmillan Publishing Company.

Photo credits: pp. 4, 5, 11, 24, 27, 39, 43, 56, 71, 83, 88, 94, 96, 107, 117, 120, 146, 153, 154, 155, The Bettman Archive; pp. 38, 49, 109, Gamma Liaison.

Printing: 2 3 4 5 6 7   Year: 1 2 3 4 5 6 7

Maxwell Macmillan International Publishing Group
ESL/EFL Department, 866 Third Avenue, New York, NY 10022

Printed in the U.S.A.

ISBN 0–02–362975–4

Contents

Acknowledgments		iv
Introduction		v
Language and Culture Sequence		vi
PROGRAM 27	"Moving In"	1
PROGRAM 28	"Just the Two of Us"	7
PROGRAM 29	"I Didn't Mean To"	13
PROGRAM 30	"A Song From Long Ago"	19
PROGRAM 31	"Recycling"	25
PROGRAM 32	"A Getaway Vacation"	31
PROGRAM 33	"It's a Deal"	37
PROGRAM 34	"The Great Northwest"	43
PROGRAM 35	"Ethnic Food"	49
PROGRAM 36	"Riverdale Day"	55
PROGRAM 37	"On the Nature Trail"	61
PROGRAM 38	"The Windy City"	66
PROGRAM 39	"Such a Good Teacher"	73
PROGRAM 40	"The Motor City"	79
PROGRAM 41	"College Bound"	85
PROGRAM 42	"The Health Run"	91
PROGRAM 43	"Continuing Education"	97
PROGRAM 44	"They're Playing Our Song"	103
PROGRAM 45	"Campus Life"	109
PROGRAM 46	"The Volunteers"	115
PROGRAM 47	"The Life of Riley"	121
PROGRAM 48	"Lost and Found"	127
PROGRAM 49	"A Dark and Stormy Night"	133
PROGRAM 50	"The Wooden Whistle"	139
PROGRAM 51	"And Justice for All"	145
PROGRAM 52	"Home, Sweet Home"	151
Answer Key		157
Useful Vocabulary and Expressions		163

Acknowledgments

The long and winding road...

This is the phrase that comes to mind whenever I think of ELTB. ELTB has been a long and winding road full of dedication, errors, learning, disappointment, amazement, and now, elation. The first materials are going public...

There have been many people who have helped us get down this road and many more who have cheered from the sidelines. I am certain that the following acknowledgments do not include everyone who has made a special contribution—I have forgotten someone. With apologies for the inevitable oversight, I would like to thank the following people:

For the early vision and risks, Robert Baensch and the late Lois Roth; for keeping us safe and continuing to believe, Jack Farnsworth; for overcoming disbelief and for always being there, Mary Jane Peluso; for dedication and day-to-day hard work, Allene Feldman; for creativity, talent, and inspiration, Howard Beckerman; for unswerving guidance, Diane Larsen-Freeman; and for understanding and support, all the members of the ESL/EFL Department: Maggie Barbieri, Gloria Cazón de Pascual, Debbie Devine, Aggie Lorenzo, and Betty Castello.

Robert Curran, Stuart Leigh, and Frank Beardsley produced a superb radio series, *Tuning In the U.S.A.* Peter Thomas and Alison Rice should be thanked for the expert knowledge they contributed to this radio program. Alvin Cooperman pulled together a great television team for *Family Album, U.S.A.* and beat the odds on costs. The Dovetail Group—Gerri Brioso, Richard Freitas, Paul Freitas, and Cynthia Vansant—made the "Focus In" segments joys to behold. Tina Peel and Greg Orr are not to be forgotten for their contribution in the rough early days.

The ELTB Advisory Board provided much support and guidance during a very long period, and its members deserve many thanks: Russell Campbell (chairman), Lyle Bachman, William Greaves, Diane Larsen-Freeman, Marc Pachter, and Chiz Schultz.

The educators, broadcasters, and publishers from around the world who provided us with invaluable insight and resources are too numerous to name.

And finally, a special thank you to all the people who helped us get ELTB off the ground. I trust that we will not have disappointed you with the fruits of our efforts.

Karen Peratt
Project Director

Introduction

Welcome to *Tuning In the U.S.A.*, the exciting new American radio series created to inspire English learning around the world. In 52 programs, you will experience English in action and learn about American culture. *Tuning In the U.S.A.* is for everyone who has studied English for at least one year and wants to improve his or her understanding of the language.

Each radio program tells a story about the Stewarts, a typical American family living in New York. You will see the family in everyday situations, and you will share their many experiences as you hear English spoken naturally. You will also travel with Richard Stewart as he visits places in the U.S. such as the Pacific Northwest, Chicago, and Detroit.

The unique format of each radio program includes the following:

INTRODUCTION	Each program begins with an introduction by a narrator. This introduction sets the scene for the drama.
DRAMA	Each program tells a complete story in two acts. Each story centers around one important event in the lives of the Stewart family. The language level in the dramas follows a sequence. Grammar and vocabulary are simpler in the earlier programs. In later programs, the language is more advanced.
FOCUS IN	After each act, a "Focus In" segment calls your attention to idioms, grammar, pronunciation, useful expressions, story comprehension, or important information about life in the U.S.

This *Listener's Guide* will help you understand Programs 27–52 of the series. On these pages, you will find a unique way to study the radio shows. Each lesson follows this simple format:

PREVIEW PAGE	Before each program, a preview page prepares you for the story as well as for the language points in the program. On this page, two key illustrations introduce you to the two acts of the drama. A summary of important language and cultural points previews the material in the *Listener's Guide* lesson.
SCRIPT AND LANGUAGE NOTES	The complete script for each program follows the preview page. The script always appears in the left column of a page. Beside the script, many useful language notes and illustrations are provided to help you understand the drama. In addition, facts about U.S. life are included. A "Your Turn" feature usually asks you to compare your own culture with aspects of American life.
FOCUS IN	At the end of each act, a "Focus In" feature allows you to practice the material you have just studied in the "Focus In" segment.
ACTIVITIES PAGE	A page of language and comprehension activities appears at the end of each lesson. These activities give you a chance to practice language and comprehension skills.
ANSWER KEY	An answer key at the back of the book lets you check your answers to the "Focus In" features and to the exercises on the activities page in each lesson.
USEFUL VOCABULARY AND EXPRESSIONS	The *Listener's Guide* ends with an alphabetical list of useful words and expressions that appear in the language notes beside the scripts. Next to each item, the program number appears in parentheses for easy reference.

You can study a program in the *Listener's Guide* before *or* after you listen to the program. It's up to you. *Tuning In the U.S.A.* is designed to be entertaining and educational in an easy-to-follow format. We hope that this *Listener's Guide* will be your companion to enjoying and understanding this exciting new radio series.

THE CHARACTERS

Here are the people you will meet in *Tuning In the U.S.A.*

MALCOLM STEWART	also known as Grandpa, 72, a retired engineer who lives with his son and his son's family in Riverdale, New York
PHILIP STEWART	Malcolm's son, 50, a doctor
ELLEN STEWART	Philip's wife, 50, a homemaker and a former music teacher
RICHARD STEWART	Philip and Ellen's older son, 30, a photographer
MARILYN STEWART	Richard's wife, 29, a salesclerk in a boutique and a clothing designer
ROBBIE STEWART	Philip and Ellen's younger son, 17, a senior in high school
SUSAN STEWART	Philip and Ellen's daughter, 28, a vice-president of a toy company, unmarried and living in an apartment in Manhattan
HARRY BENNETT	an accountant, 33, a widower who dates Susan
ALEXANDRA PAPPAS	an exchange student from Greece, 16, Robbie's friend
ANDREAS PAPPAS	Alexandra's cousin, 19, a university student from Greece who is visiting the U.S.
MOLLY BAKER	a nurse, 43, who works with Philip in the hospital
BILL MACDONALD	a reporter, 40, for the *Riverdale News*

...and other friends and business associates

Language and Culture Sequence

PROGRAM 27 "Moving In"   1

Grammar and Expressions
- the present perfect progressive verb tense
- reflexive pronouns
- Idioms: *We made it. Take your time. Come and get it. more or less*

Pronunciation
- *furniture [fûr´ ni chər]*

U.S. Life
- home ownership in the U.S.
- the Fourth of July (Independence Day)

PROGRAM 28 "Just the Two of Us"   7

Grammar and Expressions
- relative pronouns
- tag questions
- Idioms: *in spite of as long as by the way*

Pronunciation
- *quartet [kwôr tet´]*
- *exactly [eg zakt´ lē]*
- *exhibit [eg zib´ it]*

U.S. Life
- social and business occasions
- leisure activities in the U.S.

PROGRAM 29 "I Didn't Mean To"   13

Grammar and Expressions
- saying "good-bye"
- use of the word *just*
- Idioms: *I didn't mean to. I don't care. Let's just forget it.*

Pronunciation
- *ruins [rü´ inz]*
- *exposure [ek spō´ zhər]*
- *damaged [dam´ ijd]*

U.S. Life
- operating a business out of your home
- sharing household chores

PROGRAM 30 "A Song From Long Ago"   19

Grammar and Expressions
- adjectives with two meanings
- question tags
- use of *interested* and *interested in*

Pronunciation
- *antique [an tēk´]*
- *height [hīt]*

U.S. Life
- antiques
- folk music in the U.S.

PROGRAM 31 "Recycling"   25

Grammar and Expressions
- apologizing
- *so much/so many* + noun
- Idioms: *You lead the way. figured out no wonder*

Pronunciation
- *disturbed [dis tərbd´]*
- *environmental [in vī´ rən men´tl]*
- *neighborly [nā´ bər lē]*

U.S. Life
- rules about noise
- recycling and environmentalism in the U.S.

PROGRAM 32 "A Getaway Vacation"   31

Grammar and Expressions
- two ways to express the future
- telephone language
- Idioms: *Guess what? I have my fingers crossed. just like that*

Pronunciation
- *hurray! [hə rā´]*
- *glacier [glā´ shər]*
- *appreciate [ə prē´ shē āt]*

U.S. Life
- vacations in the U.S.
- U.S. national parks

PROGRAM 33 "It's a Deal"   37

Grammar and Expressions
- "I'm getting out of here!"
- *What a/an* + noun
- Idioms: *Are you interested? Let me check my calendar. whenever*

Pronunciation
- *cartoon [kär tün´]*
- *cute [kyüt]*
- *design [də zīn´]*

U.S. Life
- animation in movies: Walt Disney
- the U.S. film industry

PROGRAM 34 "The Great Northwest"   43

Grammar and Expressions
- *some* and *other*
- expressing opinions
- Idioms: *come to order come up with make a living*

Pronunciation
- *fir [fər]*
- *conservationist [kän sər vā´ shən ist]*
- *concerned [kən sərnd´]*

U.S. Life
- conservation in the U.S.
- small town democracy in the U.S.

Language and Culture Sequence ▶ vii

PROGRAM 35 "Ethnic Food" 49
Grammar and Expressions
- *Am I happy to see you!*
- negative questions
- Idioms: *Thanks, anyway. . . . changing for the better. Talk about . . . !*

Pronunciation
- *donuts [dō´nəts]*
- *mushrooms [məsh´rümz]*

U.S. Life
- ethnic foods in the U.S.
- health and nutrition in the U.S.

PROGRAM 36 "Riverdale Day" 55
Grammar and Expressions
- present perfect + *already*
- *to stop by*
- Idioms: *Give a hand. just in case How does . . . sound?*

Pronunciation
- *improvement [im prüv´mənt]*
- *energy [en´ər jē]*
- *earaches [ēr´āks]*

U.S. Life
- local government services
- community volunteer organizations in the U.S.

PROGRAM 37 "On the Nature Trail" 61
Grammar and Expressions
- uses of the verb *spend*
- ways to welcome visitors
- Idioms: *saddle up fancy-looking all the comforts of home*

Pronunciation
- *scenery [sē´nə rē]*
- *folks [fōks]*

U.S. Life
- country and city life in the U.S.
- recreational vehicles in the U.S.

PROGRAM 38 "The Windy City" 66
Grammar and Expressions
- making suggestions
- asking permission
- Idioms: *For one thing . . . Yoo-hoo! right on time*

Pronunciation
- *delighted [dē lī´təd]*
- *strength [strengkth]*

U.S. Life
- African-American music
- the history of black people in America

PROGRAM 39 "Such a Good Teacher" 73
Grammar and Expressions
- use of *"hey"*
- *such a* + adjective
- Idioms: *No way! Give me a break. close call*

Pronunciation
- *assigns [ə sīnz´]*
- *tough [təf]*
- *disgusting [dis gəs´ting]*

U.S. Life
- video games
- worries about U.S. education

PROGRAM 40 "The Motor City" 79
Grammar and Expressions
- use of *about to*
- use of *"What's it like . . . ?"*
- Idioms: *Coming right up! pretty much passing through*

Pronunciation
- *special [spe´shəl]*
- *point [point]*
- *guide [gīd]*

U.S. Life
- auto manufacturing in Detroit, Michigan
- mechanization in the U.S.

PROGRAM 41 "College Bound" 85
Grammar and Expressions
- *could have* + past participle
- Idioms: *Bless you. Feel free to . . . Help yourself.*

Pronunciation
- *real [rēl]*
- *genius [jēn´yəs]*
- *accepted [ə k sep´təd]*
- *success*

U.S. Life
- admission to American colleges
- the manufacturing and service industries in the U.S.

PROGRAM 42 "The Health Run" 91
Grammar and Expressions
- *taking a break*
- *like* and *as if*
- Idioms: *Keep it up! All right! You're almost there.*

Pronunciation
- *exhausted [ig zôs´təd]*
- *exercise [ek´sər sīz]*

U.S. Life
- stress in modern living
- marathon races in the U.S.

PROGRAM 43 "Continuing Education" 97
Grammar and Expressions
- expressions of quantity
- *There's nothing to worry about.*
- Idioms: *a great deal of   an awful lot of   Tonight's the night.*

Pronunciation
- *methods [meth´ ədz]*
- *site [sīt]*
- *realizes [rē´ ə līz əz]*

U.S. Life
- community colleges in the U.S.
- continuing education in the U.S.

PROGRAM 44 "They're Playing Our Song" 103
Grammar and Expressions
- use of *whenever*
- *How about...?*
- Idioms: *uh-huh   That's the point.   There you go!*

Pronunciation
- *Greenwich [gre´ nitch]*

U.S. Life
- music from different regions in America
- Greenwich Village; the music of Bob Dylan

PROGRAM 45 "Campus Life" 109
Grammar and Expressions
- *major* as noun or verb
- *...think so, too.*
- Idioms: *mix and match   best friends   change your mind*

Pronunciation
- *astronomy [əs trän´ ə mē]*
- *convenient [kən vēn´ yənt]*

U.S. Life
- courses of study at American universities
- social life in American universities

PROGRAM 46 "The Volunteers" 115
Grammar and Expressions
- *as long as*
- *to check*
- Idioms: *Now hold on.   any minute   get in the way*

Pronunciation
- *siren [sī´ rən]*
- *signal [sig´ nəl]*

U.S. Life
- volunteerism in the U.S.
- volunteer fire departments in the U.S.

PROGRAM 47 "The Life of Riley" 121
Grammar and Expressions
- reported speech
- telephone language
- Idioms: *take a look   You made it!   Couldn't be better.*

Pronunciation
- *retirement [rē tīr´ mənt]*

U.S. Life
- retirement and retirement communities in the U.S.

PROGRAM 48 "Lost and Found" 117
Grammar and Expressions
- *What's up?*
- indefinite pronouns: *either, neither, each, both, all, many,* and *some*
- Idioms: *Oh, no!   get used to   It's easy for you to say.*

Pronunciation
- *independent [in də pen´ dənt]*

U.S. Life
- personal banking practices in the U.S.
- credit in the U.S.

PROGRAM 49 "A Dark and Stormy Night" 123
Grammar and Expressions
- *must have* + past participle
- *the longer the better*
- Idioms: *I should say so.   You know what that means.*

Pronunciation
- *imagine [i m aj´ ən]*
- *emergency [ı mər´ jən sē]*

U.S. Life
- power failures
- emergency supplies

PROGRAM 50 "The Wooden Whistle" 129
Grammar and Expressions
- *how* + adjective
- *any minute*
- Idioms: *Once upon a time...   Not that I care.   nothing in sight*

Pronunciation
- *demonstrate [de´ mən strāt]*
- *manufacture [man yə fak´ chər]*
- *imagination [i maj ə nā´ shən]*

U.S. Life
- the "entrepreneurial spirit"
- marketing a new product in the U.S.

PROGRAM 51 "And Justice for All" 135
Grammar and Expressions
- passive voice constructions
- *guilty* and *innocent*
- Idioms: *feel sorry for   beyond any doubt*

Pronunciation
- *official [ə fish´ al]*
- *evidence [ev´ ə dəns]*

U.S. Life
- the legal system of the U.S.

PROGRAM 52 "Home, Sweet Home" 141
Grammar and Expressions
- ways to say "welcome home"
- proposing *a toast*
- Idioms: *You are a sight for sore eyes!   Hear! Hear!   all the comforts of home   Here's to you.*

Pronunciation
- *champagne [sham pān´]*
- *fascinating [fas´ ə nā ting]*

U.S. Life
- homecoming celebrations in the U.S.
- diplomatic protocol

PROGRAM 27

"Moving In"

ACT I

In this program, you will study...

VOCABULARY

Do you know the meaning of these words from Program 27?

furniture
barbecue grill
fireworks

GRAMMAR AND EXPRESSIONS

Do you know how to form the present perfect progressive tense?
Can you use these expressions correctly?

We made it.
Take your time.
Come and get it.
more or less

ACT II

PRONUNCIATION

Can you pronounce this word? The accent is on the first syllable.

furniture

 ### U.S. LIFE

How do people in the U.S. feel about owning their own home?

☞ YOUR TURN

- Do you prefer living in a house or an apartment?
- What is your favorite piece of furniture?

"Moving In" ▶ 1

Here is the complete script with study material for Program 27. Use these materials before *or* after you listen.

INTRODUCTION TO ACT I

Today on TUNING IN THE U.S.A., we are in Riverdale, where Michael and Eva Buchman have just bought the house next door to the Stewarts'. They have rented a small truck to move their furniture. As they start to carry in a large couch, Richard Stewart arrives. He introduces himself and offers to help them move their **furniture**.[1] Later, Richard's wife Marilyn appears with a gift to welcome the new neighbors.

ACT I

Michael: **Ready,**[2] Eva? One, two, three, lift.

Eva: Michael, **let me catch my breath.**[3] This couch is very heavy.

Michael: OK. **Take your time.**[4] I don't want anyone to **get hurt.**[5] Why didn't we hire a moving company to do this work for us?

Eva: We can do it by ourselves. **We'll just have to**[6] **take it slowly.**[7]

10 Michael: Ready, now?

Eva: Ready! One, two, three . . .

Richard: Hi, there!

Michael and Eva: Hello.

Richard: I'm Richard Stewart. I live right there. Next door, at my **parents'**[8] house.

Michael: Nice to meet you. I'm Michael Buchman, and this is my wife Eva.

Richard: How do you do, Eva? Are you the new owners?

20 Eva: Yes. This is **our first house.**[9] We're very excited.

Richard: **I saw you trying**[10] to lift that couch. I came to offer my help.

Michael: That's very kind of you.

Richard: **It's nothing.**[11] **Should I**[12] take this end?

Michael: That's **great!**[13] Thanks, Richard. I'm ready when you are. One, two, three. *[Michael, with Richard's help, lifts*
30 *the couch.]* Eva, go open the front door.

Richard: It's heavy. I hope this is the only couch you have.

---

[1] **furniture** [fûr´ni chər]: a singular noun referring to all objects that furnish a home; a bed, couch, tables, and chairs are *furniture*.

[2] **Ready?** = Are you ready?
This is the spoken short form.

[3] **Let me catch my breath.** = Let me rest for a moment until I'm not breathing hard.

[4] **Take your time.** = Go slowly; don't hurry.

[5] **get hurt:** injure oneself

[6] **We'll just have to . . .** = It will be necessary for us to . . .

[7] **Take it slowly.** = Do the job slowly and carefully.

[8] **parents'**
The possessive of regular plural nouns ends in s'.

[9] **our first house:** the first house we've owned

[10] **I saw you trying.**
Verbs of the senses may be followed by an object and the *-ing* form of the verb.

I saw you walking.
I heard her singing.

[11] **It's nothing.** = You're welcome; it's no trouble.

[12] **Should I . . . ?** = Do you want me to . . . ?

[13] **great:** good; fine

"Moving In" 3

	Eva:	Oh, it is.
	Michael:	**We made it!**[14] Let's set it down right here.
	Richard:	It **looks nice**[15] in front of the fireplace. Shall we bring in something else?
40	Michael:	Oh, Eva and I can finish the job. The couch was the hard part.
	Richard:	**I've got time**[16] to do more. With three of us working, we **might**[17] be done **in an hour.**[18]
	Michael:	Are you sure?
	Richard:	I'm sure. Come on. I want to help.
	[Later]	
	Eva:	Is that the last box?
	Richard:	This is it.
	Michael:	Put it right over here, Richard. **I can't believe it,**[19] Eva! We're **all**[20] moved in!
50	Richard:	Yup. You're all done.
	Michael:	Thanks for your help, Richard.
	Richard:	You're welcome.
	Eva:	I think **we're going to be**[21] very happy in Riverdale.
	Marilyn:	*[She knocks on the door and enters.]* Hello?
	Richard:	Hey! This is my wife Marilyn. Marilyn, meet Eva and Michael.
60	Marilyn:	Hi.
	Eva:	Hello, Marilyn.
	Michael:	Hi.
	Marilyn:	Hello. I brought **you all**[22] something to eat.
	Michael and Eva:	For us? How nice of you!
	Marilyn:	Welcome to the neighborhood.

END OF ACT I

[14] **We made it!** = We accomplished a difficult task.

[15] **looks nice**
The verb *look* can mean "appear" or "seem."

[16] **I've got time . . .**
You can use *have got* in place of the main verb *have*.
I've got time. = I have time.

[17] **might**
The modal auxiliary *might* expresses possibility: It's possible that we'll be done.

[18] **in an hour:** no longer than an hour from now

[19] **I can't believe it!** = It doesn't seem possible.

[20] **all:** completely

[21] **we're going to be:** we will be
The future with *going to* often indicates an action that is nearer in the future or more certain.

[22] **you all:** everybody

 **U.S. LIFE**

Home ownership in the United States is part of "the American Dream." It's something Americans expect and work hard for.

Moving into a new neighborhood is also a big event in the life of a family. Many Americans are not afraid to move far from their native home if job opportunities are available in another part of the country.

☞ **YOUR TURN**

- How many times have you moved in the last ten years?
- What was the best house or apartment you've ever lived in? Why?

You often use the words *by myself, by yourself, by himself, by herself, by itself, by ourselves, by yourselves* and *by themselves* for emphasis in actions that are done alone, without help from anyone. Sometimes these words carry a feeling of proud independence.

We can do it *by ourselves* = We don't need your help.

INTRODUCTION TO ACT II

This time on TUNING IN THE U.S.A., *we are in the Stewarts' backyard for a* **Fourth of July**[1] *celebration. Susan is cooking some hamburgers and hot dogs on a* **barbecue grill.**[2] *Robbie is playing* **volleyball**[3] *with his parents and some other neighbors. Richard and Marilyn are talking with Michael and Eva, the new neighbors. They are explaining this traditional family picnic. It happens every year on Independence Day.*

ACT II

Susan: [She rings a dinner bell.] **Come and get it!**[4] Hot dogs and hamburgers are ready!

Richard: My sister Susan does the cooking every year.

Eva: It was really nice of your family to invite us to your Fourth of July picnic. Thank you for making us feel so at home in Riverdale.

10 Richard: You're welcome. We're just happy you could join us.

Eva: Do you have this party every year?

Richard: Sure. Every Independence Day. **We've been doing it for ten or fifteen years.**[5]

Eva: Are there always this many people here?

Richard: **More or less.**[6] There's all of our family, of course, plus many of our neighbors. The Goldbergs, the
20 Lindstroms, Mrs. Romero, and the Masseys. Have you met them?

Michael: Not yet. They live across the street, don't they?

Richard: That's right. There they are. They're playing volleyball with my parents and my brother.

Michael: I'm sorry. I've forgotten your brother's name.

Richard: My brother's name is Robert. But we
30 call him Robbie.

Michael: Boy, Robbie's a good volleyball player!

Richard: He loves it. He would **rather**[7] play volleyball than any other sport.

Eva: I think he's been playing all afternoon.

Richard: I'm sure he has. But pretty soon it'll be too dark to see the ball.

Michael: What happens then?

Richard: The **fireworks,**[8] of course. **They**
40 **should be starting just as soon as it's dark.**[9]

[1] **Fourth of July:** the national holiday that celebrates the independence of the United States from Great Britain. Another name for this holiday is Independence Day.

[2] **barbecue grill:** an outdoor fireplace for cooking meat over an open flame or hot coals

[3] **volleyball:** a game played by two teams hitting the ball back and forth over a net

[4] **Come and get it!**
This is an informal call to dinner.

[5] **We've been doing it for ten or fifteen years.**
The present perfect progressive tense can be used with *for* (periods of time) or *since* (specific point in time).

We've been having these picnics *for* ten years.
We've been having these picnics *since* 1981.

[6] **more or less:** about; approximately

[7] **rather:** prefer to

[8] **fireworks:** explosive devices that make loud noises or a colorful show of lights at night. Fireworks are part of Fourth of July celebrations.

[9] **They should be starting just as soon as it's dark.**
Should be starting is the present progressive, or present continuous, used as future. A future action that causes another future action is often introduced by a time expression (*as soon as, when, until*) and put in the present form.

As soon as it *is* dark, the fireworks will begin (*should be starting*).

	So, come on. We had better get some food soon.
[Later]	
Michael:	That was a great hot dog.
Richard:	Susan is a great cook. She buys the best hot dogs from the **butcher**.10 Then she cooks them slowly over a **charcoal**11 fire.
Eva:	She told me that she made the **relish**12 herself. With vegetables from your dad's garden.
Richard:	Every year. Oop! There are the fireworks.
Eva:	The fireworks! They're beautiful.
Michael:	Red . . . green . . . blue . . . and yellow.
Richard:	You know, all across America, people will be watching fireworks tonight.
Michael:	Last year, we went to New York City for the fireworks. There's a beautiful **display**13 over the **Brooklyn Bridge**.14 People come from **all over**15 to see it.
Eva:	So, of course, the traffic there is terrible.
Richard:	Well, we don't have to travel to see great fireworks.
Eva:	You're lucky to be able to see them from here.
Richard:	But, Eva, both of us are lucky. It's your neighborhood now, too.
All:	Ah!

END OF ACT II

10 **butcher:** a person who sells fresh meat in a shop

11 **charcoal:** a carbon fuel used in barbecues which burns without a flame

12 **relish:** a pickle or mustard sauce that adds flavor to food

13 **display:** something designed for public showing (in this case, the fireworks)

14 **Brooklyn Bridge:** a famous bridge over the East River in New York City. It connects the boroughs of Brooklyn and Manhattan.

15 **all over:** everywhere

Richard says,

"We've been doing it for ten or fifteen years."

Can you find the other sentence in Act II containing the present perfect progressive tense?

 **U.S. LIFE**

On the Fourth of July, or Independence Day, Americans celebrate the signing of the Declaration of Independence on July 4, 1776. Since the holiday occurs during the summer when the weather is good, it is usually celebrated with outdoor activities, such as picnics, sporting events, parades, and fireworks displays.

☞ **YOUR TURN**

Does your country have a national holiday? If so, when is it and what does it celebrate?

Activities

Here are some activities to help you check your understanding of this program.

FOLLOW THE MAP

Look at the map of the Stewart family's neighborhood in Riverdale and fill in the blanks. Use the prepositions of place listed below.

| next door to | across from | around the corner from | in front of |

1. The Stewarts live _____ the Buchmans.
2. The Stewarts live _____ the Masseys.
3. The Lindstroms live _____ the Goldbergs.
4. The bus stops _____ the Stewarts.

POLITE EXPRESSIONS

Look at these polite expressions from Program 27. Who said them?

1. "I saw you trying to lift that couch. I came to offer my help." _____
2. "That's very kind of you." _____
3. "It's nothing." _____
4. "For us? How nice of you!" _____
5. "Welcome to the neighborhood." _____
6. "It was really nice of your family to invite us to your Fourth of July picnic." _____
7. "Thank you for making us feel so at home in Riverdale." _____

PREPOSITION DECISIONS

Richard is telling Eva about all the activities going on at the picnic. Complete his description. Use *for* or *since*.

1. Robbie's been playing volleyball _____ this morning.
2. Susan's been cooking _____ three hours.
3. Everybody's been waiting for this fireworks display _____ last year's display.
4. Those hot dogs have been cooking on the grill _____ ten minutes now.
5. We've been having these picnics _____ ten or fifteen years now.

PROGRAM 28

"Just the Two of Us"

ACT I

ACT II

In this program, you will study...

VOCABULARY

Do you know the meaning of these words from Program 28?

music hall
lobby
exhibit

GRAMMAR AND EXPRESSIONS

Do you know what these phrases or expressions mean?

in spite of
as long as
by the way

PRONUNCIATION

Do you know how to pronounce these words?

quartet
exactly
exhibit

 ## U.S. LIFE

Do you know when Americans are old enough to

- drive a car?
- go on their first date?
- vote in elections?
- get married?

☞ YOUR TURN

How old were you when you did these things?

PROGRAM 28

Here is the complete script with study material for Program 28. Use these materials before *or* after you listen.

INTRODUCTION TO ACT I

Today on TUNING IN THE U.S.A., *we're in New York City with Richard and his wife Marilyn. They are in a large* **music hall**[1] *waiting for a concert to begin. While the musicians tune their instruments, Richard and Marilyn feel happy to be together. They hope to have a quiet dinner alone after the concert. But* before *the concert even begins, their plans have changed.*

ACT I

Richard: Hmm. Let's see. Tonight they'll be playing the Hunt **Quartet.**[2] Do you remember this piece, Marilyn?

Marilyn: Of course, Richard. *[She hums the melody.]* We heard it on one of our first **dates**[3] together. We went to a concert in **Central Park.**[4]

Richard: It was a beautiful night. But then . . . do you remember?

10 Marilyn: It started to rain before the piece was half over.

Richard: And you wanted to stay and listen **in spite of**[5] the weather.

Marilyn: I put your new jacket over my head to keep the rain off me.

Richard: As I remember, it didn't keep you very dry!

Marilyn: *[She laughs.]* And you could never wear the jacket again!

20 Richard: *[He laughs.]* I think that was **the day I knew I loved you.**[6]

Marilyn: Really?

Richard: Well, that was the *first* day I knew I loved you. *Now* I know it every day.

Marilyn: Oh, Richard, this is so much fun, going to a concert . . . and **just** *being* **with you.**[7]

Richard: You mean **being** *just* **with me.**[8]
30 We don't have enough time to be together—only the two of us.

Marilyn: I know.

Richard: But tonight is different. So, what shall we do after the concert?

Marilyn: Well . . . how about that nice restaurant down by the Brooklyn Bridge? We can sit at a table for two, and **look into each other's eyes . . .**[9]

[1] **music hall:** a very large room for musical events
[2] **quartet [kwôr tet´]:** a group of four musicians playing music together, or a piece of music composed for a quartet to play
[3] **dates:** meetings between two people who have a romantic interest in each other
[4] **Central Park:** the large park in the center of Manhattan, in New York City

[5] **in spite of:** even though
In spite of introduces a noun.
Even though introduces a clause.

In spite of the rain, we went to the park.
Even though it rained, we went to the park.

[6] **the day I knew I loved you:** the day (that) I knew (that) I loved you. (See **Focus In** for Act I.)
[7] **just** *being* **with you:** the fact of being together with you
[8] **being** *just* **with me:** being with only me
[9] **look into each other's eyes:** exchange romantic glances at each other

40	Richard:	Unless Susan and Harry are there.
	Marilyn:	Susan and Harry? What do you mean?
	Richard:	Well, if Susan and Harry are there, it would be **rude**[10] for us just to look into each other's eyes.
	Marilyn:	Richard, **what are you talking about?**[11]
	Richard:	Look at the couple sitting two rows in front of us.
	Marilyn:	Susan and Harry!
	Richard:	And I thought we were alone.
50	Susan:	[calling] Richard, Marilyn! What are you doing here?
	Richard:	The same thing you're doing, I think. Waiting for the music to begin.
	Susan:	Oh, Richard, I meant that we didn't know that you were going to be here.
	Marilyn:	We just got tickets this morning.
	Susan:	Can you join us after the concert?
	Richard:	Well . . . we **sort of**[12] had some plans.
	Susan:	Come on, you two. We're going to a great party.
60	Richard:	Well, I don't know.
	Susan:	Marilyn, remember the hat designer I was telling you about? She'll be there. Come on, say yes.
	Richard:	Well, Marilyn?
	Marilyn:	Sure. Let's go to the party with Susan and Harry. It'll be fun. **As long as**[13] we're together–that's the important thing.
70	Susan:	Well? Can you come?
	Richard:	Sure.
	Susan:	Terrific! **We'll meet you**[14] in the **lobby**[15] after the concert!

END OF ACT I

[10] **rude:** not polite
[11] **What are you talking about?** = What do you mean?
[12] **sort of:** more or less
This is an informal use.
[13] **as long as:** provided that
[14] **We'll meet you . . .** = We'll wait for each other . . .
[15] **lobby:** the entrance area to a large hall or theater

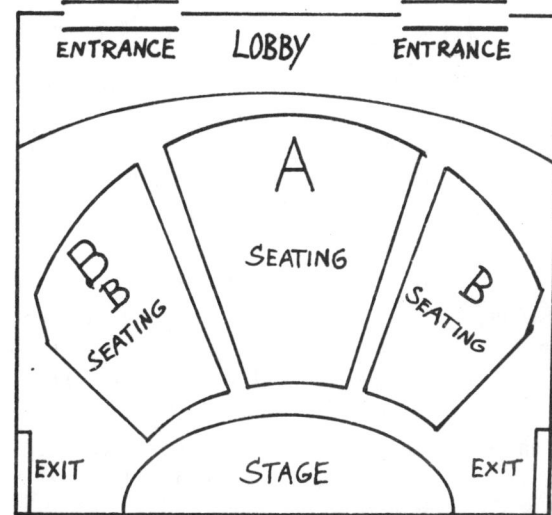

 **U.S. LIFE**

Many Americans use social occasions, such as going to a music hall, a theater, or a party, to meet people in their profession who can help them in their careers. Many business deals have been made at a dinner party Other Americans avoid *mixing business with pleasure*. They prefer to keep social functions separate from their working lives.

☞ **YOUR TURN**

• Do you ever *mix business with pleasure*?
• What types of social activities do you and your friends participate in?

Richard says,
(I think) that was the day I knew I loved you.
This sentence contains two relative clauses (*I knew* and *I loved you*). Relative clauses are usually introduced by the relative pronouns *who, that, whom,* or *whose*. In spoken English *whom* can be omitted. *That* and *who* can be omitted unless the relative clause begins with a verb.

Here is the letter *that* came for you.
I know the man *who* lives there.

Whose can never be omitted.
There is the boy *whose* dog ran away.

INTRODUCTION TO ACT II

This time on TUNING IN THE U.S.A., *Richard and Marilyn are in New York City at a party with Susan and her friend, Harry Bennett. It's a nice party, but it's very crowded. And Richard and Marilyn had not **exactly**[1] planned to go a large party on their evening out together. They wanted to be alone. But they won't be alone until the end of the night, as they **head**[2] home to Riverdale.*

ACT II

Susan: Judy, Robert, Anne, and Tom, **this is**[3] my sister-in-law Marilyn. She's married to my brother Richard. He's over there by the food table.

Marilyn: Hi. **How do you do?**[4] Robert, Judy . . . *[She laughs.]* I'm sorry. I'll never remember all your names.

Robert: Oh, that's all right. **Learning**[5] a lot of new names is never easy. It's nice to meet some of Susan's family. She talks about you **all the time**.[6]

Marilyn: Richard and I went to hear a concert. We didn't know Susan and Harry would be there, too.

Susan: **We begged them to come**[7] along with us.

Richard: Hi, everybody.

Marilyn: This is my husband, Richard. And this is . . .

Susan: A nice group of my friends. Richard, you'll have to make your own introductions. I just saw Kathy, and **I want Marilyn to meet her.**[8]

Marilyn: See you later, Richard.

Susan: *[calling]* Kathy! Wait a minute!

Robert: Susan **tells me**[9] you're a photographer, Richard. I'm the photo editor at an art magazine. Have you seen the **exhibit**[10] at the photography center? Oh, by the way, my name is Robert.

[Later that evening, Richard and Marilyn are standing at a bus stop.]

Richard: Is this bus going to Riverdale?

Bus Driver: Yup. I'm headed that way.

---

[1] **exactly** [eg zakt´lē]: entirely; quite

[2] **head:** to travel in a certain direction

[3] **this is . . .**
The demonstrative pronouns *this, that, these,* and *those* are used as personal pronouns.

In telephone conversations:

Hello, *this* is Jane Astin. = I am Jane Astin.

In introductions:

This is my sister-in-law. = Here is my sister-in-law.

[4] **How do you do?** = How are you?
How do you do? is a polite expression. You use it when meeting someone for the first time.

[5] **learning**
The *-ing* form of a verb may be used as a noun. In this case, it is called a gerund.

[6] **all the time:** frequently

[7] **We begged them to come.** = We asked them many times to come.

[8] **I want Marilyn to meet her.**
Some verbs may be followed by an indirect object and an infinitive.

	verb	indirect obj.	infinitive
(want)	I want	you	to wait here.
(tell)	I told	her	to be quiet.

These use the infinitive without *to*.

| (make) | We made | him | tell the story. |
| (let) | She let | them | watch the program. |

[9] **tells me:** has told me

[10] **exhibit** [eg zib´it]: a collection of art or other things on display for people to see

	Richard:	Good. Marilyn? **After you.** 11
	Marilyn:	Hmm. The bus is almost empty. Do you want to sit here?
	Richard:	That's fine. *[He sits down.]* Well, I think we **escaped.**12
40	Marilyn:	"Escaped" is **the right word.**13 That party might go on all night! Can you believe it? Susan and Harry wanted us to go dancing! I can **hardly**14 stand up. I'm so tired.
	Richard:	It's almost midnight.
	Marilyn:	Yes, but the dance clubs in the city are just getting started. You didn't want to go dancing, did you?
	Richard:	Oh, no. Not really. Remember the concert?
50	Marilyn:	**The concert? That seems like yesterday.**15
	Richard:	I know. But remember, at the concert we were talking about our plans for the evening.
	Marilyn:	That's right. Weren't we planning a quiet evening with just the two of us?
	Richard:	Something like that.
	Marilyn:	It didn't quite happen like that.
	Richard:	Not yet.
	Bus Driver:	*[calling]* **George Washington Bridge.**16
60	Passenger:	Oh! Thank you, driver! **I get off here.**17
	Richard:	Not until right now. You see, here we are. Just the two of us . . . riding the midnight bus to Riverdale.
	Marilyn:	Isn't it nice to be alone?

END OF ACT II

Marilyn says,

You didn't want to go dancing, did you?

The phrase *did you?* is called a **tag question** because it makes a question out of the negative statement *You didn't want to go dancing.* Tag questions are often formed from the auxiliary of the verb in the main clause (in this case *did*). A negative verb takes an affirmative tag.

You haven't seen the movie, have you?

An affirmative verb takes a negative tag:

You've seen the movie, haven't you?

11 **After you.** = Please enter (the bus) before me. This is a polite expression. You use it when two people are about to enter a doorway.

12 **escaped [ɪs kɑpt´]:** got away without anyone seeing us
Escaped is normally used for getting out of jail, or prison. By exaggerating, Richard is expressing his feeling of relief at leaving the crowded party.

13 **the right word:** the perfect word

14 **hardly:** with difficulty

15 **The concert? That seems like yesterday.**
This means that so many things have happened since we attended the concert tonight that it feels like the concert was yesterday.

16 **George Washington Bridge:** a bridge over the Hudson River, in Manhattan

17 **I get off here.** = This is my stop.

 **U.S. LIFE**

Although Americans have more leisure time than their grandparents had, single-parent families and families with two working parents seem to have less and less leisure time. When a married couple tries to plan an evening out together, it is often difficult to decide whether to spend it with friends or just to be alone together.

☞ **YOUR TURN**

- How do you spend your free time? Do you spend it alone or with friends?
- Would you say the quality of your life is improving or getting worse?

Activities

Here are some activities to help you check your understanding of this program.

WHICH CAME FIRST?

Here are the events of Richard and Marilyn's evening. Number them in the order they happened. The first answer is given.

_____ Susan noticed Richard and Marilyn at the concert.
_____ Richard and Marilyn left the party.
_____ Richard met Robert, the photography editor at the magazine.
___1___ Richard and Marilyn were talking about their first dates together.
_____ Susan invited them to a party after the concert.
_____ Richard and Marilyn rode the bus home to Riverdale.

IN-LAWS

Use the words in the box to fill in the blank lines.

sister-in-law	brother-in-law	mother-in-law	daughter-in-law	son-in-law	father-in-law

RICHARD   MARILYN   SUSAN   HARRY   PHILIP   ELLEN

1. Ellen is Richard's mother. She is Marilyn's _____.
2. Marilyn is Richard's wife. She is Ellen's _____.
3. Philip is Ellen's husband. He is Marilyn's _____.
4. Susan is Ellen's daughter. If Susan gets married, Ellen will have a _____.
5. If Susan marries Harry, Harry will be Richard's _____.
6. Susan is Richard's sister. Richard's wife Marilyn is Susan's _____.

TAG QUESTIONS

Make questions out of these statements. Add a tag question after each one. Write your answers on the lines below.

1. Richard and Marilyn didn't go dancing, _____?
2. They did go to the party, _____?
3. Robert doesn't know Richard, _____?
4. This bus isn't going to Riverdale, _____?
5. We have never met before, _____?

PROGRAM 29

"I Didn't Mean to"

ACT I

In this program, you will study . . .

VOCABULARY

Do you know the meaning of these words from Program 29?

basement
darkroom
upstairs

GRAMMAR AND EXPRESSIONS

Do you know what these phrases or expressions mean?

I didn't mean to.
I don't care.
Let's just forget it.

PRONUNCIATION

Can you pronounce these words?

ruin
exposure
damage

ACT II

 ## U.S. LIFE

Have many Americans set up businesses in their own homes?

☞ YOUR TURN

Do you have a business in your home? If yes, what kind of business is it?

"I Didn't Mean to" ▶ 13

14 ◀ PROGRAM 29

Here is the complete script with study material for Program 29. Use these materials before *or* after you listen.

INTRODUCTION TO ACT I

Today on TUNING IN THE U.S.A., *Richard is in the **basement**[1] of the Stewart home. He's working in his photography workshop—his **darkroom**.[2] Richard hasn't had much success today. He has been working hard to develop some pictures of a **cattle auction**[3] from his trip out West. Finally, Richard feels that he has solved his problems with the picture. But at that moment, Robbie opens the darkroom door and lets in the light. And the light **ruins**[4] Richard's photograph.*

ACT I

Richard: [*He speaks to himself.*] OK. Now. I'm going to try to develop this photograph one more time.

Ellen: [*She knocks on the door.*] Richard? Are you in the darkroom?

Richard: Yeah, Mom. But don't open the door!

Ellen: I won't. **I know better than to do that.**[5]

Richard: I know you do, Mom.

10 Ellen: **How's it coming?**[6]

Richard: I've been trying to develop this picture all day. I haven't had much success. But I think I've solved the problem.

Ellen: Good. **I'm glad to hear it.**[7] Marilyn and I are leaving now to go to the city.

Richard: OK. Have a good time. And **give my best to Susan.**[8]

Ellen: I will. And **good luck with your work!**[9] We'll be back after dinner.
20

Richard: OK. See you then. [*He speaks to himself.*] OK. Now, where was I? Oh, yes. I was about to refill this tray . . . And now, **I should be ready**[10] to **print a picture.**[11] . . . [*He counts.*] One, two, three, four. OK, now. That was four seconds of **exposure.**[12] So, I take the photographic paper, and I drop it in the **developing solution.**[13]
30

[1] **basement:** the lowest part of a house, usually below ground level

[2] **darkroom:** a room for developing photographs where no outside light enters

[3] **cattle auction:** a sale to sell cattle (cows, bulls, steers, or oxen) to the person offering the highest price

[4] **ruins** [rü´inz]: spoils; destroys

[5] **I know better than to do that.** = I am aware that I must not do that.

[6] **How's it coming?** = How is your work going?

[7] **I'm glad to hear it.** = I'm happy to know that.

[8] **Give my best to Susan.** = Say hello to Susan for me.

[9] **Good luck with your work!** = I hope your work goes well.

[10] **I should be ready.** = I will probably be ready. In this sentence, the modal *should* conveys probability.

[11] **print a picture:** the stage in developing a photograph when the image appears on photographic paper in its finished form

[12] **exposure** [ek spō´zhər]: the time needed for light to reach the photographic paper

[13] **developing solution:** a chemical liquid used to produce the photo image

		And picture number two goes into the **developing bath**[14] with picture number one. It's a great photograph. The Denver cattle auction. I have a feeling that this one is going to be a **prizewinner!**[15] ... Hmm. **I'd better**[16] set the timer to ring in one minute and ten seconds. That should be the perfect amount of time for the print to develop. *[He hums the tune to the song "She'll Be Coming 'Round the Mountain When She Comes."]*
	Robbie:	*[calling]* Hey, Richard!
	Richard:	I'm down here, Rob. *[He hums.]* Hmm. Only one minute more. *[He hums.]*
	Robbie:	*[He enters the darkroom.]* Richard, there's a phone call for you ...
50	Richard:	Robbie, you **jerk!**[17] **How could you be so stupid!**[18]
	Robbie:	Oh no! I forgot!
	Richard:	**I'll say you forgot!**[19] **You should pay more attention.**[20] You opened the door, and the light ruined my work.
	Robbie:	**I didn't mean to.**[21] I thought ...
	Richard:	**I don't care.**[22] Just **get out of here**[23] and leave me alone.
	Robbie:	**You don't have to scream at me!**[24] I didn't know that you were working.
60	Richard:	*[calling]* Hey! Hey, Robbie!
		END OF ACT I

One way to say good-bye is to say

Have a good time.

What could you say to someone who says

I'm going to the movies.

14 **developing bath:** the tray containing the chemical solution used to develop photographs

15 **prizewinner:** something that or someone who wins a prize in a contest

16 **I'd better ...** = I ought to ... ; I should ...
The structure *had better* + infinitive (without *to*) indicates an action that you ought to take in order to avoid a negative consequence.

17 **jerk:** a stupid or foolish person
This is an extremely insulting word.

18 **How could you be so stupid!** = Why were you so careless!
These expressions are formed as questions, but they are not real questions. They are strong criticisms.

19 **I'll say you forgot!** = I agree that you forgot!
This expression also expresses strong criticism.

20 **You should pay more attention!** = You should be more careful about your actions!
In this sentence, the modal *should* conveys obligation.

21 **I didn't mean to.** = I didn't do it intentionally.
In other words, it was an accident.

22 **I don't care.** = It doesn't matter to me.

23 **Get out of here.** = Leave; Go away.

24 **You don't have to scream at me!** = I feel bad about my mistake, so it's not necessary to shout at me.

 **U.S. LIFE**

A part of the American economy that has grown very rapidly in recent years is information gathering and processing. In many professions, the equipment needed to do this type of work has become less expensive. Computers, tape recorders, and photography and video equipment are now cheap enough to allow many people trained in these skills to set up businesses in their own homes.

☞ YOUR TURN

- Do you know someone who works in the information industry? If yes, what kind of work does he or she do?
- What are some other problems with having a business in your own home?

INTRODUCTION TO ACT II

This time on TUNING IN THE U.S.A., *we are with Robbie in the kitchen of the Stewart home. He's making dinner, but he's upset because his brother Richard is angry with him. Robbie opened the door to Richard's darkroom, and the light damaged[1] Richard's photographs. Now, as Robbie prepares dinner, he cuts his finger. But Richard is there to help him.*

ACT II

Robbie: *[He makes dinner and speaks.]* **How was I supposed to know[2]** he was **in the middle of developing[3]** some photographs? I didn't mean to ruin his pictures. And now I have to make dinner . . . *[He cuts himself with a knife by mistake.]* **Ouch![4]** Oh no! Now I've cut my finger. *[He washes his finger.]* I guess Richard was right. I am a jerk. I open the darkroom door and ruin his photography work. And then I cut my finger with a knife.

Richard: *[calling]* Robbie? Where are you?

Robbie: Oh, great. *[calling back]* I'm in here, Richard. In the kitchen.

Richard: *[He enters.]* What happened?

Robbie: Nothing.

Richard: If nothing happened, why are you standing at the sink and holding your hand under the running water?

Robbie: I told you. Nothing happened. I'm OK.

Richard: Robbie, you're **bleeding![5]**

Robbie: It's only a little cut.

Richard: Here. Let me see. That looks like a bad cut. *[He turns off the water.]*

Robbie: Yeah. Pretty **stupid,[6]** wasn't it?

Richard: Hey, forget about that. Let me put some pressure on the cut. That'll help stop the bleeding. OK? I'll try not to hurt you.

Robbie: OK.

Richard: How did you do this?

Robbie: You want the **truth,[7]** Richard? I wasn't paying attention. Just like you said. I was a stupid jerk.

Richard: Stop it, Robbie! Listen. I came **upstairs[8]** to say I'm sorry. **I lost my temper.[9]** You didn't ruin *all* my work.

[1] **damaged** [dam´ijd]: harmed; partially destroyed
The word *damage* usually applies to material things. The word *injure* applies to living things.

[2] **How was I supposed to know . . . ?** = Nobody could expect me to know (that).

[3] **in the middle of developing:** busy developing

[4] **Ouch!** = That hurts!
This exclamation is how English speakers express pain.

[5] **bleeding:** state of losing blood through an opening in the skin

[6] **stupid:** thoughtless; careless

[7] **truth:** what really happened

[8] **upstairs:** the upper floor of a house

[9] **I lost my temper.** = I got very angry.

40	Robbie:	I didn't?
	Richard:	Well, not *all* of it. You **messed up**[10] the **stuff**[11] I had in the developing tray, but I was able to make another print. And it's **just**[12] as good as the first one.
	Robbie:	**You're not just saying that.**[13]
	Richard:	No. It's really just as good. I'm sorry I yelled at you. But, next time, please be more careful, will you?
50	Robbie:	OK. I'm real sorry I opened the darkroom door. I'll be more careful **from now on.**[14] **Honest,**[15] I will.
	Richard:	All right. Hey, this cut is going to need a good **bandage.**[16]
	Robbie:	Did your pictures really **come out**[17] OK?
	Richard:	**Wait'll you see them.**[18] I've got four or five terrific photographs of the cattle auction in Denver.
60	Robbie:	I'm glad they're OK. I'm just sorry I made so much **extra**[19] work for you.
	Richard:	Hey. **Let's just forget it.**[20] How are you **making out**[21] with dinner?
	Robbie:	Not so well, as you can see. Since no one is home tonight, either you or I will have to cook. And now with this cut on my finger . . .
	Richard:	**Say no more,**[22] Robbie. Should I finish **chopping**[23] the broccoli?
70	Robbie:	**That'd be great.**[24] **I've had enough of knives for one day!**[25]

END OF ACT II

[10] **messed up:** ruined
[11] **stuff:** things
[12] **just:** equally as (someone or something else)
[13] **You're not just saying that.** = Do you really mean that, or are you saying it to make me feel better?
[14] **from now on:** in the future
[15] **honest:** sincerely
[16] **bandage:** a cloth wrapping put on a cut to keep it clean
[17] **come out:** to develop
[18] **Wait'll you see them.** = You'll be surprised when you see them.
Wait'll means "wait until."
[19] **extra:** more
[20] **Let's just forget it.** = Let's not talk about it anymore. Richard feels bad about the argument and would like them to put it out of their minds.
[21] **making out:** succeeding; progressing
[22] **Say no more.** = You don't have to explain any further because I understand.
[23] **chopping:** cutting into pieces
[24] **That'd be great.** = That would be helpful.
[25] **I've had enough of knives for one day!** = I don't want to look at another knife for a while because I have already cut myself.

U.S. LIFE

Since more and more American women are working these days, many men are expected to do their share of household work. Such chores include housecleaning, shopping, child care, and cooking.

☞ YOUR TURN

Do you think that men and women should learn each other's roles? Why, or why not?

One meaning of the word **just** is "equally as."
We use the word **just** to make the meaning stronger. In this sentence, what does **just** mean?

I'm just as strong as you.

Activities

Here are some activities to help you check your understanding of this program.

MAKE A MATCH

Draw a line from the word at the left to its meaning at the right. All the words come from the script of this program.

1. basement
2. darkroom
3. ruins
4. prizewinner
5. damaged
6. upstairs

a. something able to win a contest
b. partly destroyed
c. the upper floor of a house
d. a room for developing photographs
e. the part of a house usually below ground level
f. spoils or destroys

TWO USES OF SHOULD

As we saw in this program, the modal *should* can be used to express obligation or probability. Label each sentence below with an *O* for *obligation* or a *P* for *probability* to show how *should* is being used.

1. Jeff should be here soon. He left an hour ago. _____
2. Children shouldn't be left at the swimming pool without a parent. _____
3. The average child should be able to walk by the age of fourteen months. _____
4. You should find my keys in the car. I'm sure I left them there. _____
5. You should leave a light on in the house when you go away. _____
6. People should be more careful. Look at the litter on this beach. _____
7. I should see a doctor. I haven't felt well for three days. _____
8. We should be able to see the ocean when we get to the top of this hill. _____

AM I GETTING THROUGH TO YOU?

Often during arguments, people say things to each other that hurt feelings. Sometimes they are able to remain calm and say things that are helpful rather than hurtful. Some of the sentences below are hurtful, and others are helpful. On each blank line, write the word *helpful* or *hurtful* to describe each phrase or sentence.

1. You jerk! _____
2. I'm sorry. I didn't mean to disturb you. _____
3. How could you be so stupid! _____
4. That's OK. Let's just forget it. _____
5. How careless of me! I hope it's not serious. _____
6. It's OK. Nothing serious. _____
7. Why don't you pay more attention? _____
8. You never watch what you're doing! _____

PROGRAM 30

"A Song from Long Ago"

ACT I

ACT II

In this program, you will study...

VOCABULARY

Do you know the meaning of these words from Program 30?

I'll do my best.
I haven't either.
You've got it.

GRAMMAR AND EXPRESSIONS

Each of these adjectives has two opposites. Do you know them?

old
right
short

PRONUNCIATION

Do you know how to pronouce these words?

antique
height

 ### U.S. LIFE

Do you know what pop singer has used a harmonica in many of his songs since the early 60's?

☞ YOUR TURN

- Do you know how to play a musical instrument?
- Which instrument do you think would be easiest to learn to play?

"A Song from Long Ago" ▶ 19

PROGRAM 30

Here is the complete script with study material for Program 30. Use these materials before *or* after you listen.

INTRODUCTION TO ACT I

Today on TUNING IN THE U.S.A., Ellen Stewart is shopping for an **antique**[1] **piano bench.**[2] Ellen wants a fine old bench to sit on when she plays the piano. She goes to Mr. Rosen's antique store in Riverdale and finds a beautiful bench. And when she looks under the seat, she discovers old **sheets of music.**[3] Mr. Rosen is happy to sell Ellen the bench. And, yes, she can have the music, too!

ACT I

Ellen: *[She speaks to a cat.]* Nice kitty. Are you lost? Let me **check**[4] the **tag**[5] on your **collar.**[6] It says your name is Cleo. It says you live at Benjamin Rosen's antique store. Nice Cleo.

Mr. Rosen: *[He comes out of the store.]* Hello there! I see you have met Cleo.

Ellen: Oh, hello. I was worried that she was lost.

10 Mr. Rosen: She's not lost. She lives in my antique store.

Ellen: Then *you* must be Mr. Rosen. I was just looking at that piano bench when I **noticed**[7] her.

Mr. Rosen: Are you interested in it?

Ellen: Yes, **in fact,**[8] I am.

Mr. Rosen: Then why don't you come inside? Maybe you would like to buy the piano as well?

20 Ellen: I already have a piano.

Mr. Rosen: Ah, but this piano is a **player piano!**[9] Come inside, please. *[He speaks to the cat.]* Come on, Cleo.

[They go inside the store.]

Mr. Rosen: *[to Ellen]* Watch this. You put the paper **piano roll**[10] in here. And then you push this **button.**[11]

[The piano begins to play.]

Ellen: **That brings back memories.**[12] My
30   grandparents had a player piano when I was a child. It seemed like magic when the **keys**[13] went up and down all by themselves.

[1] **antique** [an tēk´]: very old
An *antique* is a piece of furniture or other object made many years ago.

[2] **piano bench:** a four-legged seat used to sit on when playing the piano

[3] **sheets of music:** pieces of paper with musical notes written on them

[4] **check:** look at to find out something

[5] **tag:** a plastic or metal marker with a pet's name and owner's identification on it

[6] **collar:** a leather or plastic band for the neck of a cat or dog

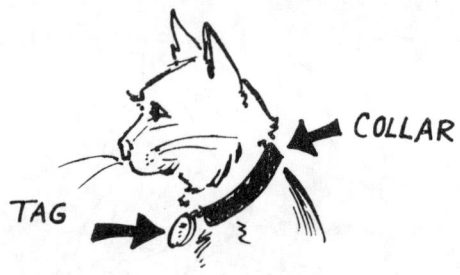

[7] **noticed:** saw

[8] **in fact:** in truth; actually

[9] **player piano:** a mechanical device that causes a piano to play a tune by itself

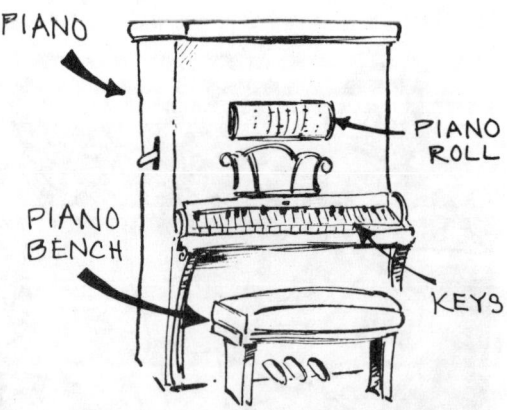

[10] **piano roll:** a musical selection in the form of paper with holes punched in it that is "read" by the player piano

[11] **button:** a mechanical switch you push to turn on a machine

[12] **That brings back memories.** = That reminds me of pleasant events from the past.

[13] **keys:** the black and white flat parts that are pressed down to play a piano
When they are struck they produce notes of differing pitch.

"A Song from Long Ago" 21

Mr. Rosen: If you're **interested,**[14] I can give you a very good price on this.

Ellen: Thank you. But **I'm not interested in buying**[15] a piano. I am interested in the bench.

[The music stops.]

Mr. Rosen: Well, they do **go together.**[16] But maybe I can sell you just the bench. **Move aside,**[17] Cleo. There. Now you can see the bench better.

Ellen: *That* is a lovely bench. And it's long enough for two. *[She looks at the price tag.]* Oh, and I see it's not too expensive.

Mr. Rosen: I think the top of the seat picks up like a **lid.**[18] Underneath it, you can store sheets of music. *[He picks up the top of the seat.]* I **guess**[19] nobody has opened it **for a while.**[20]

Ellen: **Why,**[21] look. There's a piece of music inside.

Mr. Rosen: Sure is. I **bet**[22] it's been there a long time.

Ellen: *[She sings.]* Da-da-da-da-da. Roses are the loveliest of . . .

Mr. Rosen: Hey, you're pretty good at **that.**[23]

Ellen: Thanks. I'm a music teacher. Does the music go with the bench?

Mr. Rosen: I'll make you a deal. You buy the bench, and I'll give you the music—for **free!**[24]

Ellen: *[She laughs.]* Oh, Mr. Rosen, **you've got yourself a deal.**[25] *[She sings.]* Roses are the loveliest of flowers . . . da-da-da-da-da-da-da-da-da.

END OF ACT I

[14] **interested:** have interest in

[15] **I'm not interested in (buying):** I do not want to buy
The expression *to be interested in* is followed by a gerund (the *–ing* form of a verb).

[16] **go together:** should be sold together

[17] **Move aside.** = Get out of the way.

[18] **lid:** cover

[19] **guess:** suppose

[20] **for a while:** for a long time

[21] **Why . . .** = Well . . .
The word *why* is not used here as a question word. It is simply a way to begin a remark.

[22] **I bet . . .** = I'm sure . . .

[23] **that**
Here, *that* refers to sight reading music.

[24] **free:** at no charge

[25] **You've got yourself a deal.** = I'll buy it on those terms.
This is a popular expression when a buyer and seller agree on the terms of a sale.

 **U.S. LIFE**

Americans love antiques—objects from the past. The pace of change is so rapid in the U.S. that antiques help give Americans a sense of being connected to their past, to a time when "things were made to last." For older Americans, antiques bring back memories of childhood.

☞ **YOUR TURN**

- Do you like antiques?
- How old does something have to be before you consider it an antique? Fifty years? Seventy-five years? A hundred years?

Look at the words *interested* and *interested in*.
Mr. Rosen says,

If you're interested, I can give you a very good price on this.

Ellen responds by saying,

Thank you. But I'm not interested in buying a piano.

After the idiom *interested in*, you often use a gerund (the *–ing* form of a verb).
Now, how would you complete this sentence:

I'm not interested in _____ to play the guitar.
(learn)

INTRODUCTION TO ACT II

This time on TUNING IN THE U.S.A., *Grandpa, Marilyn, and Richard are waiting for Ellen to return home from a shopping trip. When she arrives, she has a new piano bench. Actually, it's a very old piano bench. She bought it in an antique store. At the store, Ellen discovered a piece of music hidden under the seat, and the shop owner gave it to her. When Ellen plays the tune on the piano, Grandpa remembers it from **long ago.**1*

ACT II

Richard: [He plays the harmonica.] I'm getting better, aren't I, Grandpa?

Grandpa: Richard, it **sounds like**2 you've been playing harmonica for years.

[Richard and Marilyn laugh.]

Grandpa: It's almost five o'clock. **I'm surprised that your mother isn't home yet.**3

Richard: Marilyn, Mom said she was going to town, didn't she?

Marilyn: That's right. Ellen told me that she wanted to look for a new piano bench.

Richard: What was **wrong**4 with the **old**5 one?

Grandpa: Hmm, I can answer that. It was uncomfortable. And it was the wrong **height.**6

[A car horn sounds.]

Richard: **I bet that's Mom now.**7

Ellen: [She enters with a delivery person.] OK, put it there. **That's it!**8

Marilyn: Ellen, that piano bench is beautiful!

Grandpa: I bet it's as old as I am!

Richard: And almost as **good-looking.**9 **Right,**10 Grandpa?

[They all laugh.]

---

1 **long ago:** many years ago

2 **sounds like . . .** = from listening to you it seems as though . . .

3 **I'm surprised that your mother isn't home yet.** = I expected your mother to be home by now.

4 **wrong:** not satisfactory

5 **old:** former

6 **height** [hīt]: distance from the bottom to the top of an object

7 **I bet that's Mom now.** = I'm sure that Mom is arriving now.

8 **That's it!** = That's perfect!

9 **good-looking:** attractive; handsome

10 **Right?** = Am I right?
This is a short form. Both expressions mean *Am I right?*

"A Song from Long Ago" ▶ 23

	Grandpa:	Well . . . it might even be better looking. It's a beautiful piece of furniture.
	Ellen:	And there's more here than you can see.
	Richard:	What do you mean?
	Ellen:	Well, when Mr. Rosen and I lifted up the seat . . . *[She lifts up the seat.]* this was inside!
30		
	Marilyn:	It's old sheet music.
	Ellen:	Even Mr. Rosen didn't know it was in there.
	Richard:	Well, play it, Mom.
	Ellen:	All right. **I'll do my best.**[11] *[She starts to play.]*
	Grandpa:	Well, listen to that!
	Richard:	I've never heard it before.
	Marilyn:	**I haven't either.**[12]
40	Grandpa:	Ellen? How about you?
	Ellen:	I'm not sure. *[Then she remembers.]* You and Grandma **used to sing**[13] this together, didn't you?
	Grandpa:	**You've got it!**[14] *[He sings.]* "And the **garden**[15] of the roses is the garden of my dreams."
		[Ellen continues to play the piano.]
	Grandpa:	Don't stop now, Ellen. **One more time.**[16] You take Grandma's part.
	Richard:	Hey, is there a **part**[17] for a harmonica?
50	Grandpa:	Go get your harmonica! Marilyn, you can **sing along with me!**[18]
		[They sing.]

END OF ACT II

[11] **I'll do my best.** = I'll try to do the best that I can.

[12] **I haven't either.** = You haven't and I haven't.

[13] **used to sing:** sang
The structure *used to* is often employed in place of the simple past tense for actions that happened many times in the past.

[14] **You've got it!** = That's right!

[15] **garden:** area outside a house or building for growing either decorative plants or fruits and vegetables

[16] **One more time.** = Once again.

[17] **part:** place in a musical composition for the voice of a certain register or for an instrument

[18] **Sing along with me!** = Sing together with me!

 ## U.S. LIFE

America has a rich tradition of folk music. Since they could be carried from place to place, the guitar, banjo, harmonica, and flute or "penny whistle" were the most popular instruments in early American history. For many pioneers, the only form of entertainment available was the "sing-along," when family and friends would gather round a musician and try to harmonize.

☞ **YOUR TURN**

- Do you enjoy singing? What register is your voice: soprano, alto, tenor, or baritone?
- Do people in your country engage in sing-alongs?

Here is one way to ask questions:
Richard says,

Mom said she was going to town, didn't she?

He says, *didn't she?* because he thought he knew the answer, but he wasn't sure.
Here is another example:

Ellen bought an old piano bench, didn't she?

How would you complete this question?

You like TUNING IN THE U.S.A., _____?

Activities

Here are some activities to help you check your understanding of this program.

USED TO

Grandpa is telling Robbie about life in New York City when he was a boy. Change the verbs in his sentences to *used to* + infinitive. The first two are done for you.

1. "Everybody walked (**used to walk**) to school back in those days."
2. "There weren't (**didn't used to be**) many cars on the streets."
3. "We bought (_____) ice from street vendors on hot days."
4. "The fire department opened (_____) the fire hydrants so everybody could cool off."
5. "We didn't have (_____) much money to spend."
6. "I worked (_____) before school as a newspaper boy."
7. "I sold (_____) newspapers near Washington Square."
8. "I earned (_____) enough money to buy my own clothes and go to the movie house now and then."
9. "The movies didn't have (_____) sound in those days."
10. "At Christmas time we sang (_____) carols in the streets."

TOO AND EITHER

Now Grandpa is telling Robbie about two friends he had when he was young. Complete his sentences using *too* or *either*. The first two are done for you.

Grandpa: "These two friends of mine were Artie and Max. It seemed like everything about them was the same."

1. "Artie was good at football, and <u>Max was too.</u>"
2. "Artie didn't swear or smoke cigarettes, and <u>Max didn't either.</u>"
3. "Artie could speak Czechoslovak, and _____."
4. "Artie wouldn't say anything bad about anybody, and _____."
5. "Artie worked at his dad's delicatessen, and _____."
6. "I still see them from time to time. Artie's married, and _____."
7. "Artie goes to synagogue every week, and _____."
8. "Artie can still speak the mother tongue, and _____."

PROGRAM 31

"Recycling"

In this program, you will study...

ACT I

VOCABULARY

Do you know the meaning of these words from Program 31?

apologize
recycling center
environmental

GRAMMAR AND EXPRESSIONS

Do you know what these phrases or expressions mean?

You lead the way.
figured out
no wonder

PRONUNCIATION

Do you know how to pronounce these words?

disturbed
environmental
neighborly

ACT II

 ## U.S. LIFE

Do you know what a "recycling center" is?

☞ YOUR TURN

How do you get rid of trash in your country? Bury it? Burn it? Recycle it?

"Recycling" ▶ 25

26 ◀ PROGRAM 31

Here is the complete script with study material for Program 31. Use these materials before *or* after you listen.

INTRODUCTION TO ACT I

Today on TUNING IN THE U.S.A., we're in the Stewarts' garage with Robbie. He's putting trash into **metal**[1] trash cans. A neighbor, Mrs. Goldberg, tells Robbie to be quieter. Then Richard **appears**,[2] and he helps Robbie with the **trash cans**[3] in a quieter way. They take the cans to the street. And then they **notice**[4] an interesting difference between the Goldbergs' trash and their own.

ACT I

Mrs. Goldberg: *[calling]* Robbie Stewart, **what's going on?**[5]

Robbie: *[calling]* Oh, hi, Mrs. Goldberg. I'm putting the trash in the trash cans. We sure have a lot of trash this week.

Mrs. Goldberg: Do you have to make so much noise? My bedroom window is right here, you know. You woke me up with all your noise.

10 Robbie: I'll try to be quieter. I'm sorry if I **disturbed**[6] you.

Mrs. Goldberg: Saturdays, I like to sleep late. Ah, but today's a nice day. Maybe it's good to be up early. I'll see you later, Robbie.

Robbie: Good-bye, Mrs. Goldberg. *[He speaks to himself.]* She thinks this is noisy? Wait till I empty the trash from the basement. Then she'll get some real noise.

20 Richard: Hey, Robbie. Who are you talking to?

Robbie: Oh, hi, Richard. I'm talking to myself.

Richard: Yourself?

Robbie: *[He remembers.]* Oh, and to Mrs. Goldberg. She thinks I'm making too much noise. She called from her window just to tell me **so**.[7]

Richard: **Maybe she has a point**.[8] It is only eight thirty-five.

Robbie: Hey, Richard, **whose side are you on?**[9]

30

Richard: You were a little **loud**.[10] We're all part of a neighborhood, you know.

Robbie: You're right. I guess I wasn't being very **neighborly**.[11]

Richard: **Can I help you**[12] carry those trash cans to the street?

Robbie: Sure. Thanks, **I can use**[13] the help. *[He drags the cans.]*

Richard: Wait! Don't **drag**[14] it across the **driveway**.[15]

[1] **metal:** hard substance used in construction of durable items like cars and machinery: aluminum, steel, tin, copper, etc.

[2] **appears:** arrives

[3] **trash cans:** containers for refuse usually kept outside the house and taken to the street once a week for pickup by the city sanitation department

[4] **notice:** see

[5] **What's going on?** = What is happening?

[6] **disturbed** [dis tərbd´]: bothered; annoyed

[7] **so:** that
So can be used as a pronoun. In this sentence it refers back to the clause *I'm making too much noise*.

[8] **Maybe she has a point.** = Maybe she's right.

[9] **Whose side are you on?** = You should agree with me!
This expression shows our disappointment when a friend or family member doesn't take our side in an argument with an outsider (in this case, Mrs. Goldberg).

[10] **loud:** noisy

[11] **neighborly** [nā´bər lē]: friendly; considerate

[12] **Can I help you . . .** = Let me help you.
This is a polite way to offer to help someone.

[13] **I can use . . .** = I need . . .

[14] **drag:** pull along the surface without lifting

[15] **driveway:** the paved surface connecting the street to the garage

"Recycling" 27

40	Robbie:	You're right. Mrs. Goldberg will be out here in a second.
	Richard:	Let's pick up the trash can and carry it together. You **grab**[16] the **handle**[17] on one side. I'll grab the handle on the other. *[He helps Robbie carry the trash cans.]*
		[A little later]
	Richard:	There you go, Robbie. Four trash cans, **stuffed**[18] full and neatly **lined up**[19] on the **sidewalk**.[20]
50	Robbie:	Thanks for your help.
	Richard:	It's okay.
	Robbie:	Hey, Richard. Have you ever noticed something **strange**[21] about the Goldbergs' trash?
	Richard:	Something strange about the Goldbergs' trash? No. What's strange about it?
	Robbie:	There isn't any.
	Richard:	Come on. They have trash. I can see it.
60		
	Robbie:	There's only one black plastic **garbage**[22] bag. Where's the rest? They should have two full trash cans, at least!
	Richard:	Robbie, I don't have time to worry about the size of the Goldbergs' trash **pile**.[23] I've got to **get going**.[24] I have a job today—a little **photojournalism**.[25] Want to come along?
70	Robbie:	Photojournalism? You bet, I'd like to come along!
		END OF ACT I

[16] **grab:** grasp; hold onto
[17] **handle:** protrusion used to hold onto an object (see drawing on previous page)
[18] **stuffed:** packed full
[19] **lined up:** placed in a row
[20] **sidewalk:** paved surface along the side of a street where pedestrians walk
[21] **strange:** unusual; curious
[22] **garbage:** throwaway food items
The word *trash* refers to non-food throwaway items. The words *garbage* and *trash* can be used interchangeably.
[23] **pile:** things gathered at random and heaped up in a mound
[24] **get going:** leave
The expression conveys a sense of urgency.
Let's *get going.* = We'd better leave now.
[25] **photojournalism:** the photography which may or may not be accompanied by a printed news story in a magazine or newspaper

Robbie apologizes to Mrs. Goldberg by saying, "I'm sorry if I disturbed you." Here are three common expressions used for apologizing:

A. I'm sorry if I (disturbed you).
B. I'm sorry. I didn't mean (to disturb you).
C. Please excuse me for (disturbing you).

Note the use of the past tense in A, the infinitive in B, and the gerund in C.

 **U.S. LIFE**

In most American neighborhoods, there are unwritten rules about making too much noise early in the morning, late at night, and on Sundays. Ten o'clock in the evening is considered to be the time when people should turn down stereos and TVs. Good neighbors usually inform their neighbors in advance when they are planning a party for the weekend.

☞ **YOUR TURN**

- Is your neighborhood noisy, or are your neighbors considerate?
- What are the "quiet hours" in your neighborhood?

INTRODUCTION TO ACT II

This time on TUNING IN THE U.S.A., *Richard and his brother Robbie are visiting a trash* **recycling center**[1] *with Betty Reynolds, a writer for an* **environmental**[2] *magazine. As Richard is taking photographs to go with Betty's story, Robbie sees his neighbor Mrs. Goldberg. And she helps him learn more about recycling trash and protecting the environment.*

ACT II

Richard: Maybe Betty **got lost.**[3] Look for her car, Robbie. There's a sign on the door that says *"Hudson Valley Monthly."*

Robbie: *Hudson Valley* **Monthly?**[4] What's that?

Richard: It's an environmental magazine. Betty Reynolds is a friend of Marilyn's. She needed a photographer for a story she was writing.

Robbie: And that's the reason you got this job. Where are we going?

Richard: We're going to a recycling center.

Robbie: Recycling? You mean, "reusing things"?

Richard: Right. Reusing them so that we don't always have to keep making more. We make so much trash, we're going to **run out of**[5] land.

[Betty drives up and blows the horn.]

Richard: There's Betty now.

[They all drive to the recycling center, and Betty begins to explain the recycling process to Richard and Robbie.]

Richard: So the glass **gets separated by**[6] color.

Betty: That's right. There's a **container**[7] for brown glass, green glass, and clear glass. Then it gets **melted down**[8] and made into new glass.

Robbie: Hey, that person is just **smashing**[9] it up!

Betty: You're supposed to do that. Broken bottles **take up less room**[10] than unbroken bottles.

Robbie: I guess that's right. It sort of looks like fun.

Betty: Richard, let's go get some photographs of the area where they recycle old newspapers.

[1] **recycling center:** a place where trash is sorted into paper, metal, and glass, and processed so that it can be used again to make new products

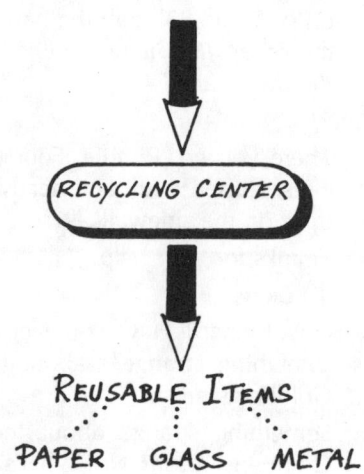

[2] **environmental [in vī´rən mənt l]:** concerning all the things that surround a living thing and influence its existence
During the last 20 years, the word *environmental* has been used to refer to the concerns of certain scientists, consumers, and politicians for the well-being of the earth as a place to support human, animal, and plant life.

[3] **got lost:** was unable to find (the center)

[4] **monthly:** (published) once per month

[5] **run out of:** use up; not have any more

[6] **gets separated by:** is sorted according to

[7] **container:** something that holds things

[8] **melted down:** changed from a solid to a liquid by heating

[9] **smashing:** striking (something) and causing it to break into small pieces

[10] **take up less room:** to occupy less volume

Richard: **You lead the way,**[11] Betty. Coming, Robbie?

Robbie: I'll be there in a minute.

Goldberg: Excuse me, young man. Could you...

40 Robbie: Mrs. Goldberg?

Goldberg: Robbie! I was just going to ask if you would help me lift a box of bottles from the **trunk**[12] of my car.

Robbie: I'd be happy to. I was pretty noisy this morning. I want to **apologize**[13] for it.

Goldberg: That's okay, Robbie. *[She opens the trunk of her car.]*

Robbie: Wow! You've got a lot of stuff here.

50 Goldberg: Mr. Goldberg and I try to recycle as much as we can.

Robbie: Mrs. Goldberg, I've just **figured out**[14] something.

Goldberg: What's that, Robbie?

Robbie: If you recycle this much trash each week, **no wonder**[15] you leave only one plastic bag for the trash collectors.

Goldberg: Oh, you noticed. There's a reason for that.

Robbie: What is it, Mrs. Goldberg?

60 Goldberg: **How long can people keep digging**[16] holes in the ground and filling them up with trash?

Robbie: I don't know the answer to **that one.**[17]

Goldberg: Well, until we get the answer to that question, would you like to help me recycle some bottles?

Robbie: Sure, Mrs. Goldberg. I'll help you smash a few!

END OF ACT II

[11] **You lead the way.** = You go first, and I'll follow.

[12] **trunk:** a large container
On a car, the large storage compartment usually located in the rear

[13] **apologize:** to explain or express regret for doing something insensitive

[14] **figured out:** managed to understand something after some effort

[15] **no wonder:** it's not surprising

[16] **How long can people keep digging...** = People cannot continue digging...
We use this question form to express our opinion that a certain activity is unwise over the long term. Richard is saying that the practice of burying trash instead of recycling it will not solve the problem of trash disposal, since we will some day run out of places to bury it.

[17] **that one:** that question (that Mrs. Goldberg asked)

U.S. LIFE

Americans have always wanted to improve "the quality of life." In the past, this has meant a nice home, modern car, nice clothes, color tv, etc. In the past twenty years, however, quality of life has come to include the idea of a quality environment. Americans want clean air and water and the protection of natural resources, such as forests and wildlife. An important part of the effort to clean the environment is to recycle waste products, and gradually more and more Americans are accepting the added work that recycling involves.

YOUR TURN

- Do you believe recycling is a good idea? Why? Why not?
- Where is the nearest recycling center to your home?

Focus In

Richard says, "We make so much trash, we're going to run out of land."
The structure *so much/so many* + noun *[that...]* expresses the consequences of an action. *Much* is used for uncountable nouns, and *many* is used for countable nouns:

I ate *so many* hot dogs that I got sick.
We wasted *so much* time that we missed the plane.

Activities

Here are some activities to help you check your understanding of this program.

PHRASAL VERBS

These two- and three-word verbs (phrasal verbs) were used in this episode. Robbie is telling Ellen about his day with Richard at the recycling center. See if you can use the phrasal verbs to fill in the blanks below. Be sure to use them in the correct tense.

wake up   line up   come along with   melt down   run out of   take up   figure out   take out   fill up

Robbie: "The day didn't start too well. I ___woke up___ Mrs. Goldberg by making so much noise when I _____ the trash cans this morning. I couldn't _____ why she never has much trash to take out. Anyway, Richard helped me _____ all the trash cans on the sidewalk, then I _____ him to the recycling center. It was really interesting. They have to smash the glass up and then _____ (it) _____ in order to reuse it. Richard says that burying trash is _____ too much land, and that recycling is a good idea. Otherwise we're going to _____ land before long. Pretty soon Mrs. Goldberg arrived. No wonder she never has much trash. She recycles it! She had three big bags that she had _____ with bottles and newspapers."

SO MUCH/SO MANY

Here is part of Betty Reynolds' article on the recycling center from the *Hudson Valley Environmental Magazine*. Fill in the blanks with *so much* or *so many*.

The River Valley Recycling Center is a smashing success. I mean bottle-smashing. I've never seen _____ broken bottles in one place in my life. You see, it's necessary to break the bottles so they don't take up _____ space. _____ people are turning to recycling. There was even a retired lady there struggling with three bags of bottles. This is why the center is having _____ success. Everybody is joining in, not just a few young environmentalists. If other people could only see the results, and talk to _____ recyclers, and find out that it doesn't take up _____ of your time to recycle!

Humor

The word "smashing" at the beginning of this article is used as a pun (see Program 8). It can mean "wonderful," "terrific," or it can have the literal meaning of breaking into small pieces.

Center cleans up Valley

APOLOGIES

Write apologies for these mistakes. If you need examples, use the expressions A, B, or C in the *Focus In* section at the end of Act I.

1. You spill soda on your host's carpet. _____.
2. You take somebody else's seat at the concert by mistake. _____.
3. You bump into somebody in a hallway. _____.

PROGRAM 32

"A Getaway Vacation"

ACT I

In this program, you will study...

VOCABULARY

Do you know the meaning of these words from Program 32?

border
working trip
glacier

GRAMMAR AND EXPRESSIONS

Do you know what these phrases or expressions mean?

Guess what?
I have my fingers crossed.
just like that

PRONUNCIATION

ACT II

Do you know how to pronounce these words?

hurray!
glacier
appreciate

U.S. LIFE

Do you know what a national park is?

☞ YOUR TURN

- Does your job call for travel?
- When you travel on business, do you have time for sightseeing?

"A Getaway Vacation"

PROGRAM 32

Here is the complete script with study material for Program 32. Use these materials before *or* after you listen.

INTRODUCTION TO ACT I

Today on TUNING IN THE U.S.A., *we are with Richard and Marilyn Stewart in Riverdale. Richard is preparing to return to Seattle, Washington. It's time for him to continue taking photographs for his book about the United States. Richard has bought Marilyn a present—an old* **music box.**[1] *Marilyn has a present for Richard, too—a sweater for his travels in the* **Pacific Northwest.**[2] *Richard asks Marilyn to join him there. She would love to—but can she* **arrange**[3] *a vacation from her job?*

ACT I

Marilyn: *[She knocks at the door.]* Richard?

Richard: Oh, Marilyn. Come in. I've finished packing my suitcase.

Marilyn: *[enters]* Do you really have to go?

Richard: I've got to go back. I need to take more photographs for my book.

Marilyn: I know, **honey.**[4] I'm going to **miss**[5] you when you're gone.

Richard: I'm going to miss you, too. I love you, Marilyn. I ...

Marilyn: Don't say any more. Or I'll start to cry.

Richard: No, no, don't cry. I bought you something. Over here.

Marilyn: A music box! *[She opens it. Music plays.]* It's lovely!

Richard: You like it?

Marilyn: I love it! And **guess what?**[6] I have something for you, too. It's in the **drawer**[7] next to the bed. Go on. Open it.

Richard: *[He opens the gift.]* Marilyn! This sweater is beautiful.

Marilyn: I made it just for you. Try it on. I'm sure it will fit.

Richard: Okay. *[He tries on the sweater.]* Ah, **sweetheart,**[8] I love it. It fits perfectly. I'll wear it every day and every night.

[1] **music box:** small ornamental box that plays a musical tune when opened

[2] **Pacific Northwest:** region of the United States at the northwest corner, comprised of the states of Oregon, Washington, Idaho, and Montana

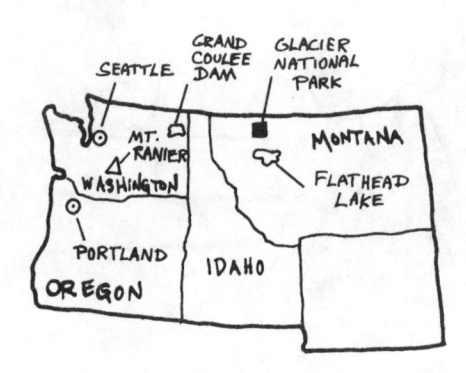

Glacier National Park

[3] **arrange:** organize

[4] **honey**
A married couple often use affectionate terms to refer to each other in place of names. *Honey* is a common term of affection.

[5] **miss:** be sad not to be with you

[6] **Guess what?** = I have a surprise for you; guess what it is?

[7] **drawer:** the sliding compartment of a chest where clothes are kept

[8] **sweetheart:** another common term of endearment

30	Marilyn:	*[She laughs.]* Well, you don't have to do that. But when you get to **Glacier National Park,**[9] you probably will wear it every night.
	Richard:	I guess it *will* get pretty cold there.
	Marilyn:	It's on the Canadian **border!**[10] And Mount Cleveland is over **ten thousand feet high!**[11]
	Richard:	How do you know all that?
40	Marilyn:	Well, I've never told you this. But **ever since**[12] I was a little girl, I've wanted to go to that park.
	Richard:	You wanted to go see the mountains?
	Marilyn:	And the icy **glaciers,**[13] the forests, the streams and rivers . . .
	Richard:	Well, Marilyn, you should be there with me!
	Marilyn:	Richard. Now, how can I do that? I have a job.
	Richard:	Call Rita Mae. Ask her to give you two weeks **off.**[14]
50	Marilyn:	*[She laughs.]* **Just like that?**[15]
	Richard:	Sure. You're the best employee she has. You worked every day this summer.
	Marilyn:	Not every day.
	Richard:	Well, you didn't take your vacation.
	Marilyn:	No, I didn't . . .
60	Richard:	Marilyn, it's perfect. Listen. I fly out today, pick up the car in Seattle, and then I'll meet you in Montana next week. C'mon, **what do you say?**[16] Let's do it!
	Marilyn:	Do you think Rita Mae will give me the time off?
	Richard:	**You'll never know if you don't ask.**[17]
	Marilyn:	I'll do it! I'll ask!

END OF ACT I

[9] **Glacier National Park:** park located in the northwest part of the state of Montana

[10] **border:** the line separating one country from another or one state from another

[11] **ten thousand feet high:** ten thousand feet above the level of the ocean (sea level)

[12] **ever since:** since
The use of *ever* conveys a sense of "a long time."

[13] **glaciers** [glā´shərs]**:** large fields of slowly moving ice

[14] **off:** time away from work
Time *off* may be due to illness, a holiday, or vacation.

[15] **Just like that?** = With no other explanation?

[16] **What do you say?** = Do you agree?
This is a common expression when we are trying to convince somebody to do something.

[17] **You'll never know if you don't ask.** = You'll never learn the answer to your question if you don't ask.

U.S. LIFE

Workers in the United States usually take short vacations. Vacation time is usually given only after a certain amount of time on the job. For example, a new employee may only receive one week of paid vacation per year. Many workers receive three and four weeks of paid vacation only after they have been on the job five or ten years. Another problem is that it is often difficult to schedule vacations to coincide with those of one's spouse.

YOUR TURN

- How much paid vacation time do you get each year?
- Do you ever take your spouse on working trips?

Focus In

There are several ways to express the future in English. Here are two from this episode:

The future with *will*: **"You'll never know if you don't ask."**

The future with *going to*: **"I'm going to miss you, too."**

INTRODUCTION TO ACT II

This time on TUNING IN THE U.S.A., *we are in Riverdale, where Marilyn Stewart is* **about to**[1] *call her employer on the telephone. She is going to ask for a two-week vacation from her job at Rita Mae Originals' clothing shop. Marilyn wants to join her husband Richard on his* **working trip**[2] *to Glacier National Park in Montana. Richard waits nervously as Marilyn makes the call.*

ACT II

Marilyn: [*She uses the telephone.*] Five, five, five.... **Wish me luck,**[3] Richard.
Richard: **I have my fingers crossed.**[4]
Marilyn: **Oh,**[5] four, seven, seven.
Richard: C'mon, Rita Mae. Say yes!
[*The phone rings.*]
Marilyn: Shhh! It's ringing.
Woman: Rita Mae Originals. May I help you?
Marilyn: Hi, Jenny. It's Marilyn. Is Rita Mae there?
10 Woman: Yes, she just came in.
Marilyn: May I speak with her, please?
Richard: Is she there?
Marilyn: [*She speaks to Richard.*] She's coming to the phone. Shhh!
Rita Mae: Hello. Rita Mae speaking.
Marilyn: Hello, Rita. This is Marilyn.
Rita Mae: Marilyn, how are you?
Marilyn: Fine, thank you. **I was wondering...**[6] could I take my vacation next week?
20 Rita Mae: Aren't you working tomorrow? Why don't we **discuss**[7] it then?
Marilyn: **If this is a bad time for you,**[8] ... I guess I could wait until tomorrow, but...
Richard: Ask her now!
Rita Mae: Marilyn, **are you there?**[9]
Marilyn: But I would rather talk about it now.
Rita Mae: Well, all right. **What do you have in mind?**[10]
30 Marilyn: I've been working so hard all summer, and I still haven't taken my vacation. I know all your workers get two weeks' vacation every year. I'd like to take my two weeks starting next week.
Rita Mae: Well... this is very **short notice!**[11]

---

[1] **about to:** going to
The expression *about to* + infinitive is used for actions in the very near future (a matter of seconds or minutes).

[2] **working trip:** a trip, usually to a vacation area, where a person goes on business but also has free time to enjoy the area

[3] **Wish me luck.** = Please hope I do well.

[4] **I have my fingers crossed.**
There is a common superstition that crossing one's fingers will bring about a desired result.

[5] **oh:** zero
In reciting phone numbers, addresses, credit card numbers, etc., the number zero is often pronounced "oh."

[6] **I was wondering...** = By the way...
This is a common way to begin a request we are not sure will be accepted.

[7] **discuss:** talk about

[8] **If this is a bad time for you...** = If you are busy right now...

[9] **Are you there?** = Are you still on the phone?

[10] **What do you have in mind?** = What do you want to talk about?

[11] **short notice:** a sudden request
Notice is the formal request by an employee to leave a job permanently or to take time off.

40	Marilyn:	I'm sorry, Rita. I know I'm not giving you much time to find someone to **take my place.**[12] But I suddenly have a chance to travel with Richard for a little while.
	Rita Mae:	Marilyn, you *are* an excellent employee. It *is* short notice, but I'm sure I can find someone.
	Marilyn:	Oh, Rita, **I appreciate it very much.**[13] Thank you. I'll see you tomorrow.
	Rita Mae:	See you then.
	Richard:	Well? What did she say?
	Marilyn:	She said yes!
50	Richard:	**Hurray!**[14] **Glacier National Park, here we come!**[15]
	Marilyn:	Richard, I've always wanted to see this park.
	Richard:	Why didn't we think of this idea earlier? You'll need to buy a few things for the trip.
	Marilyn:	I think I can get everything done in time.
60	Richard:	And I can help you. **To start with,**[16] I'll call the airline and make your reservation right now.
	Marilyn:	Good idea. Here's the phone book.
	Richard:	*[He speaks to himself as he looks in the telephone book.]* "A" is **for**[17] Airline . . . Airline . . . Airline. . . . **Here we go**[18]—Northwestern Airlines. *[He speaks to Marilyn.]* Glacier National Park *[He uses the telephone.]*—how high did you say Mount Cleveland was?
70	Marilyn:	Over ten thousand feet! Gee, maybe I should **knit**[19] myself a sweater.
	Richard:	*[He speaks into the telephone.]* Northwestern Airlines? I'd like to make a reservation. It's for Marilyn Stewart.

END OF ACT II

[12] **take my place:** replace me; do my work while I am away

[13] **I appreciate [ə prē´shē āt] it very much.** = I'd like to thank you.
This is a more formal expression of thanks.

[14] **Hurray! [hə rā´]** = Wonderful! Great!

[15] **Glacier National Park, here we come!** = We're going to Glacier National Park!
This is a popular expression of joy when the decision has been made to take a trip somewhere.

[16] **To start with . . .** = First of all . . .

[17] **for:** stands for; represents

[18] **Here we go.** = Here it is.

[19] **knit:** create a piece of clothing from threads of yarn or wool, using long needles to work the threads into a specific pattern of interconnected loops

Knitting

U.S. LIFE

Most Americans love "the great outdoors." They love to get away from the congestion of the cities and the routine of their jobs and "get back to nature." For this purpose, Congress has set aside large tracts of land called national parks where the natural vegetation and wildlife are protected. Most national parks have camping, hiking, and guided tours where visitors can learn about the natural history of the region. Glacier National Park, located in the northwest corner of the state of Montana, is known for the vast fields of moving ice that are the remnants of the Ice Age in North America.

YOUR TURN

- Have you visited any national parks in the U.S.?
- Does your country have a park system? What are some of its well-known parks?

Remember these two ways to identify yourself on the telephone:

Rita Mae: Hello. Rita Mae **speaking**.
Marilyn: Hello, Rita. **This is** Marilyn.

Activities

Here are some activities to help you check your understanding of this program.

ARTICLE *THE*

Here are some rules concerning the uses of the article *the* with geographic place names:

The is used to refer to:
1. **lake chains:** *The* Great Lakes
2. **mountain chains:** *The* Rocky Mountains, *the* Appalachians
3. **countries comprised of more than one part:** *The* United States, *the* Soviet Union, *the* United Kingdom, *the* Philippines
4. **rivers:** *The* Mississippi River

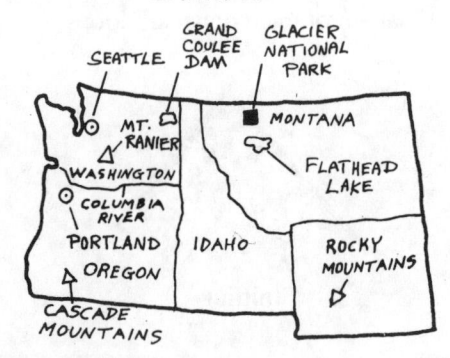

The is not used to refer to:
1. **lakes:** Lake Erie, Lake Huron
2. **individual mountains:** Mount Cleveland
3. **individual countries:** France, England
4. **continents:** North America, Australia
5. **states:** Ohio, Pennsylvania, California
6. **cities:** New York, Philadelphia, San Francisco
7. **parks:** Yellowstone, Great Smoky Mountains
8. **streets:** Broadway, Main Street, Fifth Avenue

Note: Be careful to recognize the use of these place names as **adjectives**. The noun they modify may require use of the article *the*:
The Pennsylvania Turnpike.
The Main Street Plaza.

Look at the map of the Pacific Northwest. Richard wrote a letter to Robbie telling about his trip. Put in the article *the* where needed.

Dear Robbie,
  Well, we finally made it to ____ Glacier National Park. It was a long drive from ____ Seattle. We crossed ____ Cascade Mountain Range three days ago. It was really spectacular. ____ Mount Rainer, the highest mountain in Washington, was over 14,000 feet. Later we crossed ____ Columbia River and went on to the Grand Coulee Dam. After that, we decided to visit our northern neighbors. We drove across the border into ____ Canada. Marilyn wanted to see ____ Canadian Royal Mounted Police. We came south again and then drove east towards ____ Rocky Mountains. In ____ Montana, we stayed at a lodge near ____ Flathead Lake. It was so peaceful, Robbie, you wouldn't have liked it at all. (Just kidding.)
  By the way, could you do me a favor? I need some supplies picked up at ____ Riverdale Photo Supply store. Could you do it for me? The store is on ____ Main Street, inside ____ Riverdale Mall. I'd really appreciate it. I'll write you again soon. Take care!
                                            Richard
  P.S. Marilyn sends her best.

PROGRAM 33

"It's a Deal"

ACT I

In this program, you will study . . .

VOCABULARY

Do you know the meaning of these words from Program 33?

animated movie
presentation
recognize

GRAMMAR AND EXPRESSIONS

Do you know what these phrases or expressions mean?

Are you interested?
Let me check my calendar.
whenever

PRONUNCIATION

Do you know how to pronounce these words?

cartoon
cute
design

ACT II

U.S. LIFE

What famous film animator created Mickey Mouse and Donald Duck?

☞ YOUR TURN

- Do you like American films? What kind? Science Fiction? Comedy? Drama? Horror? Crime? Adventure?
- Who is your favorite American actor or actress? International star?

"It's a Deal" ▶ 37

PROGRAM 33

Here is the complete script with study material for Program 33. Use these materials before *or* after you listen.

INTRODUCTION TO ACT I

Today on TUNING IN THE U.S.A., Susan Stewart is in her office. She's having a business meeting with a **film producer**[1] named Mike Davillo. He's making a movie. It is an **animated movie**[2] with **cartoon**[3] **characters**.[4] Mr. Davillo wants Susan to **design**[5] a toy that looks and sounds like the **leading**[6] character in his film. He shows her part of the film and invites her to come to the movie studio in California.

ACT I

Bad Character: Oh, no! It's Maxy Manners! He's coming in my direction. **I'm getting out of here!**[7]

Maxy Manners: Good-bye, Mister **Meanie**.[8] Thank you for leaving and *please* don't come back again.

Movie Announcer: So once again the **kingdom**[9] was **ruled**[10] by kind people, and Maxy Manners lived happily ever after.

10 Davillo: *[He stops the film.]* Well, that's him—Maxy Manners—our lovable little character.

Susan: He's **cute**.[11] Kids will love him.

Davillo: And he's polite! The parents will like him, too. That's the reason we call him Maxy Manners—like "maximum manners"—the most polite of all.

Susan: Mr. Davillo, you are producing a film, an animated film, that stars this
20 little character. And you want me to design a toy that looks like Maxy Manners?

Davillo: **You got it!**[12] We want the toy to be sold in toy stores at the same time that the film is shown in theaters.

Susan: Ah.

Davillo: I've heard that the Universe Toy Company makes the best-quality toys.

30 Susan: Thank you, Mr. Davillo.

Davillo: We'll need some special **engineering**[13] on this toy.

Susan: Now I'm a *little* confused. Why should this toy animal require special engineering?

[1] **film producer:** person in charge of making a movie
[2] **animated movie:** film where the illusion of movement is created by manipulation of drawings rather than by live photography

Snow White—A classic animated film by the Disney film studio

[3] **cartoon** [kär tün´]: an animated movie for children
[4] **characters:** the fictional persons in a story
[5] **design** [dē zīn´]: plan
[6] **leading:** main, principal
[7] **I'm getting out of here!** = I'm leaving!
[8] **meanie:** nasty, cruel person
Meanie is a word used mainly by children.
[9] **kingdom:** in ancient times, area governed by a king
[10] **ruled:** governed
[11] **cute** [kyüt]: attractive, especially in a childlike way
[12] **You got it!** = That's right!
[13] **engineering:** mechanical design and construction

Davillo: So it can talk, of course.
Susan: So you want a talking toy?
Davillo: Of course. He's Maxy Manners! You see, it's his voice. He says "please" and "thank you" very often. And that way of speaking helps make him special.
Susan: Mmm, I understand. Maxy Manners isn't **himself**[14] unless he can talk.
Davillo: Right! **Are you interested?**[15]
Susan: I think my company would be interested. But I'll need more information before I can make a **presentation**[16] of the idea.
Davillo: I understand. If you could come to our **studio**[17] in California, I think you could get all the information you need.
Susan: That sounds like a good idea. Let me **check my calendar.**[18] *[She checks the calendar.]* How about the first week of next month?
Davillo: **Whenever**[19] you can **make it.**[20]
Susan: OK. I'll make airline reservations for that first Monday.
Davillo: **We're all set.**[21] Thank you, Ms. Stewart.
Susan: Thank *you*, Mr. Davillo. Will I get to meet the man behind Maxy's voice?
Davillo: Ah . . . you've already met him!
Susan: *[She is surprised.]* You're Maxy!
Davillo: Yeah!
[They both laugh.]

END OF ACT I

[14] **himself:** his real identity
[15] **Are you interested?** = Do you want to do (this project)?
[16] **presentation:** demonstration (with the goal of selling something)
[17] **studio:** buildings where movies are made
[18] **check my calendar:** look at my appointment book to see if I'm free (on that date)
[19] **whenever:** anytime
[20] **make it:** come
[21] **We're all set.** = We agree.

Walt Disney

U.S. LIFE

When most Americans think of animated movies, they think of Walt Disney (1901–1966). In 1928 Disney created the cartoon character Mickey Mouse. Mickey appeared in short cartoons and became well-known by the American public. Ten years later Disney made his first feature-length animated film, *Snow White and the Seven Dwarfs*. In 1940, he produced *Fantasia*, a series of animated scenes set to classical music. In his lifetime, Walt Disney won 30 Academy Awards.

YOUR TURN

- Do you like animated films? Which one is your favorite?
- Have you seen any of the films of Walt Disney? Which is your favorite?

Focus In

Bad Character: Oh, no! It's Maxy Manners! He's coming in my direction. I'm getting out of here.

"I'm getting out of here" is one way to say "I'm leaving," usually when you want to get away fast.

It's a fire! I'm getting out of here.

INTRODUCTION TO ACT II

This time on TUNING IN THE U.S.A., *Susan Stewart is at a movie studio in Los Angeles, California. She is there to* **do business with**[1] *a film producer, Mike Davillo. But before they begin working, they watch the making of a movie. Later, Susan and Mike talk about ideas for a special toy. It will be a talking toy animal that looks like a character in Mike Davillo's new movie.*

ACT II

[*They are both walking.*]

Davillo: Can I carry that bag for you, Ms. Stewart?

Susan: Thank you. **But call me Susan, please.**[2]

Davillo: All right, Susan. And I'm Mike. Well, this bag isn't too heavy.

Susan: I've brought some things to show you. They are examples of toys that talk or make sounds.

10 Davillo: Have you ever been to a film studio before?

Susan: No. This is a big building! What happens behind all these closed doors?

Davillo: Movies are made. Do you want to **look in on**[3] one? [*He opens the door to a sound stage.*] They're about to finish shooting this picture. You might **recognize**[4] some of the stars.

20 Susan: Oh! Isn't that Linda Barrett, the actress from *Lost Romance*?

Davillo: Yeah, that's her.

Director: [*calling*] Actors, take your places!

Davillo: She's the director. Want to stay and watch a minute? We'll have to be quiet.

Susan: Yes, I'd love to.

Director: [*calling*] Quiet on the set! Take two. Cameras, roll. Action!

30 Actor: But I can't leave you here alone! It's not safe! The storm is getting worse!

[1] **do business with:** meet with for business
[2] **But call me Susan, please.** = Use my first name. This is one way Americans suggest that a relationship be put on a "first name basis."
[3] **look in on:** visit
[4] **recognize:** know on sight the identity of someone or something

Filmmaking Terms

Here are some terms used in making a movie.

places! = go to your assigned spots
set: large decorated and specially lighted soundproof room where some scenes of movies are shot
take two: the second filming of the same scene
roll: turn on (a camera or sound recorder)
Action! = Begin! (acting the scene)
Cut! = Stop!

Actress:	You have to leave me! You must go! The **rescue team**[5] will never find the **cabin.**[6] Only you know the **way.**[7]
Actor:	All right. I'll go! But just remember. I love you!
Director:	*[calling]* Cut! Let's **take**[8] that again.
Susan:	Oh, this work looks like fun.
40 Davillo:	It can be. Shall we go meet Maxy Manners now?
Susan:	**What a great idea!**[9] *[They leave to see Maxy Manners.]* I'm hungry, Mama.
Talking Toy:	*[It laughs.]*
Susan:	So, you see, there are a few ways to give sounds and voices to toys.
Davillo:	I like the way this one works.
Talking Toy: 50	I'm Captain **Xenon.**[10] Captain Xenon, here.
Susan:	The voice on that one is easy to understand. I think that's a good choice, Mike.
Davillo:	These are the drawings I promised you. I think they should give you a good **picture**[11] of Maxy Manners.
Susan:	They look fine. Can I take these drawings back to New York?
Davillo: 60	They're for you. Along with this. *[He gives her a cassette.]*
Maxy Manners:	*[He speaks on tape.]* **"It is my pleasure."**[12]
Susan:	A tape of Maxy Manners' voice. Thank you. That will help a lot.
Davillo:	You're welcome. Or, as Maxy says, "It is my pleasure."

END OF ACT II

[5] **rescue team:** professionally trained group of people who save someone in danger

[6] **cabin:** small one-story house in an isolated place usually reserved for hunting, fishing, or recreational visits to a nature area

[7] **way:** the right direction

[8] **take:** do

[9] **What a great idea!** = That's a wonderful idea!

[10] **Xenon** [zē´ nän]
This is a fictional name.

[11] **picture:** idea of what something looks like

[12] **It is my pleasure.** = You're welcome.
The usual expression is simply: "my pleasure."

Focus In

Susan says, "What a great idea!"
The structure *What a/an* + noun is a common way to show enthusiasm about something:

What a nice party!
What an interesting book!

It can also be used to show disapproval:

What a stupid movie!
What an awful way to treat a child!

U.S. LIFE

Movie making began in the United States before World War I. Since the first movies were silent, they contained no language barriers. The earliest movies served as a true international language. In 1927, Warner Brothers Studios made the first "talking picture," *The Jazz Singer*, and movies began a new era.

☞ YOUR TURN

- What is your favorite American film? What is your favorite film from your country?
- Have you ever seen a movie being made?

Activities

Here are some activities to help you check your understanding of this program.

WHO WOULD SAY IT?

Susan is a more formal person than Mr. Davillo. Look at these expressions. Do you think Susan or Mr. Davillo would say them? Write the name after the expression.

1. Wow! That's a terrific scene! _____
2. Thank you very much for your time. _____
3. Call me anytime. _____
4. Please give my best to your family. _____
5. Would you like to set the appointment? _____
6. Let's get together sometime. _____

MOVIE TRIVIA QUIZ

Check your knowledge of the movies. Take this movie trivia quiz.

1. Who was the star of *The Three Days of the Condor*?
2. What famous French film writer/director made *Beauty and the Beast*?
3. What was Mickey Mouse's first movie?
4. What American director made *ET* and *Indiana Jones*?
5. What famous Spanish filmmaker made *An Andalusian Dog*?

RETELL THE EPISODE

Here are some important events from Episode 33. Number them in the right order. The first one is done for you.

____ Susan and Mr. Davillo agreed on how to do the project.
_1_ Mr. Davillo came to Susan's office in New York.
____ Mr. Davillo told Susan he was Maxy Manner's voice.
____ Susan came out to California to visit the studio.
____ Mr. Davillo explained that he wanted the movie to be in the theaters at the same time the Maxy Manner toy was in the stores.
____ Susan watched the filming of a scene at Mr. Davillo's studio.

PROGRAM 34

"The Great Northwest"

ACT I

ACT II

In this program, you will study...

VOCABULARY

Do you know the meaning of these words from Program 34?

Douglas fir
conservationist
town meeting

GRAMMAR AND EXPRESSIONS

Do you know what these phrases or expressions mean?

come to order
come up with
make a living

PRONUNCIATION

Do you know how to pronounce these words?

fir
conservationist
concerned

U.S. LIFE

What two groups of people have very different ideas about America's national forests?

YOUR TURN

Do you think the forests should be harvested like crops or preserved in their natural state?

"The Great Northwest" ▶ 43

Here is the complete script with study material for Program 34. Use these materials before *or* after you listen.

INTRODUCTION TO ACT I

Today on TUNING IN THE U.S.A., *Richard Stewart is in the **great**[1] forests of the Pacific Northwest. Here, much of America's wood is produced. Richard is interested in photographing the trees and the men working among them. Some of the giant **fir**[2] trees he sees are hundreds of years old. But they are being cut down for sale. Richard talks to a tree cutter and learns of a meeting where the people of the town will discuss the future of the trees.*

ACT I

Richard: [*He speaks to himself.*] What a beautiful morning! . . . I love being with people, but **there's something about being alone in nature.**[3] It makes me feel so good. . . . These **Douglas fir**[4] trees are so big! [*He photographs the trees.*]
[*We hear the sound of saws.*]

Richard: Sounds like **chainsaws.**[5] Hmm. I thought this was a **public**[6] forest. I didn't think they were cutting trees here. Let's take a look.

Lumberjack: **Timber!**[7]
[*Tree falls to the ground.*]

Lumberjack: **Hey, fella!**[8] What are you doing here?

Richard: I've been hiking in these woods, and I **wondered**[9] about all this noise.

Lumberjack: Well, now you know. But you should get back over that way. It's dangerous around here.

Richard: I can see that.

Lumberjack: The **logging company**[10] doesn't allow the public up here. It's too easy for people to get hurt when we're cutting down trees.

Richard: Well, I'll be leaving then. But would you mind if I took a couple of photographs before I go?

Lumberjack: Go ahead. I don't mind. Are you a **conservationist?**[11]

---

[1] **great:** remarkable; impressive

[2] **fir [fər]:** a species of evergreen tree

[3] **There's something about being alone in nature.** =
It feels good to be alone in nature, but it's difficult to explain exactly why.
The expression *There's something about* . . . introduces a feeling that is pleasant but indefinable.

[4] **Douglas fir:** a type of large evergreen tree found in the forests of the Western U.S.

[5] **chainsaws:** large gasoline-powered saws used to cut down trees

[6] **public:** owned and managed by a government, as opposed to privately owned

[7] **Timber!** = Watch out—falling tree!
This is how tree cutters warn fellow workers that they have finished cutting a tree and it is about to fall.

[8] **Hey, fella!** = Hey, you!
Fella is an informal and old-fashioned way to refer to a man.

[9] **wondered:** asked myself

[10] **logging company:** a company that cuts trees and processes them into usable lumber.
A *log* is the trunk of a tree that has been cut down.

[11] **conservationist [kän sər vā´shən ist]:** a person who works for the preservation of natural resources

30	Richard:	If you mean, do I care about nature and the environment, then the answer is yes.
	Lumberjack:	My sister is a conservationist. And in a way, I am too. I love to **hunt**[12] and fish. And the animals have to have wildlands to live in. But this is my job. I cut trees.
	Richard:	Who do you work for?
40	Lumberjack:	The logging company that runs this **operation**.[13] They bought the **rights**[14] to cut all around here from the **Forest Service**.[15]
	Richard:	How do you choose which trees to cut?
	Lumberjack:	In some places they'll **mark**[16] this tree and that tree. In other places, like here, we cut them all down. That really angers the conservationists.
50	Richard:	I can see that it would. These are beautiful trees.
	Lumberjack:	Listen, **buddy**.[17] I've got work to do. If you want to hear more about this business, you should come to the **town meeting**[18] tonight.
	Richard:	Oh?
	Lumberjack:	Yeah, people from the logging company and from the town will be there. You'll hear all **sides**[19] of the **story**.[20]
60	Richard:	Maybe I'll do that. **So long.**[21]

END OF ACT I

[12] **hunt:** pursue and kill wild animals for sport
[13] **operation:** business
[14] **rights:** legal permission
[15] **Forest Service:** the branch of the U.S. Government which manages public forest lands

[16] **mark:** make a sign
[17] **buddy:** literally, *friend*
[18] **town meeting:** public meeting where citizens can come and express their opinions about matters concerning the town

A town meeting

[19] **sides:** points of view; opinions
[20] **story:** argument
[21] **So long.** = Good-bye.

Focus In

The lumberjack says, "In some places, they'll mark this tree and that tree. In other places, we cut them all down." The words *some* and *other* are used to divide things into groups.

Some people live in cities;
other people live in the country.

U.S. LIFE

The U.S. Forest Service is part of the Department of Agriculture. Its job is to manage the huge national forests found in many parts of the United States. The Forest Service sometimes leases (sells the right to use for a period of time) these lands to private companies for tree harvesting or energy (oil and gas) exploration. This practice has created a debate in the U.S. in recent years. How much development of public land—that is, economic use—should be permitted?

👉 YOUR TURN

Do you have publicly owned lands in your country?

INTRODUCTION TO ACT II

This time on TUNING IN THE U.S.A., *Richard is at a town meeting in the Pacific Northwest. At the meeting are many people who are **concerned**[1] about the forests. But they are worried for different reasons. Some want to **stop logging companies from cutting**[2] so many trees. Others say the cutting must continue because their jobs depend on it. It's a difficult problem—as Richard soon discovers.*

ACT II

Richard: Excuse me. Is that chair **free?**[3]

Maggie: Yes, it is. This should be an interesting meeting. Hi. I'm Maggie Wright.

Richard: Hi. My name's Richard Stewart.

Chairperson: *[She bangs the desk and speaks into a microphone.]* **Come to order!**[4] Come to order! We're here tonight to discuss the new "forest plan" for West Mountain. The Forest Service wants to hear our **comments**[5] **within the next thirty days.**[6] As you know, the Western Logging Corporation wants to start cutting trees on West Mountain . . .

Voice: Yeah, we know about that plan! It's a bad idea.

Chairperson: *[She bangs the desk.]* **Hold on.**[7] Now, there are microphones on both sides of the hall so we can hear and record all your comments. Let's **get started.**[8]

Maggie: Richard? Have you seen their plans for West Mountain?

Richard: I'm from out of town, Maggie. But I was up on East Mountain photographing this morning.

Maggie: **It's the same thing.**[9]

Ed: *[He speaks into a microphone.]* I'm Ed Anders. I'm a logger **by trade.**[10] We're cutting all over East Mountain. I see no reason not to do the same thing up on West Mountain.

Maggie: Excuse me, Richard. I need to move to the microphone.

---

[1] **concerned** [kən sərnd´]: worried

[2] **stop logging companies from cutting . . .** = prevent the logging companies from cutting . . .
The expression is *stop* (someone) *from* (doing something).

[3] **free:** not occupied

Is that chair free?

[4] **Come to order!** = Be quiet (because the meeting is about to begin).
This is the standard phrase used to open a public meeting.

[5] **comments:** opinions

[6] **within the next thirty days:** before thirty days have passed

[7] **Hold on.** = Wait a minute.
We use this expression to interrupt a speaker we don't agree with. It is not very polite.

[8] **get started:** begin

[9] **It's the same thing.** = They plan to do the same thing on West Mountain they're doing on East Mountain, that is, cut down all the trees.

[10] **by trade:** by job
A *trade* is a manual skill in the building industry such as painting, carpentry, masonry, and plumbing.

	Ed:	My family has **made a living**[11] in the woods for three **generations.**[12] We have to able to keep cutting.
40	Maggie:	[She speaks into a microphone.] I'm Maggie Wright. I understand your point, Ed. But those are **old growth**[13] Douglas firs on West Mountain. They're the last ones we have around here.
	Ed:	What do you propose we do?
	Maggie:	I think we should preserve the trees on West Mountain.
	Ed:	Come on! Seventy percent of the jobs in this town are in cutting and in forest **products.**[14]
50	Maggie:	I know. My brother is a logger, too. But the forest is a home to animals. And the land belongs to **our children,**[15] too.
	Ed:	**And what are we going to do for jobs?**[16] I don't want to move away from here or go into *any* other kind of work. I've been a logger all my life. . . .
	[The meeting ends. Richard and Maggie walk outside to the parking lot.]	
60	Richard:	Well, Maggie, you were right. It *was* interesting.
	Maggie:	Oh, here's my car. [She opens the door to her car.] We need to find other kinds of work to do around here. **We can't expect to live**[17] exactly the same way we always have—cutting and cutting. I just hope the Forest Service listens to us.
	Richard:	I'm sure they'll try to **come up with**[18] a plan that satisfies everyone.
70	Maggie:	Yup. **That's the way it works.**[19] Nice to meet you, Richard.
	Richard:	Nice to meet you, too. Good night.

END OF ACT II

[11] **made a living:** earned the money to live
[12] **generations:** the time between the birth of parents and the birth of their first child
For example, there is one *generation* between a father and son.
[13] **old growth:** original, natural growth, not planted by man
[14] **products:** consumer goods made from raw material
Here, the raw material is wood from trees.
[15] **our children:** the future generations that will live on the earth after us
[16] **And what are we going to do for jobs?** = How will we earn money?
[17] **We can't expect to live . . .** = It's unrealistic to think we can live . . .
[18] **come up with:** devise; construct
[19] **That's the way it works.** = That's the way it (the political system) operates.

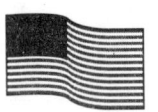

U.S. LIFE

The "town meeting" is a political tradition in American democracy dating back to the days of the Pilgrims. People come to a meeting hall to express their opinions about an issue facing the town. Even big cities hold meetings where citizens can express their views. These meetings are not always orderly, and people are not always polite. Americans, like people everywhere, can get very emotional over public policy issues.

YOUR TURN

- Do you think town meetings are a good way to decide public policy?
- What are the good aspects and bad aspects of town meeting democracy?

Focus In

Maggie says, **I think we should preserve the trees on West Mountain.**

Here are some other ways to express your opinion:

In my opinion, we should . . .
I think it would be a good idea to . . .
If you ask me, we should . . .

Activities

Here are some activities to help you check your understanding of this program.

THE TOWN MEETING

The written record of a meeting is called the *minutes*. Here are the minutes of the town meeting Richard attended. See if you can complete the entries. You may want to re-read Act II.

Woodland Town Meeting—Minutes

8:05 P.M. The chairman, Mr. Parkins, called the meeting to _____
8:10 P.M. Mr. Anders, a _____, said he thought we should _____ the trees on West Mountain.
8:20 P.M. Maggie Wright, a _____, said we should save the trees for _____

ASKING PERMISSION

Ask permission. Use *Would you mind if I . . .?* Remember to use the past tense of the verb.

1. You want to close the window on the bus. **Would you mind if I closed the window?**
2. You want to sit down here. _____?
3. You want to take a picture. _____?
4. You want to use the telephone. _____?
5. You want to use the restroom. _____?

OBJECTING

Imagine you are at a town meeting. Someone says something you think is a bad idea. Object to what they say. Use *What are we going to do for . . .?* Look at the example. Use the words listed below.

| transportation | electricity | education | recreation | wood |

1. We should eliminate the city buses! YOU: **What are we going to do for transportation?**
2. We should close the national parks! YOU: _____?
3. We should lower school taxes! YOU: _____?
4. We should stop burning coal! YOU: _____?
5. We should stop cutting down trees! YOU: _____?

PROGRAM 35

"Ethnic Food"

ACT I

In this program, you will study...

VOCABULARY

Do you know the meaning of these words from Program 35?

ingredient
diet
handful

GRAMMAR AND EXPRESSIONS

Do you know what these phrases or expressions mean?

Thanks, anyway.
... changing for the better.
Talk about ... !

PRONUNCIATION

Do you know how to pronounce these words?

donuts
mushrooms

ACT II

U.S. LIFE

What U.S. cities have the best varieties of ethnic foods? Why would these cities have great ethnic foods?

☞ YOUR TURN

What is the food dish that best represents your country's diet?

"Ethnic Food" ▶ 49

Here is the complete script with study material for Program 35. Use these materials before *or* after you listen.

INTRODUCTION TO ACT I

Today on TUNING IN THE U.S.A., *we are with Susan and her friend Harry Bennett in Chinatown, a special neighborhood of New York City. They have a list of* **fresh**[1] *foods they need to buy for a* **dinner party**[2] *that night. But Chinatown has many food markets. And the streets are very busy. And so, shopping for food in Chinatown becomes an adventure for Susan and Harry.*

ACT I

Susan: Look, Harry! These vegetables are so much fresher and nicer than the ones I usually find at the grocery store.

Harry: They're so much more unusual than the ones you usually find at the grocery store. Susan, what's that? Is that an **eggplant**?[3]

Susan: Yup, it's a Chinese eggplant. Check the list, Harry, and see if we need to buy that.

Harry: [He reads aloud.] "**Bean sprouts**,[4] **sea bass**,[5] **shrimp**,[6] eggplant!"

Susan: Ah, success! We found our first **ingredient**.[7] Oh, and there are the **mushrooms**.[8]

Harry: I know hardly anything about Chinese cooking.

Susan: That's the reason tonight will be so much fun. You'll **get to meet**[9] my friend Lily. And you'll meet her friend Ed. He's an actor. And you'll get to eat a terrific home-cooked Chinese dinner.

Harry: Sounds like fun.

Susan: Right! But only if we finish our part of the **deal**.[10] We shop. They cook.

Harry: And everyone eats.

[Harry and Susan laugh.]

Harry: Okay, next **item**[11] on the list . . . bean sprouts.

Susan: Bean sprouts, bean sprouts. Ah! Look down.

[1] **fresh:** unprocessed; raw (as opposed to processed foods which are bottled, canned, or packaged in some way)

[2] **dinner party:** a party where guests come to have dinner

[3] **eggplant:** a blackish purple, oval-shaped plant about five inches in diameter

[4] **bean sprouts:** the shoots of bean seeds

[5] **sea bass:** a type of sport fish

[6] **shrimp:** a sea crustacean with a long spiny tail

[7] **ingredient:** one of the foods or spices that go into a recipe

[8] **mushrooms** [məsh´ rümz]: a fungus with a stem and cap
Some are edible; some are poisonous.

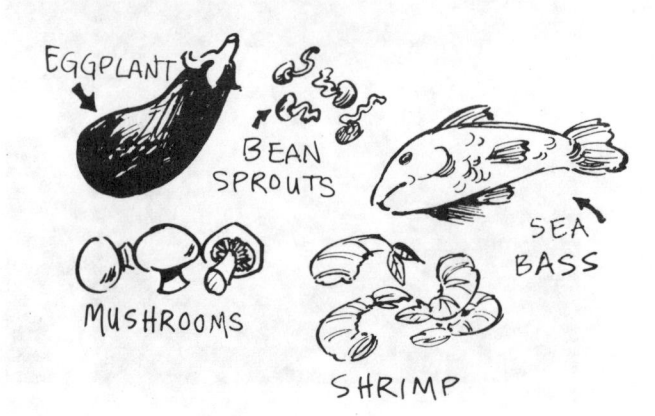

[9] **get to meet:** have a chance to meet
We use the expression *get to* (do something) to convey the idea that we are fortunate to be able to do it.
If you come to the party, you will get to meet Elizabeth Taylor.

[10] **deal:** something formally agreed upon

[11] **item:** thing

	Harry:	Oh, I see. In the **bucket**.12 Those white things must be bean sprouts. I'll just **grab**13 a **handful!**14
	Susan:	Here's a plastic bag to put them in. Oh, Harry! Look! There goes a fish seller pushing a **cart**.15
40	Harry:	He must have fifteen kinds of fish in that cart.
	Susan:	C'mon, Harry. Let's buy the shrimp and the sea bass from him.
	Harry:	Okay. You follow him. I'll get the bean sprouts and pay for the vegetables. Then I'll **catch up to**16 you.
	Susan:	All right. *[She walks away.]*
	Harry:	Susan! . . . Susan! Excuse me, officer. Have you seen a woman . . . **about this tall . . .**17 with blond hair and . . . ?
50	Policeman:	Sorry, mister. A hundred people pass this street corner every few minutes. Maybe I saw her. But I can't really say for sure.
	Harry:	I understand, officer. **Thanks, anyway.**18
	Policeman:	Good luck!
	Susan:	*[She is excited.]* Harry! Oh, there you are!
60	Harry:	Susan! Am I happy to see you! I thought I lost you.
	Susan:	And I thought I lost *you*. I went down the wrong street.
	Harry:	Well. We found each other.
	Susan:	And it's a good thing, too. We have to finish our shopping.
	Harry:	Did the man with the cart have the shrimp and the sea bass?
70	Susan:	Yes. Look in the bag. They're beautiful. And **just wait till**19 you taste Lily's cooking!
	Harry:	Susan, if eating Lily's dinner is just half as interesting as buying the ingredients for it, well . . . I'm sure it will be great!

END OF ACT I

Focus In

Susan says,
Am I happy to see you!
Am I happy to see you is different from saying "I am happy to see you." It means "I'm very, very happy to see you."

12 **bucket:** small waterproof container

13 **grab:** take with your hand
14 **handful:** the amount that you can hold in your hand
15 **cart:** a small vehicle with wheels that we use to transport goods
16 **catch up to:** meet again
17 **about this tall . . .**
This expression is used while we demonstrate a certain height with the hand.
18 **Thanks, anyway.** = Thanks even though you couldn't help.
Thanks, anyway is used in situations where the person we ask something doesn't know the answer but we thank them for the consideration they showed in listening to our request.
19 **just wait till . . .**
This expression conveys a sense of excitement about a future event.

Just wait till you see my new car!
Just wait till she hears about the new baby!

U.S. LIFE

One of the richest aspects of life in America is the wide variety of food that is available. Immigrants to the United States found a rich assortment of native American foods on their arrival here and also brought their unique dishes and foods with them. This tradition has continued to the present day with America's newest immigrants: Hispanics, Southeast Asians, Armenians, and Persians. The foods of these nations can be found at the various ethnic markets of America's major cities.

YOUR TURN

- What is your favorite ethnic food?
- What food would you consider to be distinctly American?

INTRODUCTION TO ACT II

This time on TUNING IN THE U.S.A., *we are at Susan's apartment in New York City. There's a dinner party* **going on.**[1] *Susan and her friend Harry bought the ingredients for the meal. Lily, a Chinese-American friend of Susan's, is cooking dinner. Ed, an actor, helps* **chop**[2] *the vegetables. As they discuss the American* **diet**,[3] *everyone agrees that it's* **changing for the better.**[4]

ACT II

Lily: Okay, Ed. I'm ready to **add in**[5] the eggplant.
Ed: Where is the eggplant?
Lily: Susan? Did you and Harry forget the eggplant?
Susan: Of course not, Lily. I know it's in one of these bags.
Ed: *[He looks in a bag.]* Here we are! The eggplant!
Lily: Okay. I need to start cooking it now. Ed, how quickly can you chop all of the eggplant into **thin strips**[6] about two inches long?
Ed: I'll do the best I can. *[He chops the eggplant.]*
Susan: Ed, let me and Harry help you. Here are two more knives. We'll all chop.
[Susan, Harry, and Ed chop the eggplant.]
Harry: Ed, you **handle**[7] that knife like a professional cook.
Ed: I'm a professional actor.
Harry: I thought someone said you worked in a restaurant.
Ed: I do. In between acting jobs, I'm a waiter.
Susan: A lot of actors do that kind of work, don't they—waiting on tables?
Ed: Yup. It seems like half the waiters at our restaurant are actors or singers.
Lily: Oh, Ed and I went out to eat the other day. And at the restaurant all the waiters and waitresses sang and danced in between serving dinners. It was **wild.**[8]
Harry: I guess they'd *have* to be actors to get a waiting job at *that* restaurant!
Ed: That's right. And I'll bet all of them are hoping to **be out of that job**[9] and in a great new play or a film.
Lily: That's the actor's life! Always changing.

[1] **going on:** in progress; happening
[2] **chop:** cut into small pieces using short, hard strokes with a sharp instrument
[3] **diet:** the kinds of food and drink we normally consume
[4] **changing for the better:** improving
[5] **add in:** put in; add
[6] **thin strips:** pieces that are long and not very wide
[7] **handle:** use
[8] **wild:** fun
[9] **be out of that job:** leave that job

"Ethnic Food" ▶ 53

Ed: True. But there's change in every job. I mean, look at the food and restaurant businesses. **Talk about change!**[10] The American diet is much different than it was ten years ago.

Susan: I guess people are eating more healthy foods.

Ed: Much healthier. Here's the eggplant, Lily—all chopped. Just think about it. Are any of you eating the same way you ate ten years ago?

Harry: I know I'm not. I was just starting my own business then. I didn't have much money. Once, when I was working late, I ate a whole box of chocolate **donuts.**[11]

Ed: Chocolate donuts!

Susan: [She laughs.]

Lily: Oh no! That sounds terrible!

Harry: The next day, I promised myself never to do that again.

[The tea kettle starts to whistle.]

Lily: The **tea kettle!**[12] Oh, Ed, we forgot to set out the tea cups. Would you do that, please?

Ed: **Sure thing.**[13] [He sets out the cups.] A cup for Susan. A cup for Lily. Two cups for Harry.

Harry: Two cups for Harry?

Ed: Green tea is like medicine. The Chinese believe it makes you healthy.

Harry: So? What does that have to do with me?

Ed: Aren't you the guy who ate a whole box of donuts?

[They all laugh.]

END OF ACT II

Focus In

Ed asks Harry,

Aren't you the guy who ate a whole box of donuts?

But Ed already knows the answer, and when we think we know the answer, we can ask a negative question. Harry says,

I thought someone said you worked in a restaurant.

He could ask a negative question:

Don't you work in a restaurant?

[10] **Talk about change!** = It's really changed!
We use the expression
Talk about . . . + noun or adjective to exaggerate a quality.
The World Trade Center: *talk about* tall!
An apartment in Manhattan: *talk about* expensive!

[11] **donuts** [doˊnəts]: small pastries with a hole in the middle

[12] **tea kettle:** covered pot with a pour spout used to boil water for tea

[13] **Sure thing.** = OK.

🇺🇸 U.S. LIFE

Americans have become increasingly health-conscious in the last fifteen years. Advances in food science have provided important information on the relationship of our diet to our overall health. We try to make sure we have a "balanced diet," that is, a diet that contains all of the essential food groups: vitamins, proteins, fats, and carbohydrates. At the same time, we have become more aware of the dangers of chemical additives in the food production process. Now, progress in an area of agricultural science called "biotechnology" may make it possible to produce healthier, better tasting food without the risk of toxic chemicals and preservatives.

☞ YOUR TURN

Do you try to maintain a balanced diet?

Activities

Here are some activities to help you check your understanding of this program.

A HEALTHY DIET

Susan and Harry are arguing about their diets. Use *-er than* or *more . . . than* to fill in the blanks.

Susan: "You should have more fish in your diet, Harry. Fish is much ____*(good)*____ for you than meat."

Harry: "I hate fish. It has too many bones. Meat is much ____*(easy)*____ to eat than fish. You should drink more milk. It's good for your bones."

Susan: "Oh, no. Milk is too fattening. I drink juice. Milk is much ____*(fattening)*____ than juice."

Harry: "You're much ____*(worried)*____ about how you look than how healthy you are. Women!"

Susan: "Maybe you should worry more, too, Harry."

MATCH UP

Here is a list of dishes (left) and the countries they come from (right). See if you can match the country with the dish. Write the letter of the country next to the number of the dish.

____ 1. Won Ton Soup   a. North Africa
____ 2. Couscous   b. Italy
____ 3 Paella   c. America
____ 4 Beef Burgundy   d. Germany
____ 5 Miso Soup   e. Scotland
____ 6 Tamales   f. France
____ 7 Veal Parmesan   g. Spain
____ 8 Sauerkraut   h. Japan
____ 9 Pumpkin pie   i. Mexico
____ 10 Haggis   j. China

IDENTIFY THE FOOD

Here are some common fruits and vegetables. See if you know them. Write the letter of the food on the line next to the name of the food.

____ 1. eggplant   ____ 2. carrot   ____ 3. potato

____ 4. apple   ____ 5. orange   ____ 6. peas

____ 7. banana   ____ 8. grapes   ____ 9. tomato

____ 10. watermelon

PROGRAM 36

"Riverdale Day"

ACT I

In this program, you will study...

VOCABULARY

Do you know the meaning of these words from Program 36?

scrambled eggs
tractor
lifeguard

GRAMMAR AND EXPRESSIONS

Do you know what these phrases or expressions mean?

Give a hand.
just in case
How does ... sound?

PRONUNCIATION

Do you know how to pronounce these words?

improvement
energy
earache

ACT II

U.S. LIFE

Do you know what a community project is?

Hint: It's something you don't get paid for: volunteer work.

☞ YOUR TURN

Have you ever done any volunteer work? What was it?

"Riverdale Day" ▶ 55

Here is the complete script with study material for Program 36. Use these materials before *or* after you listen.

INTRODUCTION TO ACT I

Today on TUNING IN THE U.S.A., *it's early on a Saturday morning, and Robbie Stewart and his father Philip are in the kitchen. Philip is making breakfast. Today is Riverdale Day. On this day many people of the town* **get together**[1] *to clean up the parks. Robbie and his friends will be helping. But Philip has forgotten all about Riverdale Day—until now. So when Robbie leaves, Philip makes a plan.*

ACT I

Philip: [He is breaking eggs into a bowl.] Good morning, Robbie.
Robbie: Good morning, Dad.
Philip: I'm making some **scrambled eggs**.[2] Can I make some for you?
Robbie: No, thanks, Dad. **I've already eaten.**[3] I got up early.
Philip: [He stirs the eggs.] Maybe we can do something together today.
10 Robbie: I'm sorry, Dad. But **I'm busy**[4] from morning till night.
Philip: Where are you going?
Robbie: To the park... Did you see some sandwiches? I made some sandwiches earlier. They were right here.
Philip: They're in the refrigerator. You have enough sandwiches to feed a small army.
Robbie: [He looks inside the refrigerator.] I
20 only have four. They're all peanut butter and jelly. I'm going to get hungry.
Philip: Why? What's happening at the park?
Robbie: It's Riverdale Day, Dad.
Philip: [remembering] Oh, that's right. **Today's the day when**[5] everyone helps clean up the town parks.
Robbie: That's right. They're doing something
30 special to improve the playground area.
Philip: They want to make it bigger?
Robbie: Not bigger. **Mostly**[6] they want to make it safer. Do you remember my friend Jimmy?
Philip: Sure, I do. He has a job as a **lifeguard**[7] at the town swimming pool. Right?
Robbie: That's right. He and I will be working together today.
[A car horn honks.]
Robbie: That must be Jimmy now. I've got to
40 go, Dad. [He starts to walk away.]
Philip: Let me help you carry your things out.

[1] **get together:** meet

[2] **scrambled eggs:** a breakfast dish made by mixing egg yolks and whites with milk and frying in a pan

[3] **I've already eaten.**
Already is used with the present perfect to indicate an action that we may not expect to have happened.

Boss: Would you please type these letters?
Secretary: I've *already* typed them.

[4] **I'm busy...** = I will be busy...
The present is often used for future actions.

[5] **Today's the day when...** = Every year on this day...
This expression applies to events that are repeated regularly, usually once a year.

[6] **mostly:** for the most part; mainly

[7] **lifeguard:** person trained in lifesaving techniques who is hired to watch swimmers at a swimming pool or beach

"Riverdale Day"   ▶   57

Robbie:	Thanks. You see, I'll be **doing some painting**[8] today. Can you grab my **paint brushes**?[9]
Philip:	Sure. What else are you taking?
Robbie:	Oh, **rollers**[10] and **scrapers**.[11]
Philip:	What other jobs are there to do?
Robbie:	Well, the **ball field**[12] needs work.
	[They leave the house.]
Philip:	Didn't Eric Simpson break his arm on the ball field last year?
Robbie:	Yeah, but Dave Hopper's dad is a **builder**,[13] and he's bringing a **tractor**[14] to make the **rough ground**[15] **smooth**.[16]
Philip:	*[He thinks aloud.]* Mmm-hmm. Good idea.
Jimmy:	Hi, there, Dr. Stewart!
Philip:	Good morning, Jimmy.
Jimmy:	Are you coming to the park?
Philip:	Actually, Jimmy, I forgot all about Riverdale Day. I've been so busy working this week. **But there must be something I can do to help.**[17]
Robbie:	It's okay, Dad. You've been working so hard. You should just rest this weekend.
Philip:	Well . . . here are your paint brushes.
Robbie:	*[He gets into Jimmy's car.]* Thanks a lot, Dad.
Philip:	Do a great job now!
Robbie:	We will.
Jimmy:	Bye, Dr. Stewart.
Philip:	Good-bye!
Robbie:	Bye, Dad. See you later.
Philip:	*[He speaks to himself.]* Hmmm. I think you *will* see me later.

END OF ACT I

Focus In

Today, we're going to study this kind of sentence:
Robbie: I've already eaten.

Here's another example:

**Can I make you some sandwiches?
No thanks, I've already made some.**

☞ YOUR TURN

Is there a community organization for organizing voluntary work in your neighborhood? How can you find out?

[8] **doing some painting:** will be painting
We use the expression *to do some* + gerund in familiar speech:
I did some drawings = I drew.
She does some babysitting = She babysits.

[9] **paint brushes:** tools with a wooden or plastic handle and hair bristles used to apply paint

[10] **rollers:** tools used to apply paint to a broad surface
They are easier to use than a brush but are not suitable for small areas.

[11] **scrapers:** tools used to remove old paint from a surface before repairing it

[12] **ball field:** field designed for playing football, baseball, soccer, etc.

[13] **builder:** a person whose profession is constructing buildings, bridges, roads, etc.

[14] **tractor:** vehicle designed to pull heavy loads

[15] **rough ground:** ground that is uneven and therefore difficult to walk over

[16] **smooth:** having a regular, even surface
Smooth is the opposite of *rough*.

[17] **But there must be something I can do to help.** =
I'm sure there is something I can do to help.
The modal *must* is often used to show certainty about an action.
He must be here. = I'm sure he's here.

U.S. LIFE

The cost of providing public services in America has gone up a lot in recent years. Public services include everything from police and fire protection to cleaning and repairing parks and streets, operating libraries, swimming pools, and other public sports facilities. In certain communities, the local government has had to cut back or eliminate these services completely because of lack of money. As a result, many communities have organized the kind of cooperative program you heard about in this episode. These programs have names like "Adopt a Beach" or "Adopt a Park."

INTRODUCTION TO ACT II

This time on TUNING IN THE U.S.A., it's Riverdale Day. And so, many of Riverdale's citizens are giving their time and **energy**[1] to clean up their public park. Robbie Stewart and his friends are making **improvements**[2] to the playground. Some of his friends' parents are also helping. There is much **digging**,[3] painting, and other work to do. And although Robbie's dad is late in getting there, he comes to offer his help, too.

ACT II

[We hear the sounds of a machine.]

Philip: *[calling]* Mr. Hopper! Mr. Hopper!
Hopper: Oh, hello, Dr. Stewart. How are you?
Philip: I'm just fine. How's your family?
Hopper: They're all fine. Sally still gets a few **earaches**[4]—but just now and then.
Philip: Lots of young kids get them. They'll stop soon.
Hopper: Are you looking for Robbie?
10 Philip: Not really, I just stopped by to offer my help. Is there anything I can do for you?
Hopper: Oh, no. This big machine will do all the **heavy work**.[5]
Philip: Well, maybe I can **give** someone else **a hand**.[6] Where is Robbie?
Hopper: I saw him head toward the bathrooms with Jimmy. They were carrying a can of paint and some paint brushes.
Philip: Thanks, Mr. Hopper.
20 Hopper: Okay, Dr. Stewart. Give Mrs. Stewart my best.

[The machine starts up again.]

Philip: I will. And, Mr. Hopper, the ball field looks great.
Hopper: I'm just doing my part of the work.
Jimmy: Hey, Robbie, isn't that your dad coming this way?
Robbie: Jimmy, I'm painting inside this toilet **stall**.[7] I can't see anything.
30 Jimmy: I'm sure it's your dad.
Robbie: Jimmy, it can't be. We **left him standing**[8] in the driveway.

---

[1] **energy** [en´ ər jē]: the capacity for or the doing of work

The term *energy* implies busy activity when we're talking about people.

She has a lot of energy. = She does a lot of work in a short amount of time.

[2] **improvements** [im prüv´mənts]: the results of activity to make something better

The new gymnasium is a great improvement to our school.

[3] **digging**: removing something (in this case earth) with a shovel

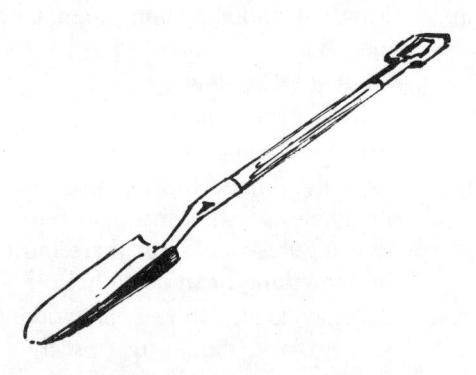

[4] **earaches** [ēr´āks]: pain in the ear

[5] **heavy work**: work that requires a lot of strength to do.

[6] **Give . . . a hand.** = Help.
The expression is *to give* (or *lend*) someone *a hand*.

[7] **stall**: a closed compartment to provide privacy in a public bathroom

[8] **left him standing**: left him (while he was) standing

"Riverdale Day" 59

Philip:	*[He approaches them.]* Hello, Jimmy. Have you seen Robbie?	
Robbie:	*[He hears Philip.]* Hey, Dad.	
Philip:	**How's the painting going?**[9]	
Robbie:	Fine. I'm painting the inside of the toilet stalls. What are you doing here?	
Philip:	It's Riverdale Day. I came to help.	
40 Robbie:	Dad, you know you don't *have* to do anything.	
Philip:	Oh, no, I want to help. I saw Mr. Hopper with his **bulldozer**.[10] And most of your friends' mothers or fathers are **involved**.[11] I want to help, too.	
Robbie:	Are you sure? Do you have time for it?	
Philip:	**I'm making time for it.**[12] I wore my old clothes. And see? I've got on my work shoes.	
50		
Jimmy:	What's that in your pocket, Dr. Stewart?	
Philip:	This? A paintbrush. I brought my own—**just in case.**[13]	
Jimmy:	Hey, you really did come prepared.	
Philip:	Why, thank you, Jimmy.	
Jimmy:	I guess doctors learn to be that way.	
60 Robbie:	Yeah. He's always trying to teach me to be prepared.	
Philip:	It's important to think ahead. To plan for the expected and the unexpected, too.	
Robbie:	That's great, Dad. So, what did you bring for lunch?	
Philip:	Lunch?	
Robbie:	Don't worry, Dad. I'm prepared this time. **How does** peanut butter and jelly **sound**[14] to you?	
70		
Philip:	It sounds great. But let's do some painting first.	
Robbie:	All right!	

END OF ACT II

[9] **How's the painting going?** = How is the painting progressing?

[10] **bulldozer:** machine used to move large quantities of earth

[11] **involved** [in vålvd´]: committed to or engaged in something
He's *involved* with the conservation movement.

[12] **I'm making time for it.** = I'm taking time from other things to do this.

[13] **just in case:** in the event that
The expression *just in case* is an abbreviation of *just in case it is necessary.*

[14] **How does . . . sound?** = How would you like . . . ?
How does a trip to Europe sound? = How would you like to take a trip to Europe?

U.S. LIFE

Community volunteer programs usually have had a hard time getting people to join in their activities. The reason is that people have so many other demands on their time. Most find the experience rewarding, however, and such activities are vital to the communities they serve.

☞ YOUR TURN

What type of work does your neighborhood need right now? Street cleaning? Graffiti removal? Park maintenance? Street lighting?

Focus In

Philip says, **"I just stopped by to offer my help."**

The expression *to stop by* is used for casual, unannounced visits. Philip is saying that he didn't plan to come and no one is expecting him.

Activities

Here are some activities to help you check your understanding of this program.

I'VE ALREADY...

Mr. Hopper is talking about some jobs that Robbie and his friend Jimmy were supposed to do. Complete Robbie's and Jimmy's answers. Use *already* and an object pronoun (it, them). Look at the example.

Mr. Hopper:	Don't forget to paint the toilet stalls, Jimmy.
Jimmy:	*We've already painted them*.
Mr. Hopper:	Well, then start doing the walls, Robbie.
Robbie:	_____.
Mr. Hopper:	OK. Go ahead and cut the grass on the ball field.
Jimmy:	_____.
Mr. Hopper:	Oh, OK. Well, there is some trash to take to the dump.
Robbie:	_____.
Mr. Hopper:	I can't believe it. You guys are fast. Here are the keys to the bulldozer. Bring it over to the football field.
Jimmy:	_____.
Mr. Hopper:	Wow! How would you like a job with my construction company?

RETELL THE STORY

Here are some things that happened in this episode. Number them in the right order. The first one has been done for you.

_____ Philip arrived at the ball field to work.
_____ Philip made scrambled eggs for breakfast.
__1__ Robbie got up early and made peanut butter and jelly sandwiches.
_____ Jimmy and Robbie were painting the bathroom stalls when Philip arrived.
_____ Philip helped Robbie out the door with his painting tools.
_____ Mr. Hopper asked Philip if he was looking for Robbie.

IDIOM REVIEW

Here are some idioms from past episodes. Use them to fill in the blanks in Robbie's letter to Richard. Be sure to use the past tense where necessary. Be sure to capitalize where appropriate.

by the way	headed	take your time	we made it.
give her best to ...	how's it going?	just wait till ...	talk about ... !
changing for the better	more or less	seems like yesterday	hardly

Dear Richard,
_____ in the Pacific Northwest? You missed Riverdale Day. You won't recognize the ball field. _____ you see how even the ground is! Jimmy and I worked all day painting. _____ work! We _____ had time to stop for lunch. Even Dad came down to help. He kept telling us to go slowly. "_____," he said. "We've got all day." I didn't think we'd ever finish. But by 6 o'clock _____. Before it got dark we stood back and looked at our work. I was remembering the time you taught me to play baseball on this same field. It was so many years ago but _____. Well, after that everybody _____ home. Everybody was tired but feeling good. You know, I think Riverdale is _____. It's grown a lot, but it's stayed _____ the same. _____, I saw your old friend Tina. She said to _____.

Yours,
Robbie

PROGRAM 37

"On the Nature Trail"

In this program, you will study...

ACT I

VOCABULARY

Do you know the meaning of these words from Program 37?

wildlife
motor home
campsite

GRAMMAR AND EXPRESSIONS

Do you know what these phrases or expressions mean?

saddle up
fancy-looking
all the comforts of home

PRONUNCIATION

Do you know how to pronounce these two words? Be careful. Both of them contain silent letters!

scenery
folks

ACT II

U.S. LIFE

Do you know what the initials RV stand for?

☞ YOUR TURN

Think about the vacations you've taken. Where do you prefer to go, to cultural places like cities, recreational resorts, or places where you can "get back to nature"?

"On the Nature Trail" ▶ 61

Here is the complete script with study material for Program 37. Use these materials before *or* after you listen.

INTRODUCTION TO ACT I

Today on TUNING IN THE U.S.A., *Richard and his wife Marilyn are visiting one of America's national parks—Glacier National Park—in the northwestern state of Montana. They are taking a* **tour**[1] *of the park* **on horseback**[2] *with a guide and a group of other visitors. They admire the* **scenery**[3]*—the tall trees, the* **streams,**[4] *the mountains, and the lovely* **wildflowers.**[5] *When Marilyn asks the guide about a particular wildflower, another park visitor has the answer.*

ACT I

Mike: All right, **folks.**[6] Before we **saddle up**[7] and begin our horseback trip through the park, **let me introduce myself.**[8] I'm Mike Swenson, and I'm your guide this morning. Let me tell you a few things about Glacier National Park. It's our most northern park **outside**[9] Alaska, *[His voice grows softer as he rides away.]* and there are more than two hundred lakes and fifty glaciers.

[Later. Marilyn and Richard are both on horseback.]

Marilyn: Richard, look at the snow on top of the mountains!

Richard: It's hard to believe, isn't it, Marilyn? Snow. And it's so sunny and warm down here. *[He takes photographs.]*

Mike: *[He speaks to Richard.]* That's a **fancy-looking**[10] camera you have there.

Richard: I'm a professional photographer, Mike.

Mike: There's lots of **wildlife**[11] in this park.

Richard: What kind of wildlife? What should I look for?

Mike: **Moose,**[12] **elk,**[13] **black bear,**[14] **eagles.**[15] *[calling]* Okay, everybody. We're going to stop and take a little rest right here. *[He gets off his horse.]* Can I help you get down, Mrs. Bella?

---

[1] **tour:** a journey around an area, usually for sightseeing
   ... a *tour* of the museum
   ... a *tour* of the gardens

[2] **horseback:** on a horse

[3] **scenery** [sē′nə rē]: natural beauties of an area

[4] **streams:** small rivers

[5] **wildflowers:** flowers that grow wild, uncultivated by humans

[6] **folks** [fōks]: people
   Folks is a very familiar term usually associated with country life as opposed to urban life.

[7] **saddle up:** put a saddle on a horse in preparation for riding

[8] **Let me introduce myself.** = Let me tell you who I am.

[9] **outside:** excluding

[10] **fancy-looking:** sophisticated
    This is another "country" term which, when used by a person from the country to describe someone from the city, has a negative connotation. See **U.S. Life.**

[11] **wildlife:** any non-domesticated animal found in nature

[12] **moose** [müs]: the largest member of the deer family
    The moose browses in meadows and ponds of the northern and western U.S. and Canada.
    Note: the plural and singular forms are the same: one *moose*, two *moose*.

[13] **elk:** another member of the deer family, but slightly smaller than the moose

[14] **black bear:** most common type of bear found in North America

[15] **eagles:** one of the largest birds of North America. The bald eagle is the national symbol of the United States.

The Great Seal of the United States

	Mrs. Bella:	Thank you, Mike.
30	Marilyn:	Excuse me. What is the name of that little pink flower?
	Mike:	We call it a **calypso,**[16] but I don't know much more than that. Why don't you ask Mrs. Bella? She knows all about wildflowers. She and Mr. Bella are **regular**[17] visitors to the park. They come every summer to spend a couple of weeks with us.
40	Mrs. Bella:	To answer your question, young lady, the calypso is a kind of **orchid.**[18]
	Marilyn:	I love the name. I'd like to **pick**[19] one.
	Mrs. Bella:	Oh, no, please! The National Park Service asks you not to pick the wildflowers.
	Marilyn:	Why? There are so many of them.
50	Mrs. Bella:	True, but there are hundreds of thousands of visitors to the park every year. And **if each one picked a flower, they would soon disappear.**[20]
	Marilyn:	I guess I don't know much about wildflowers, Mrs. Bella.
	Mrs. Bella:	If you're interested in learning more about them, I can show you some excellent books on the subject.
	Marilyn:	That's very kind of you.
	Mrs. Bella:	My husband and I have spent probably half our lives looking down at our feet.
60	Marilyn:	*[She laughs.]* You mean looking for . . . unusual types of flowers?
	Mrs. Bella:	Exactly. Perhaps you would like to stop by the **campground**[21] this afternoon? We could have a glass of **lemonade,**[22] and both of us could learn more about the calypso.
	Marilyn:	I would enjoy that very much!
	Mrs. Bella:	Then I'll see you at the campground!

END OF ACT I

Focus In

Mrs. Bella says, **"My husband and I *have spent* probably half our lives looking down at our feet."** The verb *spend* is usually associated with money, but time is also a possession we can spend: **She *spends* her time reading and listening to the news on the radio.**

We can also *spend* blocks of time: **He *spent* his life helping the poor. I *spent* the entire afternoon looking for my keys.**

[16] **calypso** [kə lip´sō]: a type of purple, yellow, and white flower

[17] **regular:** by habit; coming every year

[18] **orchid:** a type of flower that blooms once a year
There are wild and domestic varieties of orchids.

[19] **pick (a flower):** break a flower off at the stem and keep it

[20] **If each one picked a flower, they would soon disappear.**
This is a type two (unreal) conditional sentence. The sequence of tenses is:
If + past tense, (then) + present conditional
The action in the *if* clause is considered unlikely to happen and is put in the past tense:

If I took the driving test, I would fail it. (I do not intend to take the driving test.)

In a type one (real) conditional sentence, the action in the *if* clause is in the present tense. This conveys that the action is likely.

If I take the driving test, I will pass it. (I may take the driving test.)

[21] **campground:** a place specially made for camping, usually having a fireplace and public restrooms

[22] **lemonade:** a drink made from lemon juice and sugar

U.S. LIFE

There are big differences between country and city people in the United States as elsewhere in the world. Country people value their open spaces, less complicated life styles, and independence. They often resent the political decisions that are made in the big cities. These decisions and the people who make them often seem to threaten their way of life.

☞ YOUR TURN

- Which do you prefer, city or country living?
- Have you ever lived in the country? Where? Was it more difficult to earn a living there?

INTRODUCTION TO ACT II

This time on TUNING IN THE U.S.A, *Richard and Marilyn Stewart are in a campground at Glacier National Park. They are* **paying a visit**[1] *to Mr. and Mrs. Bella, an older,* **retired**[2] *couple. For several months each year, the Bellas enjoy traveling in a* **motor home.**[3] *For them, it's the perfect way to travel because it offers* **all the comforts of home.**[4]

ACT II

Marilyn: There's the campground. I can see it through the trees. Mrs. Bella wrote her **campsite**[5] number on a piece of paper. I have it somewhere. Oh! Here it is.

Richard: Hmm. Marilyn, can you imagine Mr. and Mrs. Bella sleeping in a tent? They must be seventy years old!

10 Marilyn: *[She laughs.]* Oh, no, Richard! The Bellas aren't really **"camping out."**[6] They don't sleep in a tent. They sleep in their own bed.

Richard: Their own bed? How can they do that?

Marilyn: The Bellas travel in a motor home.

Richard: Oh. They call them RVs, don't they?

Marilyn: Yes. RV **stands for**[7] "recreational vehicle."

Richard: Sort of a house on wheels.

20 Marilyn: A motor home. Mrs. Bella says that they feel like they take their home with them. They probably have a bathroom, a kitchen, a bedroom, a washer, and a dryer.

Richard: It's hard to **imagine.**[8] **But then,**[9] I've never been inside an RV.

Marilyn: Neither have I.

[A dog barks.]

Richard: I guess we'll see **the real thing**[10] in a minute.

Mrs. Bella: *[She talks to her dog.]* **That's enough,**[11] Skippy!

Marilyn: *[She approaches.]* Hello!

---

[1] **paying a visit:** visiting

[2] **retired:** no longer working
Most Americans *retire* at the age of 65.

[3] **motor home:** house on wheels

[4] **all the comforts of home:** having everything one has at home in the way of conveniences such as running water, electricity, and appliances.

[5] **campsite:** an individual camping place in a campground

[6] **camping out:** camping outdoors, sometimes without a tent
We sometimes use the expression "camping under the stars."

[7] **stands for:** means; represents

[8] **imagine:** believe

[9] **But then . . .** = On the other hand . . .

[10] **the real thing:** the true thing; the actual thing

[11] **That's enough . . .** = Stop barking . . .

Mrs. Bella: Marilyn and Richard, welcome! I'm so glad you could come.

Richard: Thanks, Mrs. Bella. It was kind of you to invite us.

Mrs. Bella: Shall we go inside? I made a **pitcher**[12] of lemonade, and I have a number of wildflower books to show you.

40 Marilyn: *[She enters the motor home.]* This is our first time inside a motor home.

Mrs. Bella: I think you'll **find it**[13] very comfortable.

Richard: It's really big in here.

Mrs. Bella: It's about thirty feet **long.**[14] As you can see, there's a kitchen and a living room, and . . . in here there's a bath with a **laundry.**[15] Let me go get my husband. He's in the bedroom watching television. *[She calls.]* Harold! The Stewarts are here!

50 Richard: Television! Marilyn, this is just **like**[16] a house!

Marilyn: Look at their library! And all these books on wildflowers.

Richard: Here's a collection of family photographs on the wall. This really looks like a home, doesn't it?

Marilyn: Yes.

Mrs. Bella: Harold will be **out**[17] in just a second.

Richard: We were just **admiring**[18] your family
60 photos. Here we are in the middle of a great national park, and you're right at home.

Mrs. Bella: Oh, yes! We can carry our home with us! So, make yourselves at home. Now I'll go and get that lemonade.

END OF ACT II

Focus In

Mrs. Bella says,

"Make yourselves at home."

This is just one way to welcome visitors to your home. Mrs. Bella is inviting Marilyn and Richard to feel comfortable, to feel relaxed in her home.

[12] **pitcher:** container for liquids

[13] **find it:** discover; decide; think
[14] **long:** in length
[15] **laundry** [lôn′drē]: small room in a house where clothes are washed
The word *laundry* may also refer to the clothes themselves:

Where is mother? She's in the laundry.
What is she doing? She's doing the laundry.

[16] **like:** the same as
[17] **out:** here (out of the room he is in now)
[18] **admiring:** looking at and thinking well of

U.S. LIFE

The RV (recreational vehicle) has become a common sight on the highways of rural America in the last 20 years. RVs are very popular with older Americans, who, living on pensions and savings, often cannot afford to pay for vacations at hotels and resorts. Another advantage of the RV is that it provides privacy in a public setting. RV users, however, are sometimes criticized by naturalists. They say the RV users avoid direct contact with nature by surrounding themselves with "all the comforts of home."

☞ YOUR TURN

- Have you ever traveled in an RV?
- Would you prefer to visit a national park in an RV, or would you prefer to camp away from areas where there are people?

Activities

Here are some activities to help you check your understanding of this program.

WHAT DOES IT STAND FOR?

Do you know what these initials stand for?

RV   stands for **recreational vehicle**.
BA   stands for _____.
TV   stands for _____.
NYC   stands for _____.
LA   stands for _____.
PD   stands for _____.

QUESTION TAG REVIEW

In Act II of this episode, Richard said, "This really looks like a home, *doesn't it*?" He adds a tag to his statement to make it a question. See if you can make questions of these affirmative and negative statements.

1. You aren't serious, **are you?**
2. You come from Spain, **don't you?**
3. You went camping last summer, _____?
4. You've seen the Empire State Building, _____?
5. You haven't finished your work yet, _____?

YOUR HOME ON WHEELS

Here is an advertisement for a luxury motor home. Fill in the blanks. Use *there is* and *there are*.

Now it's finally here! Rolling Coach RV in Cucamonga has the latest luxury model RVs in the country. Talk about comfort! _____ room for two sofas in our spacious living room. _____ a full club bar in case you want to wet your whistle after watching moose and elk out your picture window all day, and _____ a full-size laundry in case you want to wash out those hiking clothes. _____ three bedrooms, all with their own TV outlets. You don't even have to get out of bed. Just switch the remote control and see if _____ something on TV you want to watch. _____ even a walk-in clothes closet in the master bedroom. And talk about style! _____ oak cabinets in the kitchen. Hurry on down to Cucamonga RV. _____ no time to lose!

PROGRAM 38

"The Windy City"

ACT I

In this program, you will study . . .

VOCABULARY

Do you know the meaning of these words from Program 38?

nightclub
blues
jazz
soul music

GRAMMAR AND EXPRESSIONS

Do you know what these phrases or expressions mean?

For one thing . . .
Yoo-hoo!
right on time

ACT II

PRONUNCIATION

Do you know how to pronounce these two words?

delighted
strength

U.S. LIFE

Do you know what the capital of African-American blues music is?

☞ YOUR TURN

Have you ever been to a jazz nightclub?

"The Windy City" ▶ 67

Here is the complete script with study material for Program 38. Use these materials before *or* after you listen.

INTRODUCTION TO ACT I

Today on TUNING IN THE U.S.A., *Marilyn and Richard Stewart are visiting Chicago, Illinois. They have spent the day seeing the* **local sights.**[1] *When Richard tries to photograph Marilyn, they understand the reason that Chicago is often called "the Windy City." To get out of the wind, Richard and Marilyn go into a music store and meet Mr. Otis. And he invites them out for an interesting evening.*

ACT I

Marilyn: [*calling*] **Yoo-hoo,**[2] Richard! I'm over here!

Richard: [*approaching*] And we're both **right on time.**[3] Did you have fun exploring Chicago this morning?

Marilyn: Oh, yes! How was your morning?

Richard: It was fine.

Marilyn: Did you take any pictures?

Richard: Sure. I used **up**[4] four rolls of film.
10 **Speaking of pictures,**[5] let me take a picture of my beautiful wife in beautiful Chicago.

Marilyn: Oh, Richard. [*She laughs.*]

[*The wind blows.*]

Richard: I've got it. Just stand over there by the music store window. No—right there. Ready?

Marilyn: Wait a minute, Richard. The wind is **messing up**[6] my hair. It's covering my face.

20 Richard: I guess that's the reason they call Chicago "the Windy City."

Marilyn: Well, **I've had enough of this wind.**[7] Hey! Look at the music box in the window! That one is **just**[8] like the one you gave me!

Richard: Let's go inside and get out of this wind.

[*We hear guitar music. They enter the music store.*]

Richard: Excuse me, sir.

Mr. Otis: [*He plays the guitar.*] Can I help you?

30 Richard: My wife and I were admiring the music box in the window.

---

[1] **local sights:** interesting things to see in an area

[2] **Yoo-hoo . . .** = I'm over here!
This is a common way of attracting the attention of someone at a distance from us.

[3] **right on time:** exactly on time

[4] **up:** completely

[5] **Speaking of pictures . . .** = Your saying "pictures" gives me an idea . . .
The expression *speaking of* + noun is a common way to join two ideas:
Speaking of food, let's get something to eat.
Speaking of music, I just bought a new stereo.

[6] **messing up:** undoing; putting out of order

[7] **I've had enough of this wind.** = I don't want to be in this wind any longer.

[8] **just:** exactly

	Marilyn:	But please, don't stop playing. It sounds good.
	Mr. Otis:	Thank you. My name is Billy Otis. I run this shop during the day, and I play guitar in a **blues**[9] band at night.
	Marilyn:	I'm Marilyn Stewart, and this is my husband Richard. We're from New York.
40	Mr. Otis:	**Is that a fact.**[10]
	Marilyn:	That's a beautiful music box.
	Mr. Otis:	Well, would you like to hear it?
	Marilyn:	Yes!
	Richard:	Please.
	[The music box plays music.]	
	Marilyn:	Oh, it's lovely, isn't it, Richard?
	Richard:	Both of us enjoy **all kinds**[11] of music.
50	Mr. Otis:	**Since**[12] you're not from Chicago, you should hear some Chicago music while you're here. I'm playing with the band tonight. Why don't you come?
	Marilyn:	That's the one thing we *haven't* done in Chicago . . . go hear some music!
	Mr. Otis:	The **place**[13] is called Sylvester's. It's on the North Side. You can ride the el.
	Richard:	What's the el?
	Mr. Otis:	The el is the elevated train. It runs on a track high above the street.
60	Richard:	Yeah, we've seen it. But we haven't taken it yet.
	Mr. Otis:	Well, why don't you ride it to the Clark Street **stop**[14] tonight? To Sylvester's. It's at 720 Clark Street.
	Richard:	We'll see you there!

END OF ACT I

Focus In

Look at two ways of making a suggestion you heard in this episode:

Richard: *Let's* go inside and get out of this wind.

Mr. Otis: Well, *why don't you* ride it to the Clark Street stop tonight?

[9] **blues** [blüz]: a style of African-American music which evolved during the early 20th century
Blues music has a three-line musical structure in which the words of the first line are usually repeated in the second line.

> The thrill is gone,
> The thrill is gone away.
> The thrill is gone, baby,
> The thrill is gone away.
> You know you done me wrong, babe,
> And you'll be sorry some day.
>
> "The Thrill is Gone"
> B.B. King, MCA Records

[10] **Is that a fact.** = Really?

[11] **all kinds:** every type

[12] **since:** because
Since is also used as a time expression:

> I haven't seen him *since* last year.

[13] **place:** (the place where I'm playing)

[14] **stop:** small station where the train makes a stop

U.S. LIFE

One of the most important contributions to American culture by African-Americans is the various forms of African-American music. In fact, for many people, African-American music *is* American music. It has many forms: blues, jazz, gospel, funk, bebop, reggae, and others, but all African-American music expresses in some way the black man's experience in America.

☞ YOUR TURN

Have you heard any of the types of African-American music listed above? Which kind do you like best? Do you have a favorite song?

INTRODUCTION TO ACT II

This time on TUNING IN THE U.S.A., *Richard and Marilyn Stewart visit a Chicago* **nightclub.**[1] *They have come to hear some Chicago blues music. They were invited to the club by a man they met earlier that day. His name is Mr. Otis, and he is a guitar player in the band. Mr. Otis tells Richard and Marilyn about the music of Chicago. And they* **get a chance**[2] *to hear him play the blues with his band.*

ACT II

[A train goes by.]

Marilyn: There are so many nightclubs in this area. Which one did Mr. Otis tell us to go to?

Richard: Sylvester's. At 720 Clark Street.

Marilyn: That's it! See the sign?

[They enter the nightclub.]

Crowd: **Make it plain.**[3] Yeah, **brother.**[4]

Gloria: Good evening, folks. Welcome to Sylvester's Blues Club. I'm Gloria, your hostess. Would you like to sit at a table or at the bar?

Richard: A table, I guess. We would like to sit close to the musicians. We were invited by Mr. Otis.

Gloria: Oh. Sure. The guitar player. Follow me. This way, please.

Richard: This table is fine. Thank you.

Mr. Otis: Well, hello there, Richard and Marilyn. Mind if I join you?

Marilyn: We'd be **delighted,**[5] Mr. Otis.

Mr. Otis: One of the musicians broke a **string**[6] on his guitar. As soon as he puts on a new one, we'll start again.

Richard: We saw a lot of music clubs **on our way**[7] over here.

Mr. Otis: Chicago is famous for its music. You can hear everything from blues, to **jazz,**[8] to **gospel,**[9] and **soul music**[10] in this town. I'd say that we have more different types of music here than in any other American city.

---

[1] **nightclub:** a place of evening entertainment, where customers go to dance or listen to music

[2] **get a chance:** have an opportunity

[3] **Make it plain.** = Speak sincerely.
These are spontaneous words of encouragement to a musician or singer. There is no literal translation.

[4] **brother:** friend
This is an expression of comradeship from one black man to another.

[5] **delighted** [dē lī´təd]: happy (to do that)

[6] **string:** one of the six wires that run from the neck of a guitar to its body. The guitarist plucks a string to sound a note.

A common type of electric blues guitar

[7] **on our way . . .** = while we were traveling

[8] **jazz:** an African-American music that developed from blues
Jazz music has syncopated rhythms and complex harmonic structures. See **U.S. Life**.

[9] **gospel:** a jazz form sung in churches
Gospel music is a passionate choral music whose message is religious.

[10] **soul music:** a broad term covering any type of African-American music

	Richard:	Why is that?
	Mr. Otis:	**For one thing,**[11] after the First World War, lots of **black people came north**[12] to Chicago, looking for work. And they brought their music with them. And the music I play is pure Chicago.
	Marilyn:	What kind of music is that?
	Mr. Otis:	I play Chicago blues.
	Richard:	When I hear the blues, I feel sad and happy at the same time.
40		
	Mr. Otis:	Yeah, that's it. It's about **feelings.**[13] Feeling happy. Feeling sad . . . . Yeah. There's some sadness **there.**[14] But there's **strength,**[15] too. It sounds like the band is about ready to start again.
	Marilyn:	Thanks for inviting us to the club, Mr. Otis. And for that **little bit**[16] of history about Chicago's music.
	Mr. Otis:	I'm glad you came. Enjoy the music. It'll tell you more than my words ever could.
50		

END OF ACT II

[11] **For one thing . . .** = In the first place . . .

[12] **black people came north . . .**
Most black Americans lived in the southern United States until they were freed from slavery in 1864. Since then, many have gradually migrated to all areas of the country.

[13] **feelings [fē′lingz]:** emotions

[14] **there:** in the music

[15] **strength [strengkth]:** force
In this sense, the speaker means "moral strength," or fortitude.

[16] **little bit:** small amount

Focus In

Mr. Otis sees Richard and Marilyn sitting at a table in the nightclub and says, **"Well, hello there, Richard and Marilyn. Mind if I join you?"**
This is short for *Would you mind if I joined you?* It means "Is it all right if I join you?" This is a common polite way to ask permission to do something.

U.S. LIFE

All African-Americans are descendants of the African slaves who first began arriving in America in 1619. Slaves worked the farms and plantations of the southern United States until 1864, when the Emancipation Proclamation abolished slavery. But the economic condition of African-Americans did not immediately improve. Segregation (separation of whites from blacks) and discrimination practices kept many in poverty and ignorance. In the 1960s, segregation was outlawed, and the Civil Rights Act of 1963 made discrimination by race illegal. Still, the progress of African-Americans has been a long, hard struggle.

Edward Kennedy 'Duke' Ellington, 1899–1974. A famous African-American pianist, jazz composer, and band leader

☞ YOUR TURN

- Are there groups of people discriminated against in your country?
- Does your country have laws against discrimination?

Activities

Here are some activities to help you check your understanding of this program.

MAKING SUGGESTIONS

Here are some entertainment events in Chicago. You're visiting with your friend. Make suggestions of places you can go to in the evening. Use *let's . . .* or *Why don't we . . .*

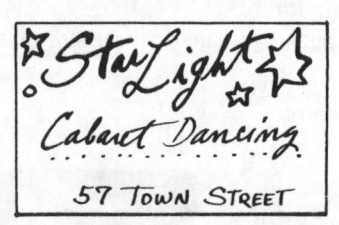

StarLight Cabaret Dancing — 57 Town Street

Sylvester's — LISTEN TO THE LATEST JAZZ PLAYERS WITH OUR NEW SOUND SYSTEM!

the GALLERY — 34 SOTO ST. — SEE OUR NEW PAINTINGS

YOU: _____.
YOUR FRIEND: No, I don't like dancing.
YOU: _____.
YOUR FRIEND: No, loud music gives me a headache.
YOU: _____.
YOUR FRIEND: No, art is boring.
YOU: Well, do you mind if I go hear some jazz at a nightclub? You can stay here at the hotel and watch TV.

SPEAKING OF . . .

The expression *speaking of . . .* + noun connects two related ideas. Match up the two parts of the sentences below. Write the letter from the right column next to the number at the left.

____ 1. Speaking of art . . .   a. let's go hear B.B. King at the Roxy.
____ 2. Speaking of animated movies . . . b. why don't we eat out tonight?
____ 3. Speaking of theater . . .   c. let's go see a play in town tonight.
____ 4. Speaking of food . . .   d. why don't we check the local galleries?
____ 5. Speaking of the blues . . .   e. there's a Disney movie on TV tonight.

MIND IF . . . ?

Request permission to do something. Make a sentence that begins "Mind if . . ." Look at the example.

You're cold. The window's open. **Mind if I close the window?**

1. You're trying to sleep. The TV in the living room is too loud.

   _____?

2. You have your camera at Glacier National Park. You see the guide on his horse.

   _____?

3. You want to sit down. There is an empty seat next to a lady.

   _____?

PROGRAM 39

"Such a Good Teacher"

ACT I

In this program, you will study...

VOCABULARY

Do you know the meaning of these words from Program 39?

video game
shopping center
arcade

GRAMMAR AND EXPRESSIONS

Do you know what these phrases or expressions mean?

No way!
Give me a break.
close call

ACT II

PRONUNCIATION

These two words have silent letters. Do you know how to pronounce them?

assigns
tough

This word has a letter pronounced like a "k."

disgusting

U.S. LIFE

Do you know what these are: Pac Man, Space Invaders, and Nintendo?

☞ YOUR TURN

Have you ever been to a video arcade?
What are some games you played there?

"Such a Good Teacher" ▶ 73

Here is the complete script with study material for Program 39. Use these materials before *or* after you listen.

INTRODUCTION TO ACT I

Today on TUNING IN THE U.S.A., *we are with Robbie and some of his friends at a* **shopping center.**[1] *They are playing games on electronic machines in a* **video game**[2] **arcade.**[3] *It's a popular activity with teenagers. The boys start talking about an English teacher at their school, and Robbie finds that he is the only one who likes the teacher. When he learns that the teacher is moving out of town, Robbie decides to visit him and say good-bye.*

ACT I

[There are the sounds of video games.]

Jimmy: Hey, Joseph, are you almost done with that video game? How about giving me a **turn?**[4]

Joseph: **No way,**[5] Jimmy. Ask Robbie. He may be done with his game.

Robbie: *[He speaks to himself.]* Hey, **yah-oh!**[6] *[He laughs.]* That was a **close call!**[7] Now watch the **kitty**[8] go! Meow!

Jimmy: Hey, Robbie. Come on and let me try that game. You've been playing **Cat and Mouse**[9] for at least fifteen minutes!

Robbie: Yeah, but the mouse was winning **up until now.**[10] **Any minute now,**[11] that cat ... is going to catch that mouse ... and **swallow** ... him ... **whole.**[12] See? He ate him!

Jimmy: Ah ... that's **disgusting!**[13]

Robbie: What's so disgusting? Cats eat mice. It's a fact.

Jimmy: Yeah, but do you have to **lick your lips**[14] when you talk about it?

Robbie: Jimmy, we are at the shopping mall, in the video arcade, playing an electronic game. That is a computer picture of a cat eating a computer picture of a mouse.

Jimmy: So? **What are you getting at?**[15]

Robbie: This, Jimmy, is only a game. In fact, some people say that life itself is just a game.

Jimmy: Yeah, **you and who else?**[16]

[1] **shopping center:** a collection of stores located together in one area, usually in a suburb

[2] **video game:** electronic game where the player interacts with a computer terminal. See **U.S. Life.**

[3] **arcade:** a covered area where shops or games are located

[4] **turn:** in a game, such as cards, where players play one after the other, the time to act
Whose *turn* is it?
It's my *turn*. I go after you.

[5] **No way ...** = Definitely not.
This is an informal way to turn down a request.

[6] **yah-oh!** = exclamation of surprise

[7] **close call:** a near miss
The cars almost crashed into each other. It was *a close call.*

[8] **kitty:** cat

[9] **Cat and Mouse:** here, the name of a video game
Cat and mouse is an expression that applies to any situation where a predator is stalking its prey.

[10] **up until now ...** = until now

[11] **any minute now ...** = in a few seconds

[12] **swallow ... whole:** swallow in one bite

[13] **disgusting [dis gəs´ ting]:** rude and in bad taste; offensive

[14] **lick your lips**
After eating a meal, an animal *licks its lips.*
Jimmy is trying to tell Robbie he shouldn't show satisfaction at saying something disgusting.

[15] **What are you getting at?** = What do you mean?

[16] **You and who else?** = Who besides you believes that?
This is a rhetorical question. It's not meant as a real question, but a statement. In other words, Jimmy means that Robbie is alone in his strange way of looking at life.

Robbie: **William Shakespeare.**[17] *[He recites.]* "All the world's a stage, and all the men and women **merely**[18] **players.**"[19]

Jimmy: Please . . . not poetry. I don't **need**[20] William Shakespeare on a Saturday morning. It makes me think of Mr. Pollard.

40 Joseph: Mr. Pollard! The English teacher? **Give me a break!**[21] He **assigns**[22] too much homework.

Robbie: Mr. Pollard's only doing his job, guys.

Jimmy: Robbie, you're wrong, and Joseph is right. Mr. Pollard is . . . unfair. His Shakespeare class is too hard. It's *impossible!*

Joseph: *Was* impossible.

50 Robbie: What do you mean "*was* impossible"?

Joseph: I mean past tense—"was," "used-to-be." What do you think I mean?

Robbie: Well, why do you say that?

Joseph: I went past Mr. Pollard's house this morning, and I saw a moving van parked out in front. There were boxes all over the place.

Robbie: Mr. Pollard must be moving.

Jimmy: You know, when I was in the school
60 principal's office on Friday, I heard some talk about one of the English teachers moving to Maryland. I guess that must be him.

Robbie: *[He is surprised.]* Mr. Pollard is leaving?

Jimmy: C'mon. **Who cares?**[23] Let's walk over to the **pizza place**[24] and buy some **sodas.**[25]

Robbie: You guys can have a soda. I like Mr.
70 Pollard. Sure, he's a hard teacher, but I've learned a lot from him. He's a good teacher.

Joseph: *[He speaks to Robbie.]* Hey, Stewart, where are you going?

Robbie: I'm going to say good-bye to Mr. Pollard.

END OF ACT I

Focus In

Hey, Joseph.
Hey, Robbie.

Jimmy uses the word "hey" to get someone's attention. We usually use this word only with people we know well.

---

[17] **William Shakespeare** [Shāk´ spir]
Shakespeare (1564-1616) was an English poet and dramatist. Many consider him to be the greatest writer in the English language.

[18] **merely** [mēr´lē]: only
[19] **players:** actors or actresses
[20] **need:** want
[21] **Give me a break!** = Stop talking nonsense!
[22] **assigns** [ə sīnz´]: gives (as an order)
The President *assigned* the job to the Secretary of Labor.
[23] **Who cares?** = I don't care.
This is another rhetorical question.
[24] **pizza place:** restaurant where pizza is served
[25] **sodas:** soft drinks

U.S. LIFE

Video games have become very popular in the United States during the last ten years, especially with teenagers. In a video game, the player doesn't compete against another player but against a computer. Most games challenge the player's hand-to-eye coordination. Action is carried on a video display screen (a TV screen). By manipulating dials and knobs, the player tries to avoid a series of accidents or to attack an enemy. The theme of many of the games is warfare. Parents often worry that the games are a poor form of recreation for their children. Many would prefer to see them play games where physical activity is involved and where they compete against other children rather than a machine. The interactive technology of video games, however, is finding new and exciting applications in education and training. It is a classic example of a new technology having both negative and positive uses.

☞ YOUR TURN

- Have you ever played a video game?
- Have you ever taken a course designed for interactive video?

INTRODUCTION TO ACT II

This time on TUNING IN THE U.S.A., *Robbie has decided to visit Mr. Pollard, a teacher who is leaving the high school. He's moving away to another state because his wife has a new job there. Mr. Pollard was a* **tough**[1] *teacher, but Robbie is sorry to see him leave because he has taught him a lot.*

ACT II

[Furniture is being loaded onto a truck.]

Robbie: Good morning. Is this the Pollard house?

Moving Man: Yeah, it is. They're moving out today.

Robbie: Where are you taking everything?

Moving Man: As soon as we get this truck loaded, we're leaving for Baltimore, Maryland. **About four hours south of here.**[2]

Robbie: Is it okay if I go in?

Moving Man: I guess so.

10 Robbie: *[He enters.]* Mr. Pollard? Mr. Pollard? It's Robbie Stewart.

Mr. Pollard: Robbie, what a nice surprise!

Robbie: Oh, hi, Mr. Pollard.

Mr. Pollard: Come on in. What are you doing here?

Robbie: I was just down at the video **arcade**[3] with a couple of friends, and someone said there was a moving van at your house. And so . . . I wondered if you were moving.

20 Mr. Pollard: I *am* moving. My wife got a new job in Baltimore. Did you come **all the way over here**[4] just to say good-bye?

Robbie: Well, yeah, I did. I hope I'm not disturbing you.

Mr. Pollard: Not at all, Robbie. I'm **pleased**[5] you're here. Sit down.

Robbie: Thank you, Mr. Pollard.

Mr. Pollard: I'm afraid I haven't much to offer you. Almost everything is packed
30 away in boxes—except my tea kettle. Can I offer you a cup of tea?

Robbie: Aw, sure, if it's not too much trouble.

Mr. Pollard: No trouble at all. Come with me into the kitchen while I put the water on to boil.

---

[1] **tough** [təf]: difficult

[2] **about four hours south of here:** four hours driving time
Distances are often expressed by the time it takes to drive them in a car. Car speed is usually considered to be 50 miles per hour on highways. A four-hour drive is therefore about 200 miles.

[3] **arcade:** game room

[4] **all the way over here . . .** = so far
The expression *all the way* is intended to exaggerate a distance.

He walked *all the way* to school!

[5] **pleased:** happy

[A little later, a tea kettle whistles.]

Robbie: And so, you see, even though a lot of kids thought you were a hard teacher...

Mr. Pollard: I guess I did ask for a lot of **written work.**[6]

Robbie: You did. But you were such a good teacher! You made us think!

Mr. Pollard: You know, Robbie, when a teacher hears a student say something like that—well, it makes being a teacher about the best job in the world. But now, tell me about you, Robbie. **Any new thoughts about your future?**[7]

Robbie: A few. I didn't think I could **put my thoughts into words.**[8] But I'm getting better at it—**thanks to you.**[9] And now, I'm even thinking that I might be a journalist and write for a newspaper.

Mr. Pollard: You'll be a good writer, I'm sure. I have something for you in this box. It's a book I think you'll like.

Robbie: A book for me, Mr. Pollard?

Mr. Pollard: If I could borrow your pen, please. I'd like to write something in it for you.

Robbie: Sure. Here's my pen.

Mr. Pollard: [He writes.] This book is called *Love of Language*. It helped me a lot with my writing when I was your age.

Robbie: Mr. Pollard, I'm really sorry you're leaving the high school. You taught me a lot. **Thanks for everything.**[10]

Mr. Pollard: You're welcome, Robbie. How about a little more tea?

END OF ACT II

[6] **written work:** homework that has to be written out on paper

[7] **Any new thoughts about your future?** = Do you know what you want to do for a career?

[8] **put my thoughts into words:** express clearly what I am thinking

[9] **thanks to you:** because of your help

[10] **Thanks for everything.** = Thank you for helping me.

U.S. LIFE

Young people in America seem to be offered more and more distractions, that is, recreational activities of no educational value. Many people in America, from parents to public leaders, are worried that because of these distractions, young people are spending too little time on study. They worry that students have lost their enthusiasm for schoolwork and their intellectual curiosity. They want to bring back what many feel is an old-fashioned respect for education and for the teacher.

YOUR TURN

Who was your favorite teacher when you were in grade school?

Focus In

Robbie says,

"But you were such a good teacher!"

He means that Mr. Pollard's teaching was so good that Robbie didn't mind working hard in his class. In fact, Mr. Pollard was such a good teacher that Robbie went to see him before he left.

Activities

Here are some activities to help you check your understanding of this program.

WHO SAID IT?

Robbie and his friends speak informally. Mr. Pollard, Robbie's English teacher, speaks more formally. Below are some pairs of expressions. Both expressions in the pair mean almost the same thing. Which one do you think is Robbie's and which one is Mr. Pollard's?

1. How about lending me your pen?　　　　　Could I possibly borrow your pen?

2. Would you mind not talking so loud?　　　Do you have to talk so loud?

3. What are you getting at?　　　　　　　　What do you mean?

4. I don't need all this noise.　　　　　　　 I'd appreciate your being quieter.

5. Would you like to see a movie?　　　　　Do you want to see a movie?

6. Here, have a donut.　　　　　　　　　　Can I offer you a donut?

7. It's no trouble at all.　　　　　　　　　　Don't mention it.

CHECK YOUR SPELLING

Here is part of a paper Robbie wrote for Mr. Pollard's class. It's about William Shakespeare. See if you can find any words misspelled. Check in your dictionary for the correct spelling and write it on the lines below.

William Shakespere wrote some pretty terific plays. He wrote *Macbeth*, who becomes king by killing all his freinds. He aslo wrote *Hamlet*. Hamlet kills his uncle Claudius and then he feels sory about it. He takes this diskusting skull in a graveyard and makes a beatiful speech about life. Hamlet was a confused guy, kind of like me.

_____　_____　_____　_____

_____　_____　_____　_____

PROGRAM 40

"The Motor City"

ACT I

In this program, you will study...

VOCABULARY

Do you know the meaning of these words from Program 40?

diner
shift
robot

GRAMMAR AND EXPRESSIONS

Do you know what these phrases or expressions mean?

Coming right up!
pretty much
passing through

ACT II

PRONUNCIATION

Do you know how to pronounce these words?

special
point
guide

U.S. LIFE

Do you know what states are in the Midwest of the United States?

☞ YOUR TURN

- Do you drive a car? What kind?
- What was the first car you ever drove?

"The Motor City" ▶ 79

Here is the complete script with study material for Program 40. Use these materials before *or* after you listen.

INTRODUCTION TO ACT I

Today on TUNING IN THE U.S.A., *Richard Stewart stops to eat at a **diner**[1] in Detroit, Michigan. It is late at night, but the diner is full of people. Richard's waitress explains that there is an automobile factory across the street. People work there in **shifts**.[2] When a shift is over, one group of workers leaves, and another group begins to work. People crowd into the diner whenever a work shift changes. Richard talks to one of the factory workers. He tells Richard a little bit about Detroit and invites him to take a tour of the automobile factory.*

ACT I

[We hear music from the radio.]

Announcer: And you're listening to radio station **WEXR**[3] in Detroit. It's twelve midnight in the **"Motor City,"**[4] and it's time for the news.

Richard: Twelve o'clock? I've been driving for seven hours! It's about time to get something to eat, and that diner looks good.

[He enters the diner and sits at a table.]

Nicole: Hi, there. Would you like to see a menu?

Richard: Yes, thank you. And I'd like to start with a cup of coffee.

Nicole: Here's a menu. Coffee's **coming right up!**[5]

Richard: Is the diner always this busy?

Nicole: **Pretty much.**[6] We're open twenty-four hours a day. And see that automobile factory right across the street? They're open twenty-four hours a day. Most of our customers work there.

Richard: Of course, you probably get most crowded when the work shift changes.

Nicole: Yup—like right now. Lots of people just **got off work.**[7] So. Are you ready to order?

Richard: Yes, I'd like the **fried egg**[8] **special**[9]

Adnan: Hey, Nicole! How about another cup of tea before I go to work?

Nicole: Just a minute, Adnan. As soon as I finish with this customer. Would you like **wheat toast**[10] with that?

[1] **diner:** a modestly priced restaurant often shaped like a passenger train car

[2] **shifts [shifts]:** the length of time a worker spends at his or her job
Factories usually divide the 24-hour day into three 8-hour shifts: day shift (7 a.m. to 3 p.m.), afternoon shift (3 p.m. to 11 p.m.), and night shift (11 p.m. to 7 a.m.)

[3] **WEXR**
Radio and TV stations in the United States identify themselves by the letter "W" or "K" and three letters.

[4] **Motor City:** Detroit, Michigan

[5] **Coming right up.** = (Your food) will be here in just a moment.

[6] **pretty much:** more or less

[7] **got off work:** finished work for the day

[8] **fried egg:** egg cooked in a pan without breaking the yolk

[9] **special [spesh´əl]:** a dish of several items served together and offered at a price less than what the items would cost if ordered separately (a la carte)

[10] **wheat toast:** grilled bread, made from unrefined flour

	Richard:	Sure. How many people work at that auto plant?
	Nicole:	Thousands. I'm sorry, but I've got a lot of customers here. But that **guy**[11] there—his name's Adnan—he can tell you anything you want to know.
40	Richard:	Hi. Adnan. I'm Richard Stewart. Is "Adnan" an Arabic name?
	Adnan:	Yes, it is. You know, Detroit has the largest Arab population of any American city.
	Richard:	Really?
	Adnan:	This must be your first trip to Detroit.
	Richard:	First time. I'm just **passing through**.[12] Do you work over there in the factory?
50	Adnan:	Yes, I do, along with my two brothers. You really should visit one of our automobile factories.
	Richard:	Maybe I should. Do they show you all sorts of new technologies—new methods of making cars?
	Adnan:	Sure. You'll see a lot of **robots**.[13] Those machines are doing more and more of the most dangerous and **boring**[14] work.
60	Nicole:	Adnan, here's your tea. *[She speaks to Richard.]* And here's your special. Fried eggs, wheat toast, and orange juice.
	Richard:	Thanks.
	Adnan:	Nicole, may I have my **check**[15] now?
	Nicole:	**Sure thing.**[16]
	[She writes his check and gives it to him.]	
	Adnan:	*[He speaks to Richard.]* You should really go see the factory. There's a tour every day.
	Richard:	Maybe I'll go tomorrow.
70	Adnan:	Well, I've got to get to work now. My shift's **about to**[17] start.
	Richard:	So long, Adnan!
	Adnan:	Okay. Good night.
	END OF ACT I	

Focus In

Adnan's shift is *about to* start. This means he's going to start working very soon.
It's twelve midnight in the Motor City.
What is *about to* happen? The news is *about to* start.

[11] **guy** [gī]: man (informal)

[12] **passing through**: traveling through
We *pass through* a place on our way to a destination.
Route 66 *passes through* St. Louis.

[13] **robots**: machines that perform work usually done by a human being

[14] **boring**: tedious and repetitive

[15] **check**: restaurant bill

[16] **Sure thing.** = Yes.
This is a cheerful informal response to a request.

[17] **about to**: going to
See Episode 32, Act II.

U.S. LIFE

Detroit, Michigan was a perfect location to begin an automobile factory. It was near the iron ore fields of Minnesota and was centrally located in the United States. And so it was that in 1908 in the Detroit suburb of Dearborn, Michigan, Henry Ford (1863–1947) began manufacturing his Model T, the first mass-produced car in the United States. Ford made his cars on an *assembly line*. Starting with raw materials at one end, the car was built (assembled) gradually as it passed along work stations. Ford's assembly line made auto production economical enough for his cars to be affordable to middle-class Americans, and Detroit soon became the "Motor Capital" of the world.

YOUR TURN

- Have you ever visited Detroit?
- What other industry has this city become famous for?

INTRODUCTION TO ACT II

This time on TUNING IN THE U.S.A., *Richard Stewart is taking a tour of an automobile factory. Richard sees a robot **spray-painting**[1] a car. The man who runs the robot is Al, an automobile factory worker for eighteen years. Al tells the tour group about changes he has seen in the factory. There are new programs to help workers learn to work with the new machines, and the **workplace**[2] is much safer now.*

ACT II

	Richard:	Excuse me. Where does the factory tour start?
	Judy:	Right here. Hi. I'm Judy, your tour **guide**.[3]
	Richard:	My name is Richard.
	Judy:	We're just starting. *[She speaks loudly.]* Ladies and gentlemen, I'd like to point out some of the special features of this automobile factory.
10		If you have any questions, please **feel free to**[4] ask.
	Tom:	Judy? Hi, my name is Tom. I'm writing a paper for my high school history class. It's about changes in the modern factory.
	Judy:	We've made a lot of changes over the years in the way we make cars.
	Richard:	You use robots now, right?
	Judy:	Right.
20	Richard:	Will we be seeing some robots?
	Judy:	Sure. Let's step over here. Now look at the painting machine. That's the robot.
	Tom:	If I had a car, I'd want it spray-painted **bright red**,[5] just like that.
	Richard:	It looks like a big mechanical arm.
	Judy:	And it can do things more easily than a person can. And faster.
	Tom:	Do you think we can talk to the
30		operator of the machine?

[1] **spray-painting:** painting by a machine that forces air and paint in a fine mist through a nozzle

[2] **workplace:** literally, the place where one works

[3] **guide [gīd]:** person who takes us through a tour of a factory, museum, or park and explains points of interest

[4] **feel free to:** don't hesitate to . . .; go ahead and . . .

[5] **bright red:** true red, rather than a shade of red

Judy:	Let's see. *[calling]* Hey, Al, can you **break**[6] for a minute or two?
Al:	*[He comes over to them.]* Hi, Judy.
Judy:	This young man's writing a paper for school. He'd like to ask you a question.
Tom:	Do you think this factory is safer today than when you first started working here?
40 Al:	**Definitely!**[7] I've been working here eighteen years, and the company's been improving safety all the time. Of course, we should *also* thank the automobile workers' **union**[8] for that.
Tom:	Why's that?
Al:	If the factory isn't safe, our union representatives tell us not to work.
Richard:	Excuse me, Al. What's it like working with a robot?
50 Al:	Well, I think it's great. See, I don't have to get so close to the paint. If you breathe that paint, you could really get sick.
Richard:	Have some of your friends lost their jobs because the robots are doing more of the work?
Al:	Well, it's true that you don't need as many workers when you **bring in**[9] robots. But there's a program to
60	**retrain**[10] workers for new jobs.
Tom:	So, you like robots?
Al:	Hey! Some of my best friends are robots.
[Everyone laughs.]	
Judy:	Ok. The next **point**[11] on our tour is over this way . . .

END OF ACT II

[6] **break:** stop what you are doing
[7] **definitely:** sure; positively
[8] **union:** workers' organization that represents them legally in negotiations with the employer for wages, benefits, and working conditions
[9] **bring in:** start using
[10] **retrain:** train a worker in a skill to do a new job
[11] **point [point]:** thing of interest

Humor
In Act II, Al, the auto worker, says, "Hey! Some of my best friends are robots." This is a common saying in America to show we are not prejudiced against any race or ethnic group. Does Al mean that robots are people, too?

The comedian Charlie Chaplin made a movie about mechanization called *Modern Times*.

U.S. LIFE

As American industry becomes more and more mechanized, fewer workers are needed to manufacture a product. It's not hard to see why labor unions have usually been against mechanization: it means fewer jobs. But in recent years the trend has been for workers displaced by mechanization to be retrained to do other, more complex skills. The idea of doing one job for a lifetime seems to be a thing of the past.

YOUR TURN

- Have you ever retrained to do another type of work?
- Do you think it's a good idea to change jobs from time to time? Why or why not?

Focus In

Richard wants to know Al's opinion, so he asks him, "What's it like working with a robot?"

**What's it like working with people?
It's okay, but I prefer working with robots.**

Activities

Here are some activities to help you check your understanding of this program.

PERFORMANCE EVALUATION

In factories, the boss sometimes evaluates his workers' performance; that is, he checks to see how well each one is working. Here are some notes comparing different workers in the auto factory. Make a sentence comparing their performance. Look at the example.

Al works carefully. Adnan works very carefully. **_Adnan works more carefully than Al._**

1. Joe works fast. Pete works very fast. ___
2. Jalil works efficiently. Medved works very efficiently. ___
3. Jack works hard. Robert works very hard. ___
4. Ed works carelessly. Paul works very carelessly. ___
5. Sal works diligently. Maury works very diligently. ___

PRONUNCIATION ROUNDUP

Here are some words from Episode 40. Circle the words that sound like the underlined word. The first one is done for you. More than one in each group may be correct.

1. *eight:* fight, meet, (late), (weight)
2. *right:* bite, ought, sight, like
3. *guy:* buy, key, high, boy
4. *break:* leak, make, seek, lake
5. *guide:* fried, skied, died, laid

GEOGRAPHY OF THE MIDWEST

Study the map again in Act II. Label the large industrial cities of the Midwest on the map below.

| Chicago | Cleveland | Pittsburgh | Milwaukee | Detroit |

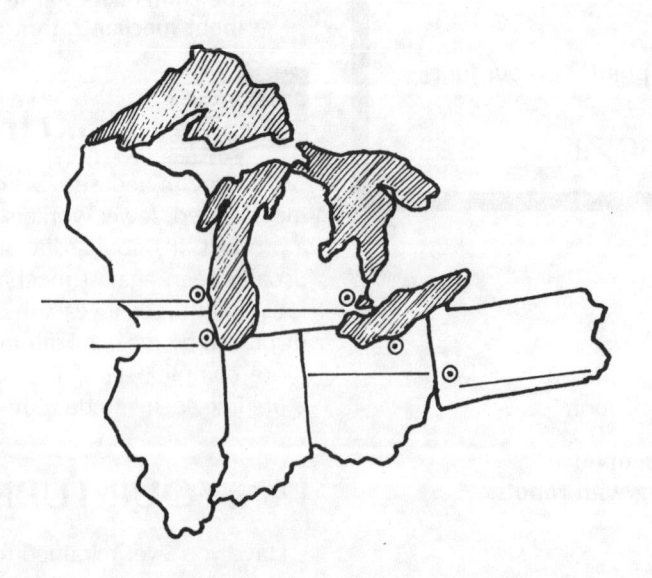

PROGRAM 41

"College Bound"

ACT I

ACT II

In this program, you will study...

VOCABULARY

Do you know the meaning of these words from Program 41?

apply
admission
catalogue

GRAMMAR AND EXPRESSIONS

Do you know what these phrases or expressions mean?

Bless you.
Feel free to...
Help yourself.

PRONUNCIATION

Do you know how to pronounce these words?

real
genius

In the following words the first "c" is hard (like k) and the second "c" is soft (like s). Can you pronounce them?

accepted
success

U.S. LIFE

Do you know the name of the test Americans take to gain admission to college?

☞ YOUR TURN

Which is more important for success in college, intellectual ability or hard work?

"College Bound" ▶ 85

INTRODUCTION TO ACT I

Today on TUNING IN THE U.S.A., we're with Robbie and Alexandra in the Stewarts' backyard. They're gathering the leaves that have fallen from the trees. Robbie is having trouble making some decisions. He must apply to college soon. But which colleges should he apply to? When Robbie's sister Susan suggests that he try asking for help, Robbie does **just that!**[1]

ACT I

Robbie: Alexandra, let's **rake**[2] the leaves together into one big pile.

Alexandra: Can you believe it, Robbie? The **fall**[3] is **half over.**[4]

Robbie: And I haven't decided what colleges I'm **applying to!**[5]

Susan: *[calling]* Rob-bie! Alex-an-dra! Do you two want some apple **cider?**[6]

Robbie: Sure, Susan!

10 Alexandra: Yes, please! Robbie, why don't you just go to a college near home?

Robbie: Some kids do that. But many don't. They choose a college for a lot of other reasons. Then they have to apply for admission. Of course, not everybody gets **accepted**[7] at the college they want.

Susan: *[She walks over and gives them the cider.]* Here you go, workers! Take
20 a break!

[They stop raking the leaves.]

Robbie: Thanks, Susan.

Susan: That's a nice pile of leaves. What were you two talking about?

Robbie: College. You know, I have to make some big decisions **real**[8] soon.

Susan: Like where to apply for admission? Mom was telling me that you weren't sure what to do.

Robbie: Well, when *you* were about to
30 graduate from high school, how did *you* **figure out**[9] where you wanted to go to college?

Susan: Let's see . . . it was pretty easy for me.

Robbie: You were a **genius,**[10] right? You probably could have gone to any college you wanted to.

Susan: Well, good **grades**[11] **didn't hurt,**[12] but just as important, I knew what I wanted to study.

---

[1] **just that:** exactly that

[2] **rake:** gather with a rake

[3] **fall:** Autumn

[4] **half over:** half finished

[5] **applying to:** formally requesting permission to enter

[6] **cider:** apple juice

[7] **accepted** [ək sep′təd]: formally approved to enter

[8] **real** [rēl]: very (adverb)
Real can also be used as an adjective to mean *true* or *authentic*.

[9] **figure out:** understand after making an effort
I finally figured out that math problem.

[10] **genius** [jēn′yəs]: a person of extremely high intellectual ability
Albert Einstein was a genius.

[11] **grades:** marks given in school to show achievement
Grades usually range from A (excellent) to F (failure).

[12] **didn't hurt:** were not a disadvantage
The expression *it doesn't hurt* is an example of understatement [the opposite of exaggeration].

It doesn't hurt = It helps . . .

40 Alexandra: Robbie knows **what he wants to be!**[13] A reporter!
   Robbie: Well, I *think* so. And I know **Columbia University**[14] has a really good journalism program.
   Susan: What about Columbia University?
   Robbie: But Grandpa and Dad both went to the **University of Michigan.**[15] They loved it! Maybe I should **carry on**[16] that family tradition.
50 Alexandra: Michigan's so far from home.
   Susan: Alexandra has a point.
   Robbie: And then, what about choosing a big school or a little one?
   Alexandra: Oh, it's so complicated in the United States! But, really, with so many choices, you're very lucky, Robbie!
   Robbie: Lucky? I dont *feel* lucky! *[He kicks the pile of raked leaves.]*
60 Alexandra: Oh, Robbie, stop kicking! You're messing up our pile of leaves!
   Robbie: But that's how I feel—messed up, confused!
   Susan: I know what to do, Robbie. Every high school has a college **advisor.**[17]
   Robbie: Yeah, I know. There's one at Riverdale High.
   Susan: Now *that* person knows all about different colleges. In my senior year in
70   high school, mine really helped me. Ask your college advisor for help.
   Robbie: Maybe I should.
   Susan: Sure. Asking for help won't hurt you.
   Robbie: Really?
   Susan: Of course.
   Robbie: Well, then, Susan, **we could sure use some of your help**[18] raking up these leaves.
   [They all laugh.]
   Susan: Oh, Robbie . . .

   END OF ACT I

[13] **what he wants to be:** what career he wants to have
[14] **Columbia University:** university located in upper Manhattan in New York City and established in 1754
[15] **University of Michigan:** university located in Ann Arbor, Michigan, and established in 1817
[16] **carry on:** continue
[17] **advisor:** a person whose job it is to give advice or counsel in a special area
[18] **We could sure use some of your help.** = (informal) We would appreciate your helping us.

U.S. LIFE

Unlike many countries, the United States does not have a national college preparatory curriculum. Admission to college is based on two things: a student's secondary (high school) grades, and his score on the SAT (Scholastic Aptitude Test). High school grades are a measure of a student's achievement, that is, what he or she has actually learned in school. The SAT is a measure of a student's aptitude, that is, what he or she is intellectually able to accomplish. The SAT measures two types of aptitudes: verbal or language ability, and mathematics ability. In addition, non-native speakers of English may be required to take a TESOL test (Test of English as a Second Language).

☞ YOUR TURN

Do you think it is a good idea to go to college immediately after graduating from secondary school? Why? Why not?

Focus In

Robbie says, **"You probably could have gone to any college you wanted to."** The past modal *could have* + past participle indicates something that was possible in the past but that did not happen.
She *could have gotten* married, but she decided to go to school instead.

INTRODUCTION TO ACT II

This time on TUNING IN THE U.S.A., *we are at Robbie's high school. He's meeting with his school's college advisor, Ms. Lubecki. She's helping him decide which colleges he should apply to. Robbie needs the help. He's confused about the choices he has to make about his future education. Too bad he has such a bad cold. It doesn't help him to choose a college—or does it?*

ACT II

[Robbie knocks at the door.]

Ms. Lubecki: Yes? Come in.

Robbie: Ms. Lubecki?

Ms. Lubecki: Yes. Hello! *[She recognizes him.]* You're Robert Stewart.

Robbie: That's right . . . um, Robbie.

Ms. Lubecki: Well, Robbie, do come in. Shut the door behind you, please.

[Robbie shuts the door and enters her office.]

Ms. Lubecki: And **have a seat.**[1] Good. Now, Robbie, when you made this appointment, you said you wanted to talk about choosing a college.

Robbie: *[He sneezes.]* **Ahh-chew!**[2]

Ms. Rubecki: Oh! **bless you!**[3]

Robbie: Thank you. I guess **I'm coming down with a cold.**[4]

Ms. Lubecki: There's a box of **tissues**[5] on the shelf beside you. **Feel free to**[6] **help yourself.**[7]

Robbie: Uh, thanks.

Ms. Lubecki: **Not at all.**[8] Now, Robbie, I'm going to ask you some questions, and we'll put your answers into the computer. You just need to tell me a few things that you're looking for. But the more information we can give the computer, the better. Then it will give us a list of colleges that **fit your needs.**[9]

Robbie: *[He sneezes.]* Ker-chew! Ah, sorry.

Ms. Lubecki: No problem. Shall we begin? **Major field of study.**[10] *[She types on the computer.]*

Robbie: I think that might be journalism.

Ms. Lubecki: Location of college. Is it important to you to stay near home? Or are you **willing**[11] to live anywhere?

---

[1] **Have a seat.** = Sit down.

[2] **Ahh-chew!**
This is one way we spell out in English the sound made when we sneeze.

[3] **Bless you.** = (May God) bless you.
This is the traditional polite expression used when someone sneezes. It really carries no religious connotations.

[4] **I'm coming down with a cold.** = I'm getting a cold.

[5] **tissues:** soft paper used to wipe the nose

[6] **Feel free to . . .** = Don't hesitate to . . . ; go ahead and . . .
The expression *feel free to . . .* is a polite way to offer something.

[7] **Help yourself.** = Take what you want.

[8] **Not at all.** = You're welcome.

[9] **fit your needs:** have what you are looking for

Columbia University

[10] **major field of study:** a student's main subject in college or university: mathematics, literature, journalism, science, economics, etc.

[11] **willing:** agreeable

	Robbie:	I don't know. I don't think it matters to me.
40	Ms. Lubecki:	That's a good answer. I'll mark the space that says "unimportant." Now, size of college? I can give you some choices here: five hundred to two thousand students. Two thousand to six thousand students. Six thousand to twelve thousand students. More than twelve thousand.

[She gives the computer printout to Robbie.]

	Ms. Lubecki:	Here you go, Robbie. This is the list of colleges that offer the things you want.
50	Robbie:	There are at least twenty listed here.
	Ms. Lubecki:	Those colleges are a good place to begin your **search.**[12]
	Robbie:	*[He reads.]* Boston College. University of Michigan. My father and grandfather went there.
	Ms. Lubecki:	An excellent university. Of course, it's very large.
60	Robbie:	Most of these colleges are located in the **Snow Belt.**[13] *[He sneezes and blows his nose.]*
	Ms. Lubecki:	You're right. *[She reads.]* "Michigan, Iowa, Indiana." They are pretty far north. Winters are long and cold. Oh, here's "University of Florida." That's in the South. Would you like to live in the **Sun Belt?**[14]
	Robbie:	I'm not . . . sure . . . about . . . Fl . . . *[He sneezes.]*
70	Ms. Lubecki:	It sounds like your cold is getting worse.
	Robbie:	I think so, too. Ms. Lubecki, maybe I *should* take a look at the University of Florida **catalogue.**[15] The Sun Belt sounds pretty good right now. *[He sneezes.]*

END OF ACT II

[12] **search:** act of looking for
The verb form also is *search,* to look intensively for something

[13] **Snow Belt:** regions where the winters are cold and a lot of snow falls

[14] **Sun Belt:** regions where the winters are mild and it almost never snows

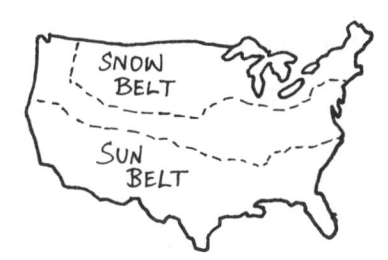

[15] **catalogue** [kat´ə log]: book with detailed information on a given subject

U.S. LIFE

During the last 20 years the U.S. economy has changed from an economy based on industry and manufacturing (making things) to an economy based on providing services. As a result, some cities in the American Midwest, which was once a powerful industrial region, have lost population. Many people have moved from these "Snow Belt" states to the "Sun Belt" states of the southern and western United States, where there are a large number of service industry jobs. Economists and others worry about this trend. They believe that a country's economic strength must be based on industrial production.

☞ YOUR TURN

- Do you work in the manufacturing sector of your economy or in the service industry?
- Do you agree that manufacturing is important to a country's economic health?

Focus In

Ms. Lubecki says, "**There's a box of tissues on the shelf beside you. Feel free to help yourself.**"
The phrase *feel free* is another way to give permission.

Feel free to ask me any question about English.

Activities

Here are some activities to help you check your understanding of this program.

REGRETS

Now that he is applying to college, Robbie is worrying about his high school grades. He is telling Susan about the things he *could have done*. Look at the example. Make more sentences with *could have* + past participle.

Robbie: "I didn't study hard enough. *I could have studied harder.*"

1. "I didn't get an A in American History. _____."
2. "I didn't make an effort in math. _____."
3. "I didn't take good notes in English class. _____."
4. "I didn't get up early enough. _____."
5. "I didn't use my time well in school. _____."

WHO SAID IT?

Here are some quotes from Episode 41. Write the name of the person who said them on the line at the left.

1. "Robbie, why don't you just go to a college near home?" _____
2. "I have to make some big decisions real soon." _____
3. "Ask your college advisor for help." _____
4. "... the more information we can give the computer, the better." _____
5. "The Sun Belt sounds pretty good right now." _____

PERSONALITY QUIZ

Ms. Lubecki gave Robbie a personality test to find out more about his likes and dislikes. Robbie responded enthusiastically to everything. Make more sentences like the one in the example. Use the comparative form (-er or *more*).

Ms. Lubecki: "Robbie, do you like warm weather?"
Robbie: "*Sure. The warmer the better.*"

1. Ms. Lubecki: "Robbie, do you like long classes?"
Robbie: "_____"
2. Ms. Lubecki: "Robbie, do you like difficult tests?"
Robbie: "_____"
3. Ms. Lubecki: "Robbie, do you like challenging subjects?"
Robbie: "_____"
4. Ms. Lubecki: "Robbie, do you like hard math problems?"
Robbie: "_____"
5. Ms. Lubecki: "Robbie, do you like early morning classes?"
Robbie: "_____"

PROGRAM 42

"The Health Run"

ACT I

ACT II

In this program, you will study...

VOCABULARY

Do you know the meaning of these words from Program 42?

snack-food
cheer
marathon

GRAMMAR AND EXPRESSIONS

Do you know what these phrases or expressions mean?

Keep it up!
All right!
You're almost there.

PRONUNCIATION

Do you know how to pronounce these words?

exhausted
exercise

Hint: we pronounce the letter "x" like "gz".

U.S. LIFE

Do you know the name of a long race held in many large cities in the U.S.?

☞ YOUR TURN

What kind of racing is the most popular in your country? Bicycle racing? Car racing? Horse racing?

"The Health Run" ▶ 91

Here is the complete script with study material for Program 42. Use the materials before *or* after you listen.

INTRODUCTION TO ACT I

Today on TUNING IN THE U.S.A., we are with Philip Stewart at the hospital. While Philip is buying some fruit juice from the **snack-food**[1] **machines**,[2] he talks with a friend, Dr. Mary Steer. They discover that they have a few things in common. Like Philip, Mary is **watching her diet**[3] and being careful about what she eats. Both of them are also exercising more. And they both are planning to run in a race next Saturday.

Act I

[We hear a voice on the loudspeaker.]

Philip: *[He puts coins in a snack-food machine.]* Good morning, Mary.

Mary: And a good morning to you, too, Philip. Are you taking a **midmorning**[4] **coffee break**[5] or an early lunch?

Philip: Actually, I'm taking a midmorning *juice* break.

Mary: A juice break? I thought I was the only person who took juice breaks instead of coffee breaks.

Philip: These days I'm only drinking one cup of coffee a day—at breakfast.

Mary: These days? Anything new these days?

Philip: I'm watching my diet. I'm being careful about what I eat. And I'm exercising more. *[He puts coins in one of the snack-food machines.]* Hmm. What should I get to drink? Apple juice? Grape juice? Ah, orange juice has a lot of **vitamins**.[6] I think I'll try that today.

Mary: It sounds like you've started an **exercise program**.[7]

Philip: Yes, that's right.

Mary: I think I could have **guessed**[8] that, anyway.

Philip: How?

Mary: Well, you've been wearing your **running shoes**[9] to work.

Philip: You're a good **detective**,[10] Mary. But these also happen to be my most comfortable shoes.

Mary: May I try another guess about you?

Philip: Go right ahead.

---

[1] **snack-food:** light food eaten between regular meals

[2] **machines** [mə shēnz´]: (vending) machines
These machines usually dispense candy or soft drinks.

[3] **watching her diet . . .** = choosing carefully the kinds of foods and the amount of food she eats . . .

[4] **midmorning:** literally, in the middle of the morning

[5] **coffee break:** a short time away from work in order to have a cup of coffee

[6] **vitamins** [vɪ´tə mnz]: organic substances that are contained in the food we eat and that are necessary for good health
Vitamin A, Vitamin B₁, etc. Citrus fruits contain Vitamin C.

[7] **exercise** [ek´sər sīz] **program:** daily or weekly physical exercise whose purpose is to keep the body in good condition

[8] **guessed:** imagined

[9] **running shoes:** shoes with a soft cushion sole which are made specifically for running exercise

[10] **detective:** person hired to find out information about someone
The comic strip Dick Tracy is about a police detective.

	Mary:	You're planning to **take part**[11] in the Riverdale **Health Run**[12] this weekend.
	Philip:	How do you know that?
40	Mary:	*[She laughs.]* I saw your name on the list of runners. I'm running in it, too.
	Philip:	**It's a small world!**[13]
	Mary:	Yes, and there seem to be more and more runners in this small world! *[She hears her name announced over the loudspeaker.]* Ah, that's my call. I'll see you later, Philip. And good luck with your **training!**[14]
50	Philip:	Thanks, Mary. And the same to you.
	[Later. Philip enters the house after he has gone running.]	
	Philip:	*[He calls.]* I'm back.
	Ellen:	Hi, Philip!
	Philip:	Hi, Ellen. **Boy,**[15] do I feel great! I think I was a bit faster tonight than I was last night.
	Ellen:	Good for you. Here's a towel to put around your shoulders. I hope all this running isn't **too much for you.**[16]
60	Philip:	Not at all. I feel better now than I've felt in years.
	Ellen:	Philip? Are you still thinking that you might try to run in that race on Saturday?
	Philip:	I'm not thinking I *might try* to run. I *am* going to run. And you'll be there to watch me cross the **finish line,**[17] right?
	Ellen:	You know I'll be there. Now, go take a hot shower and get ready for dinner.

END OF ACT I

[11] **take part:** participate

[12] **Health Run:** a race in which most of the runners take part not so much for competition but to keep physically fit

[13] **It's a small world!** = What a coincidence!
This expression means literally that the world is really a small place and it is not strange that people have things in common.

I'm in the same history class with my ex-girlfriend. It's a small world.

[14] **training:** exercise program
Training can be any program where a skill is learned, for example, a salesmanship training program or a teacher training program.

[15] **boy . . .** = wow . . . ; hey . . .

[16] **too much for you . . .** = too hard for you . . .

[17] **finish line:** the stretched string that marks where a race ends
Paula crossed the finish line in 3 hours 21 minutes and 10 seconds.

U.S. LIFE

A key word in the modern American vocabulary is "stress." Stress is the feeling of anxiety and exhaustion that comes from the pressures of modern living. Stress is such a common problem today that many people are turning to one of its most common cures: physical exercise. People of all ages and types are exercising: jogging, weight lifting, swimming, and even just plain old walking! Is this just a fad, or will it last?

☞ YOUR TURN

- What is your favorite form of physical exercise?
- Do you feel relaxed afterward?

Focus In

Mary asks,

"Are you taking a midmorning coffee break or an early lunch?"

Philip is *taking a break*; he has stopped working for a while to rest and drink some juice. He is *taking a juice break*.

INTRODUCTION TO ACT II

This time on TUNING IN THE U.S.A., *Ellen and Grandpa Stewart are standing on a street corner in Riverdale. They are waiting for Philip at the finish line of the Riverdale Health Run, a six-mile race. This is Philip's first time running in a race. Ellen and Grandpa have seen many runners finish the race. But Philip has not been among them.*

ACT II

[People are calling to the runners.]

Grandpa: It doesn't look like that **fellow**[1] is in very **good shape**,[2] does it, Ellen?

Ellen: No, Grandpa. He's **exhausted**.[3] He can hardly walk. *[She is worried.]* Do you think Philip is having as much trouble? Where is Philip?

Grandpa: He's all right, Ellen. Pretty soon, he'll come running right past where we're standing. And we can give him a big **cheer**.[4]

[A woman calls to a runner.]

Mary: *[She breathes a bit hard.]* Ah! Excuse me! You're Ellen Stewart, Philip Stewart's wife, aren't you?

Ellen: Yes, I am.

Mary: Hi, I'm Mary Steer. I work in **pediatrics**[5] with your husband.

Ellen: Oh, yes, Mary. Hi. I saw you finish the race. Nice job.

Mary: Thanks.

Ellen: Did you see Philip while you were running?

Mary: Yes, I just saw him a few minutes ago.

Ellen: How's he doing?

Mary: He's just fine. We ran together for a while. He's having fun. He'll be finishing soon.

---

[1] **fellow** [fel´ ō]: man
This is an old-fashioned word used mainly by the older generation.

[2] **good shape:** good physical condition

[3] **exhausted** [ig zôs´təd]: extremely tired physically

[4] **cheer:** shout of encouragement to someone competing in a game or performance

[5] **pediatrics** [pē dē a´triks]: the field of medicine having to do with children

30	Grandpa:	Here he comes now, Ellen, around the corner! There's my boy, Philip! [calling] Come on, Philip! **Keep it up!**[6]
	Ellen:	[calling] Come on, Philip!
	Mary:	[joining in] **All right!**[7] **You're almost there,**[8] **Doc!**[9]
	All:	Come on! Come on! Come on! You're almost there! Come on, Doc! Yea!
		[At the Stewarts' house a little later. Philip is soaking his sore feet.]
40	Philip:	[He groans.] Oooh, more hot water. Oh, that feels so good on my **aching**[10] feet. Thank you, Ellen.
	Ellen:	That's better, isn't it? It looked like you had a lot of fun today.
	Philip:	I really did. [He laughs.] Even if I was one of the last to finish the race.
	Ellen:	That really doesn't matter, does it?
	Philip:	Not at all. I was just trying to **do my best.**[11] There was one point where everything seemed so easy. I wasn't even tired. It was terrific.
50	Ellen:	Well, now that the race is over, will you still be running every night after work?
	Philip:	I think so. I'm going to try to keep it up. You know, it's almost as much fun training as it is running in a race.
	Ellen:	Really?
	Philip:	Yes. Maybe you should run with me, Ellen. You'd see how good it can make you feel.
60	Ellen:	All except your feet! Have you forgotten about those?
	Philip:	For a moment I did. How about a little more hot water?

END OF ACT II

[6] **Keep it up!** = Go on! Keep going!
These are words of encouragement to a runner.

[7] **All right!** = Great!
These are words of approval for someone who has just performed extremely well.

[8] **You're almost there.** = You've almost finished. (there = the finish line)

[9] **Doc:** Doctor
This abbreviated form is used only when one has a very close friendship with a doctor.

[10] **aching:** sore; painful
An ache is muscle soreness usually caused by vigorous activity.

[11] **do my best:** perform the best that I can

U.S. LIFE

Many major cities in the United States have an annual "marathon" race. The race is named after the city in Greece where a long distance runner arrived to bring the news that the Greeks had defeated the Persians in 490 B.C. The marathon race is usually over 20 miles long. Another type of sporting event that has grown in the last 10 years is athletic competition for the handicapped. Wheelchair races and swimming events are becoming more and more common. These events are usually put on to support a charity or some other worthy cause. Sponsors (companies) donate equipment and a small cash prize for the winner.

YOUR TURN

- Have you ever seen a marathon race?
- Have you ever competed in one?

Focus In

Grandpa says, "It doesn't look like that fellow is in very good shape." The words *as if* can be substituted for *like*.

My feet feel *like* they ran 100 miles.
My feet feel *as if* they ran 100 miles.

96 ◀ PROGRAM 42

Activities

Here are some activities to help you check your understanding of this program.

WHO IS IT?

Complete each sentence with the correct name. Write the names on the lines below.

1. _____ is watching (his/her) diet.
2. _____ has started an exercise program.
3. _____ told Philip she would watch him run.
4. _____ shouted encouragement to Philip in the race.

THINGS IN COMMON

Reread Act I. List below the things that Mary and Philip *have in common.* Start with "They both . . .

Example: They both are doctors.

1. _____
2. _____
3. _____

THE HANDICAPPED TRIATHLON

Read this short article about an athletic event for handicapped athletes. Then answer the questions below.

THE RIVERDALE TRIATHLON

The first annual handicapped triathlon of Riverdale was a huge success Sunday. Athletes from outside the state were on hand to swim, race, and throw the javelin. Betty Morovitz of Scottsdale, Arizona took first place in the women's competition. Betty lost both her legs in an automobile accident in 1986. She said, "I've been training for this triathlon for two years. I could hardly believe it when I saw the finish line just ahead!"

True or False?

1. A triathlon is an athletic event with three different types of competition. _____
2. Athletes came from the northeast part of the U.S. to compete. _____
3. Men and women compete against each other in the same events. _____
4. Betty was sure she would win the race. _____

PROGRAM 43

"Continuing Education"

ACT I

In this program, you will study...

VOCABULARY

Do you know the meaning of these words from Program 43?

construction
materials
systems

GRAMMAR AND EXPRESSIONS

Do you know what these phrases or expressions mean?

a great deal of
an awful lot of
Tonight's the night.

PRONUNCIATION

Do you know how to pronounce these words?

methods
site
realizes

U.S. LIFE

Do you know what a community college is?

☞ YOUR TURN

How many years were you out of school after you graduated from high school or college?

ACT II

"Continuing Education" ▶ 97

INTRODUCTION TO ACT I

Today on TUNING IN THE U.S.A., we're in Riverdale, at the Hawthorne **Construction**[1] Company. Grandpa Stewart has volunteered to talk to a group of high school students about careers in construction. But Grandpa needs to know about the new methods of building that have been developed since he retired. So Grandpa meets the construction supervisor, Bill Myers. And Mr. Myers invites Grandpa to attend a **continuing education**[2] class where he can learn more.

ACT I

[There are the sounds of construction.]

Grandpa: I'm looking for Bill Myers. He's a supervisor with Hawthorne Construction Company?

Bill: I'm Bill Myers. Nice to meet you, Mr. . . . ?

Grandpa: My name is Malcolm Stewart. I telephoned this morning and made an appointment.

Bill: Yes, of course. Let's **step**[3] into my office. It's much quieter.

[They step inside his office.]

Bill: That's better. Now, how may I help you?

Grandpa: Well, Bill, I had my own construction company for a number of years.

Bill: **Oh, you did?**[4]

Grandpa: Yes. In fact, that's why I called you. I've been asked to visit some local high schools and talk to youngsters about my career in construction.

Bill: That sounds like a great thing to do.

Grandpa: I want to be able to talk about the **latest**[5] methods in construction. So, I came down here because I heard you are using many new methods on this job.

Bill: Yeah, we sure are. Excuse me, Mr. Stewart.

Grandpa: What's that?

[The computer prints out something.]

Bill: New **drawings**.[6] I asked for some changes this morning.

Grandpa: And the drawings are already done?

Bill: Sure. The computer gives us a lot of help with our drawings.

Grandpa: The construction business has changed **a great deal**[7] in the last few years.

---

[1] **construction** [kən struk´ shən]: the building of large structures, such as houses, buildings, bridges, and highways

[2] **continuing education**: education designed for people who have already completed a basic program of education leading to a degree

[3] **step**: enter

[4] **Oh, you did?** = Is that right?
This is a form of question tag. It is not a real question, but an informal way of responding to a statement that surprises or interests us.

[5] **latest** [lā´təst]: current; up to date

[6] **drawings**: construction plans; blueprints

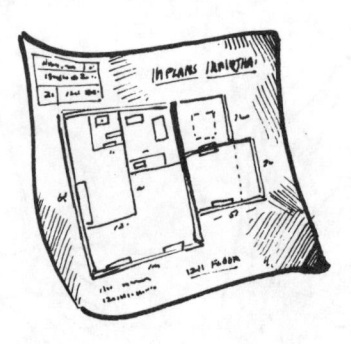

[7] **a great deal**: a lot of

	Bill:	Yes. We're using new **materials**[8] and new **methods**[9] that make the job go a lot faster. But let me show you around the construction **site**.[10]
40	Grandpa:	Great! Let's go
	[They go outside to the construction area.]	
	Grandpa:	It looks like you have **an awful lot**[11] of work to do before you're finished.
	Bill:	Well, this entire job should be finished **within six months.**[12]
	Grandpa:	Hu Ho! Buildings **go up**[13] much faster **nowadays.**[14] It used to take us much longer. You know, Bill, I want the kids I talk to to get the latest information. I would like to learn
50		more.
	Bill:	I have an idea. I teach a class in modern construction methods at the **community college**[15] on Thursdays at six o'clock. **You're welcome to attend**[16] any time you'd like.
	Grandpa:	Well, I've already got my engineering degree.
	Bill:	Lots of my students already have their degrees. I teach a continuing
60		education course.
	Grandpa:	Oh, really?
	Bill:	It's for people who want to keep learning about new things, even after they graduate from school.
	Grandpa:	*[He thinks.]* Huh! Maybe that would be good for me. **Perhaps**[17] I'll see you in class!

END OF ACT I

[8] **materials:** construction items such as concrete, wood, steel, and plastic
[9] **methods** [meth´ədz]: ways of doing something (in this case, ways of constructing)
[10] **site** [sīt]: an area designated for a special purpose: construction site, campsite, dumping site, etc.
[11] **an awful lot:** very much
[12] **within six months:** before six months have elapsed
[13] **go up:** are built
[14] **nowadays** [nau´ə dāz]: at the present time
[15] **community college:** a college where only the first two years of a college program are taught
A community college is sometimes called a "junior college." See **U.S. Life**.
[16] **You're welcome to attend . . .** = I invite you to attend. . .
[17] **perhaps:** maybe

U.S. LIFE

A very important part of the American educational system is the community college. These community-supported, two-year colleges serve many purposes. They provide the first two years of college courses for high school graduates who may not be able to afford to move out of their parents' homes to live at a four-year college, or who are not sure what subject area they wish to specialize in. Community colleges also offer a wide range of evening courses for working people who want to improve or "upgrade" their education, or who want to make a career change.

☞ YOUR TURN

- What type of courses are available in your country for people who want to change careers?
- Have you ever attended a community college in the U.S.? What courses did you take?

Focus In

An awful lot, like *a lot of*, is a quantitative expression that can be used with mass or count nouns in the affirmative:

a lot of coffee (mass noun)
a lot of chairs (count noun)

A great deal is used only with mass nouns.

a *great deal* of money (mass noun)

Remember that in the negative and the question forms we distinguish between mass and count nouns with the words *much* and *many*:

**How much coffee did you buy? I didn't buy *much*.
How many chairs do we need? We don't need *many*.**

INTRODUCTION TO ACT II

This time on TUNING IN THE U.S.A., we are at the Riverdale home of the Stewart family. Ellen Stewart is **at her sewing machine.**[1] Grandpa Stewart is on his way to a continuing education class. Grandpa is worried that he will be the oldest person in the class. Ellen tells him that age doesn't matter when it comes to learning. Once the class starts, Grandpa **realizes**[2] that he will enjoy continuing his education.

ACT II

[Ellen is using her sewing machine.]

Grandpa: *[calling]* Ellen!

Ellen: **Just a minute,**[3] Grandpa. I can't stop sewing right now.

Grandpa: *[He enters the room where she is sewing.]* Ellen, have you seen my blue shirt?

Ellen: Here it is. I was just fixing the front pocket.

Grandpa: Oh, I was looking **all over**[4] for it.

10 Ellen: You seem a little nervous. Is something wrong?

Grandpa: I don't know. I'm on my way to that class tonight at the community college.

Ellen: Oh, that's right! **Tonight's the night!**[5] You'll enjoy going back to school.

Grandpa: I may **find**[6] that I'm a little old for homework and studying.

Ellen: You're never too old to continue
20 your education, Grandpa.

Grandpa: I know.

Ellen: **You'll see.**[7] You'll be ahead of the younger students in one area.

Grandpa: And what might that be?

Ellen: You've had a **lifetime**[8] of **learning experiences.**[9]

Grandpa: *[He laughs.]* You're great, Ellen! And thanks for fixing my shirt pocket.

Ellen: Have a good time, Grandpa.

30 Grandpa: OK. See you later. *[He leaves.]*

---

[1] **at her sewing machine:** (working) at her sewing machine

[2] **realizes** [rē´ə līz əz]: discovers; understands

[3] **Just a minute.** = (informal) One moment, please. We use this expression to ask someone we know to wait while we do something.

[4] **all over:** everywhere
All over can also mean "finished."

The marathon race is *all over.*

[5] **Tonight's the night.** = short for: Tonight is the night you are going to school.
This expression refers to something already known by the person we are speaking to, and so there is no need to repeat it.

So, today's the day (you are getting married)!

[6] **find:** learn

[7] **You'll see.** = short for: "You'll see that I'm right."

[8] **lifetime:** the duration of a person's life

Margaret Mead devoted a lifetime to the study of primitive cultures.

[9] **learning experiences:** events in real life which teach us something (as opposed to learning in a created environment like a classroom).

[At the school, later that evening]

Bill: I'd like to welcome two new **members**[10] to our class tonight. Mildred Stern and Malcolm Stewart. Would each of you tell us a little about yourself and let us know why you're here.

Grandpa: [He clears his throat.] Hello, everyone. My name is Malcolm Stewart.

[They all greet him.]

Grandpa: I had my own construction company. I'm retired now. I'm about to start visiting high schools to discuss careers with young people. I met Bill earlier this week, and he invited me to learn more about **today's**[11] construction methods. So, that's why I'm here.

Bill: Thank you, Malcolm. Mildred?

Mildred:: I'm Mildred Stern. And I'm sixty-five years old. My husband and I have always wanted to buy an old house and fix it up. And we just bought one!

Bill: **Good for you,**[12] Mildred. Now, I want to begin tonight's class with a discussion of modern **heating**[13] technologies. There are two basic **systems**[14]...

[Later, at the Stewarts' house]

Grandpa: [He enters.] Hello, Ellen. I thought I might find you here—at the sewing machine.

Ellen: Oh, Grandpa! How was your class?

Grandpa: It was fine. [joking] I thought I'd be fifty years older than everybody in the class. But I wasn't at all. There was a woman named Mildred Stern, and she just bought a house...

END OF ACT II

[10] **members:** persons who belong to an organization, in this case, a class

[11] **today's:** modern

[12] **Good for you.** = Congratulations.

[13] **heating:** providing warmth to a home or building through some energy source such as natural gas, coal, oil, or electricity.

[14] **systems [sisˊtəmz]:** methods
A *system* is a group of components working together for a common purpose: communication *system*; sewage *system*; planetary *system*, etc.

U.S. LIFE

In the United States the attitude that learning stops when we graduate from high school or college has given way to the idea that education is a goal in itself and can be a lifelong experience. During the past 20 years, continuing education departments (also called adult education) have sprung up in school districts all over the country. Grade school and high school buildings that were normally closed in the evenings and on weekends have opened their doors to evening and weekend classes for curious, motivated, career-minded students, many of whom have not seen the inside of a classroom for 15 to 30 years!

☞ YOUR TURN

Do you think education is for the young only or also for "the young at heart"?

Focus In

Ellen says,

"You seem nervous. Is something wrong?"

After Grandpa explains why he's nervous, Ellen says,

"There's nothing to worry about."

If you want someone to feel better, one way to do it is to say "There's nothing to worry about."

Activities

Here are some activities to help you check your understanding of this program.

THE OLD DAYS

Grandpa is telling the class about the old days when he had his own construction company. He is remembering some of the people who worked for him. See if you can fill in the blanks from the words provided below.

| was careful | knew big machines | put in long hours | knew architecture |

1. Grandpa: "When it came to *drawing plans*, nobody _____ as well as Charlie Peterson."
2. Grandpa: "When it came to *operating heavy equipment*, nobody _____ as well as Big Bill Olmstead."
3. Grandpa: "When it came to *working overtime*, nobody _____ as well as Walt Campbell."
4. Grandpa: "When it came to *walking on girders high above the street*, nobody _____ like Jimmy Little Bear."

THE CLASS SCHEDULE

Grandpa liked the community college so well he signed up for some more classes. Here is his weekly schedule. Use it to answer the questions below.

	MON	TUES	WED	THURS	FRI	SAT
6 P.M.	Construction Methods		Construction Methods		Construction Methods	Modern Marketing
7 P.M.		Computer Literacy		Shakespearean Poetry		
8 P.M.						
9 P.M.						

1. Which class meets three times a week? _____
2. Which class is the longest? _____
3. Which class meets the most hours per week? _____
4. How many hours does Grandpa attend school each week? _____

A GREAT DEAL OF/AN AWFUL LOT OF/MUCH/MANY

Here are some notes Grandpa took in his Construction Methods class. Use the words above to fill in the blanks.

- _____ improvements made recently in modern construction methods
- used to take _____ time to put up a building
- doesn't take as _____ time anymore
- companies don't use as _____ men as they once did
- construction now requires _____ money

PROGRAM 44

"They're Playing Our Song"

ACT I

In this program, you will study...

VOCABULARY

Do you know the meaning of these words from Program 44?

fiddle
string quartet
whenever

GRAMMAR AND EXPRESSIONS

Do you know what these phrases or expressions mean?

uh-huh
That's the point.
There you go!

ACT II

PRONUNCIATION

Do you know how to pronounce this word?

Greenwich

Hint: The "w" is silent.

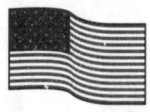

U.S. LIFE

Do you know what kind of music comes from New Orleans? From the Appalachian Mountain region? From the plains states?

☞ YOUR TURN

Think of a type of music specific to your *country*. Is there one city or region it makes you think of when you hear it?

"They're Playing Our Song" ▶ 103

Here is the complete script with study material of Program 44. Use these materials before *or* after you listen.

INTRODUCTION TO ACT I

Today on TUNING IN THE U.S.A., Alexandra and her cousin Andreas are listening to some tape recordings. Andreas made the tapes on his recent trip around the United States. He explains to Alexandra how he discovered America through its many kinds of music. He plays a tape of some music from San Antonio, Texas. Then he remembers one important place he forgot to record.

Act I

Andreas: Ready for a surprise, Alexandra?
Alexandra: **Uh-huh.**[1]
Andreas: **Tah-dah!**[2] Music from all around America.
Alexandra: Andreas! There must be a hundred cassette tapes in this suitcase.
Andreas: Eighty-six, to be exact. What would you like to hear?
Alexandra: *[reading the labels on the tape recordings]* Well . . . "West Virginia: **fiddle**[3] music." "Colorado: **Boy Scout**[4] Jam-bor-ee?"
Andreas: That means, "get-together," "festival."
Alexandra: Hmm. Andreas, there are so many different kinds of music here. **I don't know where to begin.**[5]
Andreas: **Pick**[6] anything. Music is the universal language. That's what I tell my radio audience.
Alexandra: Hey, **you just gave me an idea.**[7] I'll **pretend**[8] I'm a student back in Greece, and I'm **tuning in**[9] to listen to my favorite college radio show.
Andreas: Oh, you mean *my* radio show?
Alexandra: Right. Pretend you're at the radio station.
Andreas: Okay. Listen. "Good evening, everyone. Recently, I took a trip and tried to discover America through its music." *[He puts a tape into the cassette player.]* "It had been a hot,

[1] **uh-huh** [ə hə´]: slang for "yes"
[2] **Tah-dah!** [ta da] = Here it is!
[3] **fiddle:** violin
[4] **Boy Scout**
The Boy Scouts of America is an organization for young men which teaches leadership and social responsibility.

[5] **I don't know where to begin.** = I don't know how to go about it (getting the music I want).
[6] **pick:** choose; select
[7] **You just gave me an idea.** = What you said made me think of a solution.
[8] **pretend:** act as if; make believe
[9] **tuning in:** turning on the radio and finding the program you want

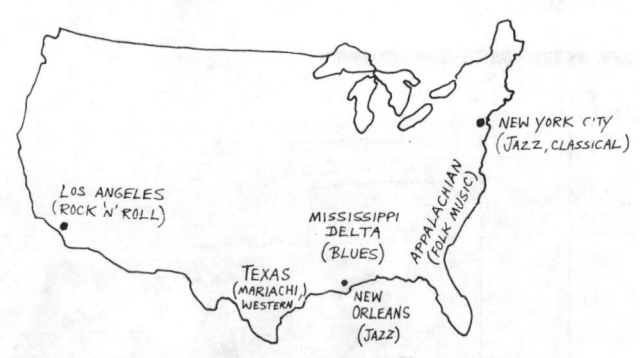

Some of the regions of the U.S. and the music associated with them

dry day, and I decided to take a **stroll**[10] in the park after dinner. There were lots of other people who **had the same idea,**[11] including this group of musicians..."

[Mexican music]

Alexandra: [She interrupts.] They sound Mexican.

Andreas: They are. **I was just getting to that part.**[12] "San Antonio has a very big Mexican population. Just listen to that sound."

[The music continues.]

Andreas: "And now, **adios**[13] from San Antonio, Texas!"

Alexandra: It'll be a great radio show, Andreas!

Andreas: Thanks. You know, **whenever**[14] I hear that music, I feel as if I *am* in San Antonio. I can remember what the air smelled like, what the food tasted like.

Alexandra: I felt I was there, too. Where else do you have music from?

Andreas: All over. Pick a place.

Alexandra: Let me think. **I've got it.**[15] I want to hear the music that will make me think of New York City.

Andreas: New York City? Alexandra, I forgot to record New York City!

Alexandra: But, Andreas, you're going back to Greece the day after tomorrow. You can't go without recording New York!

Andreas: You're right. Grab your coat. Let's go to the city.

END OF ACT I

[10] **stroll** [strōl]: a leisurely walk for exercise or to see sights

[11] **... had the same idea** = ... were doing the same thing

[12] **I was just getting to that part.** = I was about to explain that.

[13] **adios:** Spanish for "good-bye"

[14] **whenever:** any time

[15] **I've got it.** = I have an idea.

U.S. LIFE

Just as they brought their cuisine, customs, and language with them to the places they settled in, immigrants to America also brought their music. Immigrants to the mid-Atlantic seaboard and Appalachian Mountains, many of whom came from the British Isles, brought their Celtic folk music and dances. You might still hear and see a "Virginia reel" being danced at a festival in this region. The southern states, where blacks were prominent, heard the lament of "the blues." From the vast central region of the country came "country and western," a folk music form made popular in the social protest songs of Woodie Guthrie. These regional musical forms were the basis for much of America's popular music, including rock 'n' roll.

YOUR TURN

- Why do you think American music has become popular in other countries of the world?
- Which musical forms do you think are truly international? Rock 'n' roll? Classical? Jazz? Country and western?

Focus In

The word *whenever* means "it's not important when."

Andreas: You know, *whenever* I hear that music I feel as if I am in San Antonio.

So, *whenever* Andreas wants to feel like he is in San Antonio, he can play that music.

When can he play that music?

Whenever ... right now, or *whenever* he wants to.

INTRODUCTION TO ACT II

This time on TUNING IN THE U.S.A., *Alexandra and her cousin Andreas are in New York City. Andreas is planning to return to Greece soon. He has his tape recorder with him. And he's recording music for his radio program in Greece. Andreas is searching for the music that will represent New York, the most famous of all American cities.*

ACT II

[*Traffic noise. Alexandra and Andreas are walking.*]

Alexandra: Where are we going now, Andreas?

Andreas: I thought we'd head downtown to **Greenwich Village.**[1] You're getting tired, aren't you, Alexandra?

Alexandra: I'm not getting tired, but I'm confused. We don't know what kind of music we're looking for.

Andreas: **But that's the point!**[2] We're here to *discover* the music. Sometimes you just have to let the music find *you*.

Alexandra: It's not that. The problem is that **every time we turn around,**[3] we find a different kind of music.

Andreas: I know. [*He laughs.*] It seems that every neighborhood has a sound of its own.

Alexandra: Why are you laughing? It's not funny. We've almost used up all your blank recording tape.

Andreas: I can always get more tape. Remember that **string quartet**[4] we heard playing Mozart on Fifth Avenue?

Alexandra: Yeah. And then we sat in Central Park, and there was that guy playing the harmonica.

Andreas: How about Greenwich Village? Who knows what we'll hear if we go there?

Alexandra: OK. I'm just worried that you won't find *the one* sound that will always mean New York when you hear it. And Andreas, **what about your radio show**[5] back in Greece?

Andreas: Alexandra, I already have all the music I'll need right here.

---

[1] **Greenwich Village** [gre´nitch vil´ij]: neighborhood that includes the lower west side of the borough of Manhattan in New York City

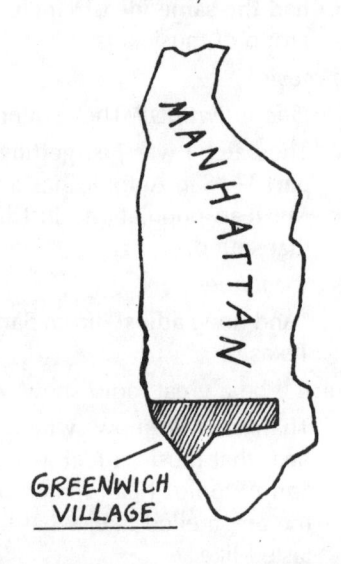

[2] **But that's the point.** = That's exactly what I am trying to say.
This expression is a way of resolving a disagreement between two people by redefining the problem.

A: I don't want to waste money on a new TV.
B: But *that's the point!* If we don't buy a new TV we'll waste a lot of money repairing this old one.

[3] **every time we turn around:** constantly
This expression conveys frustration at not being able to keep up with events.

Every time I turn around there are more weeds in the garden!

[4] **string quartet:** a musical ensemble composed of only stringed instruments, usually a violin, a viola, a cello, and a bass violin

[5] **What about (your radio show)?** = What will happen (to your radio show)?

Alexandra: But we've recorded so many different kinds of music today. What kind of New York radio program will that be?

40 Andreas: A great New York radio program—**that's what it will be.**[6] Look around you. What kind of person do you see?

Alexandra: Well, from this street corner I see . . . people from all over the world.

Andreas: **There you go!**[7] Just like the music we've heard. Come on, Alexandra. Let's take a subway ride downtown. *[They enter a subway station.]*

Andreas: Downtown trains—that way.

50 Alexandra: Hey, look, Andreas! More musicians. Come on.

Andreas: *[He speaks to a musician.]* Hello there. Are you going to sing right here?

Musician: Yup. This is our **regular spot.**[8]

Andreas: Would you mind if I recorded your music?

Musician: OK. Just don't expect to get the whole song.

Andreas: Why not?

60 Musician: You'll see. *[He speaks to his band.]* Ready, everyone? One, two, three . . .

[The musicians begin to sing and play a song. However, after a little while, a train pulls into the station and drowns out the music.]

END OF ACT II

[6] **That's what it will be.**
The use of *that's what* + (repeat of an antecedent clause) is used to make an answer more emphatic.
Q: What will I do if I lose my job?
A: You'll find another job, *that's what you'll do!*

[7] **There you go!** = That's right!

[8] **regular spot:** usual place

U.S. LIFE

Greenwich Village, the area in lower Manhattan around Washington Square, has been the home of many artists and musicians over the years. In the early 1960s, a young man from a small town in Minnesota came here to play his unique music in the coffee houses of "the Village," as it is popularly known. Bob Dylan's music was a unique blend of country and blues, and his words seemed to remind America of a time when life was simpler and material possessions were not important. Whether such a time ever existed is hard to say, but Dylan's music, inspired by America's regional folk music heritage, connected the country to its past.

Focus In

Sometimes we can make a suggestion with the words *how about*. When Andreas says, "How about Greenwich Village," he is asking Alexandra, "Do you want to go to Greenwich Village?" We can often leave out the verb with *how about*:

How about Greenwich Village? =
How about going to Greenwich Village?

☞ YOUR TURN

- Have you ever visited Greenwich Village?
- Have you heard street musicians there or in the subways?

Activities

Here are some activities to help you check your understanding of this program.

AN AMERICAN FOLK SONG

Here are the lines to a well-known American folk song, "Bicycle Built for Two," composed in the 1890s by Harry Dacre, an English immigrant to the U.S. Use the phrases in the boxes below to fill in the blanks in the song.

| On the seat, | I can't afford a carriage, | I'm half crazy, | All for the love of you! |

Daisy, Daisy

Give me your answer, do!

_____

_____

It won't be a stylish marriage,

_____

But you'll look sweet,

_____

On a bicycle built for two!

DO YOU KNOW *WHAT THE QUESTION WAS?*

Answer these questions with "I don't know . . ." Look at the example. Be sure to use affirmative word order in your answers.

1. What does "jamboree" mean? *I don't know what "jamboree" means.*
2. Where does Bob Dylan live now? _____.
3. How many songs did he write? _____.
4. Why can't you sing in tune? _____.
5. When does the concert begin? _____.

AMERICAN MUSICOLOGIST

A musicologist [myü´zi käl´ə jəst] is someone who studies about music. Take this quiz on American music and see how good a musicologist you are.

1. Music which came from America's black culture is:
    a. the blues   b. country and western   c. mariachi
2. The city where many country and western recording artists record their music is:
    a. Detroit   b. Nashville   c. New York City
3. Bob Dylan is a:
    a. concert pianist   b. folk and pop music artist   c. native of New York City
4. The music of the American Southwest is heavily infuenced by:
    a. Puerto Ricans   b. Italian immigrants   c. Mexicans

PROGRAM 45

"Campus Life"

In this program, you will study...

ACT I

VOCABULARY

Do you know the meaning of these words from Program 45?

major subject
dormitory
exchange student

GRAMMAR AND EXPRESSIONS

Do you know what these phrases or expressions mean?

mix and match
best friends
change your mind

PRONUNCIATION

Do you know how to pronounce these four-syllable words?

astronomy
convenient

Hint: The accent is on the second syllable in each word.

ACT II

U.S. LIFE

Do you know who stays in a dormitory?

☞ YOUR TURN

Have you ever shared an apartment with roommates? What did you like/dislike about it?

"Campus Life" ▶ 109

110 ◀ PROGRAM 45

Here is the complete script with study material for Program 45. Use these materials before *or* after you listen.

INTRODUCTION TO ACT I

Today on **TUNING IN THE U.S.A**, *Robbie and Alexandra are visiting Teresa Molina at Columbia University. Alexandra is living with Teresa's family in Riverdale while she is going to high school in the United States. She is curious about American colleges, and Robbie thinks that he might like to attend this college. After going to Teresa's* **astronomy**[1] *class, they eat lunch in the college cafeteria and talk about college life.*

ACT I

Professor: All right, class. We know that the earth is the **fifth largest**[2] planet and that it's the third planet from the sun. *[She writes on the blackboard.]* What about the temperature of the earth's interior? *[She calls on Teresa to answer the question.]* Teresa Molina.

Teresa: It's extremely hot. Scientists know that the temperature of the earth rises one degree **for every**[3] one hundred and fifty feet in depth. At the **core**[4] of the earth, the temperature is extremely high. Right now, estimates are that the temperature may be . . .

[After class, in the cafeteria]

Alexandra: Teresa, you sure were **good**[5] in that astronomy class.

Teresa: Thanks, Alexandra. I'm glad you and Robbie could visit today.

Robbie: Alexandra says you're planning to study astronomy as your major subject.

Teresa: Right now, I think I want to be an astronomer.

Robbie: Maybe after you graduate, you'll work in the **space program!**[6]

Teresa: Maybe. But I'm only a first-year student. I have almost four years left until I get my degree.

Robbie: That is a long time. What happens if you **change your mind**[7] and decide not to be an astronomer?

Teresa: Then I change my **major subject**[8] and study something else. Until then, I'm taking a lot of science courses. I have to learn physics and mathematics. And some people say I should study chemistry—and even biology.

Robbie: Biology? Plants and animals?

---

[1] **astronomy** [əs trän′ə mē]: the field of science which deals with the planets and stars

[2] **fifth largest**: ranking fifth in size of all planets

[3] **. . . for every . . .**
This expression establishes a mathematical one-to-one relationship between two things.

The Recycling Center pays one cent *for every* can you turn in.

[4] **core**: center

[5] **good**: intelligent

[6] **space program**: the program of the United States run by the National Aeronautics and Space Administration (NASA) for space exploration

[7] **change your mind**: change your attitude, plans, or opinion about something

I'm glad she *changed her mind* about getting married after she finishes high school.

[8] **major subject**: area of study one concentrates in
His *major subject* is World Literature.

	Teresa:	Well . . . some astronomers **design**[9] experiments to look for life on **other**[10] planets.
40		
	Alexandra:	Life on **another**[10] planet? What does your professor say about that?
	Teresa:	Not much. We haven't gotten to that yet.
	Robbie:	Hey, speaking of life on another planet, this tomato soup was out of this world.
	Teresa:	[She laughs.] I'm glad you liked it. The food here is good.
50	Robbie:	And it's cheap. My whole lunch cost only three dollars.
	Teresa:	Well, this *is* a university cafeteria. There are no waiters. You get the food yourself. And when you're done, you **clean up after yourself.**[11] So it's not very expensive here.
	Alexandra:	Teresa, does every college student eat in a cafeteria and live in a **dormitory**?[12]
60	Teresa:	Oh, no! Fewer than half the students live in dormitories. I like living in a dorm. It's so **convenient.**[13] It's close to everything on campus.
	Paul:	[passing by] Hey, Teresa!
	Teresa:	Hi, Paul! See you in physics class! [She speaks to Alexandra and Robbie.] That's my **lab**[14] partner. Now, he lives at home with his parents. Next year, he'll get an apartment and share it with a roommate.
70		
	Alexandra:	**I wish we could meet your roommate.**[15]
	Teresa:	Well, actually, I've got three roommates. Let's **clear off the table**[16] and go to the dorm. We'll see who's there.

END OF ACT I

[9] **design** [də zīn´]: create a plan for something

[10] **other/another**
Note that *other* is used with plural nouns (*other planets*) and *another* is used with singular nouns (*another planet*).

[11] **clean up after yourself:** to clean up yourself a mess you make
She always made her children *clean up after themselves*.

[12] **dormitory:** a large residence hall for students at a college or university

PLAY ON WORDS

Robbie says, "Hey, speaking of life on another planet, this tomato soup was out of this world." We use this expression to say that something is so wonderful or strange that it must have come from beyond our world. Robbie is making a **play on words.** Astronomy class is about stars, which are literally "out of this world," and tomato soup is so good it's figuratively "out of this world" too!

[13] **convenient** [kən´vēn´yənt]: easy to use

[14] **lab:** laboratory

[15] **I wish we could meet your roommate.**
The verb *wish* is usually followed by a subordinate clause in which the verb is in the past tense (for present time actions) and in the past perfect tense (for past time actions).

I *wish* I knew her name. =
I would like to know her name. (present time)

I *wish* I had studied harder for the test. =
I'm sorry I didn't study harder for the test. (past time)

[16] **clear off the table:** remove the dishes from the table

U.S. LIFE

American universities offer students a wide variety of courses to choose form. In addition to courses in the major field of study, the student may choose *electives*, that is, courses that are not required. The first two years of study (freshman and sophomore years) are the same for most students. In their third and fourth (junior and senior) years, students take more courses in their major field and fewer electives.

YOUR TURN

What was your favorite subject in school?
Do you remember the teacher who taught you?

Focus In

When you study at an American college or university, your most important subject of study is your *major* subject. But *major* can also be a verb.

I'll change my major subject. = **I'll major in something else.**

INTRODUCTION TO ACT II

This time on TUNING IN THE U.S.A., *Robbie and Alexandra are visiting Teresa Molina at college. She shows them her room in the dormitory and introduces them to her roommate, Charlotte Washington. Teresa and Charlotte come from different parts of the United States and from very different* **backgrounds,**[1] *but they have become best friends. Robbie and Alexandra discover how new and exciting college life can be.*

ACT II

[Violin music]

Teresa: [She speaks to Robbie and Alexandra.] That's my roommate, Charlotte, playing the violin. **She's a music major.**[2]

[They knock on the door and enter Teresa's room.]

Teresa: Charlotte?
Charlotte: Oh, hi, Teresa.
Teresa: Charlotte, I want you to meet Alexandra Pappas.
Alexandra: Hello.
10 Charlotte: Hi. Come on in.
Teresa: She's a high school **exchange student**[3] from Greece. And she lives with my family. This is her friend Robbie Stewart.
Robbie: How do you do?
Charlotte: I'm Charlotte Washington.
Alexandra: This is a very nice room.
Teresa: This is just our **sitting room.**[4] It's part of a **suite**[5] of rooms. Behind
20 those doors there are two bedrooms. Charlotte and I share one. Serena and Cathy share the other.
Alexandra: They're your other roommates.
Teresa: Yes.
Charlotte: I call our suite of rooms "the little U.N."
Robbie: The little United Nations?
Charlotte: Yes. We come from so many parts of the country—and the world. You
30 see, Serena is from England. Cathy's family is Chinese-American. Teresa—well, you know Teresa. And, of course, my family is **African-American**[6]—from North Carolina.
Robbie: That's interesting.
Charlotte: The university thinks so, too. They try to **mix and match**[7] roommates.

[1] **backgrounds:** origins; prior situations
Our background is our personal history, which is considered to have a strong influence on the way we behave, think, and feel.

[2] **She's a music major.** = She's majoring in music. College students often identify each other by what subject they are majoring in.

He's a math major. She's an art major.

[3] **exchange student:** student from another school or country
The word *exchange* comes from the idea that two students from different countries *exchange* places with each other in their schools, although this is not always done.

[4] **sitting room:** living room; place where visitors are received and entertained

[5] **suite** [swēt]: collection of rooms in a hotel or dormitory all part of the same residence

[6] **African-American:** American whose ancestors came from Africa

BOOKER T. WASHINGTON   MARTIN LUTHER KING

GEORGE WASHINGTON CARVER   SOJOURNER TRUTH

Famous African-Americans

[7] **mix and match:** to put together objects of different types

40		The four of us come from different places, but we're interested in a lot of the same things. And we all get along well.
	Teresa:	Actually, Serena and Cathy are so busy with classes, they're **hardly ever**[8] here. Most kids only use their room at night for studying and sleeping.
	Charlotte:	Except music students like me. *[She starts to play the violin again.]*
	Robbie:	You play beautifully. Do you come from a family of musicians?
50	Charlotte:	**Good heavens,**[9] no! My parents are factory workers in North Carolina. I'm the first **trained musician**[10] in the family.
	Teresa:	She's also the first to go to college.
	Charlotte:	*[She is slightly embarrassed.]* Teresa . . .
	Teresa:	I'm sorry. I didn't mean to embarrass you. *[teasing]* But you're my favorite roommate.
60	Charlotte:	*[She laughs.]* The fact is, we *are* **best friends.**[11] Oh, Teresa, it's almost two o'clock! Don't you have a class?
	Teresa:	I sure do. See you later, Charlotte. Come on, Robbie, Alexandra! We've got to **get going.**[12]
	Charlotte:	And I've got to practice. I'm glad to have met you.
	Robbie:	Nice to meet you, too.
	Alexandra:	Bye, Charlotte.
	[They leave and shut the door.]	
	Robbie:	You know, college looks really great.
70	Teresa:	It's a chance to get to know people very different from yourself.
	Alexandra:	People from different kinds of families and different parts of the world.
	Teresa:	Charlotte and I will be friends **forever.**[13]
	Robbie:	Hey, Alexandra. You know what?
	Alexandra:	No. What, Robbie?
	Robbie:	That sounds like us.

END OF ACT II

[8] **hardly ever:** almost never

[9] **Good heavens!**
This is a polite exclamation of surprise.

[10] **trained musician:** musician who has been educated in music technique and theory, as opposed to one who learned informally

[11] **best friends:** each other's favorite or most highly esteemed friend
Many people identify one friend above all others as being their *best friend*.

[12] **get going:** (informal) leave

[13] **forever:** without end

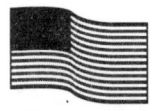

U.S. LIFE

A big part of the college experience is living on campus with other students. Many students love the freedom of living away from home in a dormitory with other students. Others find dormitory life regimented and have a hard time retaining their individuality. Fraternities, sororities (men's and women's social organizations), and other campus clubs offer students a chance to develop their own special interests and to socialize with students who have similar interests. This can be important at a university of 40,000 students—about the population of an average size town!

☞ YOUR TURN

- Do you belong to any social organizations?
- Do you think a college student should spend time in social organizations as well as "hit the books"?

Focus In

Charlotte says, "**The university *thinks so, too*.**"
This is a way to agree.

**She plays the violin well.
I think so, too.**

Activities

Here are some activities to help you check your understanding of this program.

ROBBIE'S WISHING WELL

In Episode 41 we saw that Robbie was worried about college. He's so worried now that he's talking to himself. Make sentences that start with "I wish..." Look at the example.

Robbie: "I didn't study hard in high school." **I wish I had studied hard in high school.**

1. Robbie: "I can't decide which college to attend."_____.
2. Robbie: "I don't have enough self-confidence."_____.
3. Robbie: "There are too many colleges to choose from."_____.
4. Robbie: "I didn't use my time well in school."_____.

SOCIAL REGISTER

There are many expressions in English that mean the same thing. The greeting "Hi" means the same thing as "Hello," but it is *less formal than "Hello."* Look at the categories below. Under each one are three expressions that all mean about the same thing. Label them 1 (most formal), 2 (less formal) and 3 (informal).

Greetings
____ Hi.
____ How are you today?
____ Hello.

Introductions
____ I'd like you to meet Mary.
____ This is Mary.
____ Meet Mary.

Requests
____ Please turn the music down.
____ Would you please turn down the music.
____ Would you mind turning down the music.

Surprise
____ My goodness!
____ Wow!
____ That's amazing!

Apologies
____ Oops.
____ Sorry.
____ I'm so sorry.

Salutations
____ Nice meeting you.
____ It was a pleasure meeting you.
____ So long.

PROGRAM 46

"The Volunteers"

In this program, you will study . . .

ACT I

VOCABULARY

Do you know the meaning of these words from Program 46?

general store
alarm
volunteer

GRAMMAR AND EXPRESSIONS

Do you know what these phrases or expressions mean?

Now hold on.
any minute
get in the way

PRONUNCIATION

Do you know how to pronounce these words?

siren
signal

ACT II

U.S. LIFE

Do you know which state of the United States is called "The Volunteer State?"

☞ YOUR TURN

Have you ever had to call the fire department in an emergency?

"The Volunteers" ▶ 115

Here is the complete script with study material for Program 46. Use these materials before *or* after you listen.

INTRODUCTION TO ACT I

Today on TUNING IN THE U.S.A., *Richard is in a **general store**[1] in a small town in Pennsylvania. He's buying some rolls of film. Just as he is about to leave the store, there is a sudden **alarm**[2]—a **siren**.[3] It's the **signal**[4] sent out to all the **volunteer**[5] firefighters from the local fire station. The store owner is a volunteer fireman, and he must leave quickly to help put out the fire. Richard asks to go along with him.*

ACT I

Store Owner: There you go. *[He counts the rolls of film.]* Eight, nine, and ten. You got my last ten rolls of photographic film. This is a small town here. I've never sold so many rolls in one day.

Richard: And I've never **run out**[6] of film so quickly. I guess that's because there are lots of interesting things to photograph in Pennsylvania.

10 Store Owner: Is taking pictures **your business**?[7]

Richard: Yes. I'm a professional photographer. I'm working on a book about America. I've been traveling around the country for over a month.

Store Owner: Just taking pictures?

Richard: Just taking pictures.

Store Owner: Hmm. Where are you from?

Richard: New York.

20 Store Owner: The Big City.... Now, there's a different way of life.

Richard: Mmm-hmm. It's no small town!

Store Owner: Let me **ring up**[8] your order. *[He uses the cash register.]* All right. Ten rolls **at**[9] three dollars and fifty cents a roll. That's thirty-five, plus tax, **makes**[10] thirty-six, seventy-five.

Richard: Here you go. Thirty-six dollars and seventy-five cents... exactly.

30 Store Owner: Thank you for shopping at Elmer's General Store. I hope you come back sometime.

[A fire alarm sounds.]

Richard: What does that siren mean?

Store Owner: *[He is serious.]* That's a fire. *[His beeper sounds.]* And that's my call from the firehouse. I'm going to have to **close up**[11] the store right now.

---

[1] **general store:** country store that stocks a wide variety of items

[2] **alarm [ə lärm´]:** loud noise made by an electronic instrument to alert people to a danger: fire *alarm*; burglar *alarm*; car *alarm*

Types of alarms

[3] **siren [sī´rən]:** a type of alarm that makes a shrill whistle that varies in pitch

[4] **signal [sig´nəl]:** a sound or gesture that has a special meaning
With a silent wave of his hand, the lieutenant gave his men the *signal* to go forward.

[5] **volunteer [vä lən tēr´]:** person who performs a service without pay

[6] **run out:** to use up

[7] **your business:** what you do for a living

[8] **ring up:** record on the cash register

[9] **at:** at the price of

[10] **makes:** adds up to

[11] **close up [klōz əp]:** close to business
Remember that the adjective *close* (near) is pronounced [klōs].

"The Volunteers" ▶ 117

Richard:	Are *you* going to **fight a fire?**[12]
Store Owner:	Yup. I'm a volunteer fireman. **Now hold on.**[13] **Any minute**[14] they'll be telling me the location of the fire.

[He waits for the beeper.]

Voice on beeper:	Structure fire at 37 Cooper Street.
Store Owner:	That's it!
Voice on beeper:	That's 37 Cooper Street. Structure fire.
Richard:	You're going there right now?
Store Owner:	Just as fast as I can drive there.
Richard:	Would you mind if I came with you?
Store Owner:	Are you trained to fight fires, too?
Richard:	No. But I'm trained to photograph them.
Store Owner:	Well, as long as you're careful and you don't **get in the way,**[15] I guess it's okay. Let's get going.

[They leave the store and get into the store owner's car.]

Voice on beeper:	Structure fire at 37 Cooper Street.
Store Owner:	All over town, men—and even a few women—are answering this call. They're stopping work and **jumping in**[16] their cars, all heading to the same place.
Richard:	How many volunteers are there in this town?
Store Owner:	About thirty. We could use a few more. We're all volunteer firefighters. We don't get paid for what we do. In a town **this size,**[17] there isn't enough money to pay full-time firefighters.

[A car approaches.]

Store Owner:	See this car passing us just now?
Richard:	It says Fred's Pizza on the side. Is he a firefighter, too?
Store Owner:	Freddy? He's our **fire chief.**[18]

END OF ACT I

Focus In

Sometimes *as long as* means *if*.

Richard: Would you mind if I came with you.
Store Owner: Well, as long as you're careful . . .

This means Richard can come along *if* he's careful.

[12] **fight a fire:** try to put out a fire
[13] **Now hold on.** = Wait a minute.
[14] **any minute . . .** = very soon
[15] **get in the way:** obstruct the work (of someone); be a nuisance to (someone)
 Be careful not to *get in the way* of the tree cutters. You might get hurt.
[16] **jumping in:** getting into
[17] **this size:** this small
[18] **fire chief:** head of the fire department

U.S. LIFE

Volunteerism—performing social service for a community or a worthy cause—has played a large part in the development of the United States. One state—Tennessee—is nicknamed "The Volunteer State." Almost every city and town in the country has its social service clubs and organizations that sponsor fund-raising activities such as dinners, picnics, and festivals to raise money for hospitals, schools and other charitable causes. The Federal Government recognizes the value of volunteerism and encourages it actively. Donations to charities are tax-deductible; that is, the dollar value of the donation is subtracted from the giver's taxable income.

Some of the voluntary service organizations in a U.S. city

☞ YOUR TURN

Do you believe that some services should be provided by social service organizations, or do you think the services should be provided by government agencies with money obtained through taxes?

INTRODUCTION TO ACT II

*This time on TUNING IN THE U.S.A., Richard is in a small town in Pennsylvania. He has the chance to photograph some volunteer firefighters at work. They are putting out the flames of a fire in Amy Clark's kitchen. The firefighters save Amy's house. And she is very **thankful**[1] —so thankful that the volunteer firefighters will gain a new member.*

ACT II

[The sound of sirens]

Store Owner: Here we are. I know this **place**.[2] This is Amy Clark's place. Uh-oh, it looks like her kitchen **caught on fire**.[3]

Freddy: *[calling]* Hey, Elmer! You got an **extra**[4] pair of gloves with you?

Store Owner: Sure thing, Chief. Here in the back of my truck. There should be a pair. . . . Yes, here they are. Is it Amy's kitchen?

Freddy: Yup. She was cooking something, and she had a kitchen fire.

Store Owner: It looks like **the fire's almost under control**.[5]

Freddy: It was a small fire. And the **pumper**[6] truck got here really fast. We've got it under control. I just have to check the electrical wires before I can **make out**[7] my report. Thanks for the gloves, Elmer.

Store Owner: Right, Chief. *[He speaks to Richard.]* Well, Richard, a little kitchen fire. **It's not much for picture-taking.**[8] I hope you're not disappointed.

Richard: I'm not at all disappointed. It's a **happy ending**[9] to a story that might have been unhappy.

Store Owner: It could have been a lot worse!

Richard: Hey, there's an idea for a picture! See? That volunteer has a **kitten**.[10]

Store Owner: Where?

Richard: There—leaning out of the smoky window with a kitten. I've got to get that picture! *[He starts to take photographs.]*

---

[1] **thankful** [thank´fəl]: grateful

[2] **place:** home

[3] **caught on fire**
To catch fire or *to catch on fire* are the most common expressions to say that a fire started somewhere.

[4] **extra** [ek´strə]: in addition to the minimum necessary
Luckily, we had some *extra* water to give the neighbors after the earthquake.

[5] **The fire's almost under control . . .** = The fire is not out, but it is manageable.

[6] **pumper:** the fire truck that pumps water through hoses to put out a fire

[7] **make out:** fill out; complete

[8] **It's not much for picture-taking.** = It doesn't provide interesting subjects for pictures.
The informal expression *not much for* + noun indicates that someone or something is not suitable or inclined for a given purpose:

She's not much for dancing. (She isn't good at dancing, or: she doesn't like dancing.)

[9] **happy ending:** the successful solution to a problem or a dilemma in which someone was in danger

The movie had a *happy ending*.

[10] **kitten:** a young cat

	Amy:	It's lucky the fire was only in the kitchen.
	Freddy:	And your cat will be just fine, Amy.
40	Amy:	Freddy—**or should I say**[11] Chief? I want you to tell all your men and women how much I appreciate what they did.
	Freddy:	I'll be sure to tell them.
	Amy:	They saved my house! I tried to **slow down the fire**[12] by myself, but I couldn't stop it. You firefighters got here so fast! You know, last month, Elmer came around asking for a **donation.**[13] **I'm awfully glad**[14] I gave some money.
50	Store Owner:	And we appreciate your donation. It helped us buy our new communications system.
	Amy:	And that helped save my house!
[Her cat starts to meow.]		
	Amy:	And my cat.
	Store Owner:	Oh, this is my friend . . . uh . . .
	Richard:	Richard Stewart.
	Store Owner:	He's a photographer—a professional—from New York.
60	Richard:	I took a picture of one of the volunteers saving your cat.
	Amy:	You know, I've thought of joining the volunteer fire department. But I never **felt**[15] that I had the time.
	Freddy:	A lot of people say that. But someone has to do it. **We make time for it.**[16]
	Amy:	And, thank goodness, you do, Chief. You know, I think I'll make time for it now.
[Richard takes a picture of them.]		
70	Chief:	That would be great, Amy. We practice **fire drills**[17] first Wednesday of every month. We hope to see you at the firehouse next week—right after **supper.**[18]

END OF ACT II

Focus In

The word *check* sometimes means "see" or "examine." Freddy says, **"It was a small fire . . . I just have to check the electrical wires before I can make out my report."** This means he has to see if the wires are okay.

[11] **or should I say . . . ?** = should I call you . . . ?
[12] **slow down the fire:** keep the fire from spreading, from growing bigger
[13] **donation:** money or object given at no cost to a charity or other social organization
He always gives a large *donation* at Christmas time to the Children's Hospital.
[14] **I'm awfully glad . . .** = I'm very glad . . .
[15] **felt:** thought
[16] **We make time for it.** = We fit it into our schedule.
[17] **fire drills:** exercises in which firefighters practice their response to a fire
Fire drills are also held in offices and public buildings. In this case the occupants of the building practice filing out of the building in an orderly and pre-planned way.
[18] **supper:** a late afternoon or evening meal
Supper and *dinner* are often used interchangeably.

U.S. LIFE

A volunteer fire department (VFD) can be an important organization, especially in rural areas far from state or county fire stations. Volunteer fire departments are staffed by local residents who go through a training program usually conducted by a professional firefighter. The VFD raises money for its operations through donations and fund-raising activities. State or county fire departments usually donate older trucks and equipment to the VFD. VFDs are often staffed by retirees or older residents of a community because young people may work longer hours and not have time. A VFD in a community can lower the rates residents pay for their fire insurance, because the insurance company considers the area to have a lower fire risk.

YOUR TURN

Have you ever seen a VFD in action? Did the firefighters manage to put out the fire?

Activities

Here are some activities to help you check your understanding of this program.

CAPTION THE PHOTOS

Here are some of the photos Richard has taken during his trip around America. Can you think of captions for them? The first one is done for you. Your answers may vary.

1. In the Northwest, you can go for trips on horseback.

2. With a _____, you can _____.

3. A recycling center makes it possible to _____.

4. In a National Forest, _____.

5. In a small town in the Northwest, _____.

6. In _____, in "the Motor City," _____.

PROGRAM 47

"The Life Of Riley"

In this program, you will study . . .

ACT I

VOCABULARY

Do you know the meaning of these words from Program 47?

retirement community
activity room
active

GRAMMAR AND EXPRESSIONS

Do you know what these phrases or expressions mean?

take a look
You made it!
Couldn't be better.

PRONUNCIATION

Do you know how to pronounce this word?

retirement

ACT II

U.S. LIFE

Do you know what a retirement community is?

☞ YOUR TURN

What plans do you have for your retirement?

"The Life Of Riley" ▶ 121

Here is the complete script with study material for Program 47. Use these materials before *or* after you listen.

INTRODUCTION TO ACT I

Today on TUNING IN THE U.S.A., *Grandpa and Ellen learn that some older neighbors are moving to a retired persons' community. The neighbors, Sam and Pauline Wolf, come to say good-bye. Grandpa is happy that he lives with his family, and he doesn't think that he would like to live in a* **retirement community.**[1] *But when the Wolfs invite him to come visit them at their new home, Grandpa decides to go* **take a look.**[2]

ACT I

[Ellen plays the piano.]

Grandpa: *[He speaks into the telephone.]* Oh, no, Sam. Sure we are. Please, come on over. We'll be here. Good-bye. *[He hangs up the phone.]* Well, that's a shame.

Ellen: *[She stops playing the piano.]* Is something the matter?

Grandpa: That was Sam Wolf on the phone. He says he and Pauline are moving to a retirement community. A place called Cedar Hills.

Ellen: It's probably a very nice place.

Grandpa: Well, I'm glad I'm living with my family, Ellen. I don't think I'd be as happy in a retirement community.

Ellen: *[She laughs.]* Oh, Grandpa, **what do you know about**[3] retirement communities. They're probably wonderful places to live. *[She continues to play the piano.]* Did I hear you ask Sam and Pauline to stop by?

Grandpa: Yes, they want to **pay us a visit**[4]—to say good-bye. I'm going to **miss**[5] them.

Ellen: What time will they be here?

Grandpa: Oh, in a few minutes. They said they were leaving the house now.

Ellen: I'm going to the kitchen to make a **fresh**[6] pot of coffee. *[She leaves.]*

[The doorbell rings. Grandpa goes to the door and opens it.]

Grandpa: Come in. Come in. Pauline, Sam, how are you?

---

[1] **retirement** [rē tīr′mənt] **community:** a private community for retired people. See **U.S. Life.**

[2] **take a look:** to go see for oneself; to check on something that one is curious about

[3] **What do you know about . . . ?** = You aren't qualified to say that . . .
We use this expression to criticize people who are expressing an opinion about something they know nothing about.

[4] **pay . . . a visit:** to visit

[5] **miss:** to be sad at no longer seeing someone or someplace
I sure *miss* Grandpa.
I *miss* Ohio in the springtime.

[6] **fresh:** (in reference to food) new; ripe; not preserved: *fresh* strawberries, *fresh* coffee, *fresh* fruit, *fresh* fish

	Pauline:	We're fine, and we're pretty excited about moving.
	Sam:	We hope this isn't **good-bye,**[7] Malcolm.
	Grandpa:	Come and sit down. Ellen is in the kitchen making some coffee.
40	Ellen:	*[She enters.]* No, she's not. She's right here, and the coffee is **brewing.**[8] Sam and Pauline, you two look great. You know, the neighborhood will **not be the same without you.**[9]
	Pauline:	Thank you, Ellen. But **it's time for us to move on.**[10] Both Sam and I are seventy years old. Our house is too large for just the two of us.
	Grandpa:	So, where is this retirement community?
50	Pauline:	It's not far away, Malcolm. Cedar Hills is just **an hour's drive**[11] from here.
	Sam:	It's a nice place, Malcolm. There are lots of things to do.
	Grandpa:	Tell me about it.
	Sam:	It's like many retirement communities. It offers special activities that older people might like—golf, discussion groups . . .
60	Pauline:	And it has services that older people need, like a food service . . . and a nursing service.
	Grandpa:	Oh. That makes you sound so old! And I don't **think of you as old**[12] yet.
	Sam:	Well, someday we will be old. But, Malcolm, before that happens, we want you to come and visit us there. See it for yourself.
70	Grandpa:	All right. I think I'd like that.

END OF ACT I

[7] **good-bye:** as in: good-bye forever; farewell
[8] **brewing [brü´ ing]:** word used for the process of preparing coffee, tea, or beer
[9] **. . . not be the same without you.** = We will miss you when you are gone.
[10] **It's time for us to move on.** = It's time for us to begin another stage of our lives.
[11] **an hour's drive:** a car trip that takes one hour
[12] **think of you as old:** consider you old

U.S. LIFE

Older people (senior citizens) have important decisions to make after their children have left home. They may find their homes too large to care for themselves. And, if they are living on retirement incomes (fixed incomes), they may not be able to afford the help required to maintain their houses properly. If one of them should pass away, the surviving person often becomes lonely living by him or herself. The choice may be to move in with a son or daughter, like Grandpa did, or to move to a retirement community, like the Wolfs did.

☞ YOUR TURN

Do you know any older persons who live alone? How well are they able to manage for themselves?

Focus In

In Act I, you heard this line of dialogue:

> **Grandpa:** "They said they were leaving the house now."

Grandpa is using **reported speech**; that is, he is reporting what someone else said. It is common to use the past tense *said* or *told me* in reported speech. The verb in the following clause is then changed to the past tense (they *were* leaving).

INTRODUCTION TO ACT II

This time on TUNING IN THE U.S.A., Grandpa is visiting his friends Sam and Pauline Wolf at their new retirement home. The Wolfs used to be neighbors of the Stewarts in Riverdale. But they decided to leave their large house and join other older people at a retirement community. This is Grandpa's first visit to such a place. And what he finds there is very **different from what he expected.**[1]

ACT II

Guard: *[She walks over to Grandpa.]* Hello. May I help you?

Grandpa: I'm here to visit some friends. **They're expecting me.**[2]

Guard: Let me call them for you. What are their names?

Grandpa: Sam and Pauline Wolf.

Guard: Who should I say is calling?

Grandpa: Malcolm Stewart.

[The guard buzzes the Wolfs on the intercom.]

10 Sam: Hello?

Guard: *[She speaks into the intercom.]* Mr. Wolf? You have a visitor, Malcolm Stewart.

Sam: Malcolm! Tell him to stay right where he is. I'll come down to meet him.

Guard: *[She speaks to Grandpa.]* **He'll be right down.**[3] Won't you take a seat?

Grandpa: I'll tell you the truth. I'd rather stand right there next to that open
20 **doorway.**[4]

Guard: Why don't you? I know Mr. Freeman won't mind if you listen in. He leads the Cedar Hills Community Singers. That's who you hear singing right now.

[We hear the singers.]

Grandpa: They're very good.

Guard: We think so, too.

Sam: *[He comes out of the elevator.]* Malcolm! **You made it!**[5]

30 Grandpa: It was **an easy drive**[6] from Riverdale. I'm glad to see you, Sam. I've missed you. But where's Pauline?

[1] **different from what he expected**
Grandpa thought the retirement community was going to be a certain way. He was surprised by the way it really was.

[2] **They're expecting me.** = They know that I'm coming.

[3] **He'll be right down.** = He'll be here in a moment.

[4] **doorway:** the opening left by an open door

[5] **You made it!** = You arrived safely!

[6] **an easy drive:** a short, uncomplicated trip with not too much traffic

Sam: She's down in the **activity room.**[7] She's planning to meet us there at noon. Come on. We have just enough time for me to **show you around**[8] the place.

[They go outside.]

Sam: I'm so glad you're here. Did you see the community garden?

40 Grandpa: I saw it. It looks well **cared for.**[9]

[They arrive at an exercise class.]

Sam: Well, here we are.

Instructor: One, two, three, **reach.**[10] One, . . .

Sam: Oops. Wrong door. I thought that was the activity room.

Grandpa: They sure are **active**[11] in that class! Does everyone here have to do exercises?

Sam: Only if you want to. You don't have to do anything. That's the nice part.
50 But there are plenty of activities, if you want to be active.

Grandpa: Whatever happened to old folks just taking it easy?

Sam: There are nice big comfortable chairs everywhere—around the swimming pool—everywhere. Here we are. *[He opens the door to the activity room.]* And here's Pauline.

Pauline: Hi, Malcolm! How nice to see you!

60 Grandpa: Pauline, how are you?

Pauline: **Couldn't be better.**[12]

Grandpa: Sam was just giving me the grand tour. *[He laughs.]* **This is quite a place.**[13] And I'm glad to see you so happily settled.

Sam: Shall we take a walk in the garden?

Grandpa: Why not?

END OF ACT II

[7] **activity room:** room designated for physical recreation activities
[8] **show you around:** take you to see the different areas (of a house, grounds, etc.)
[9] **cared for:** maintained
[10] **reach:** extend the arms (as in a physical exercise routine)
[11] **active:** energetic
[12] **Couldn't be better.** = I'm very well.
[13] **This is quite a place.** = This is an impressive community.

U.S. LIFE

Retirement communities are places where retirees live with other people their age in a setting that corresponds to their needs. Meals, recreational and social activities, travel, and even continuing education are provided at a fixed cost. Members may own their own apartment or condominiums, or they may rent them. Maintenance and upkeep are provided as part of the contract. Retirement communities provide their members a chance to continue to grow and mature in their "golden years."

☞ YOUR TURN

Do you think you would like to live in a retirement community? Why or why not?

Focus In

The guard asked, "**Who should I say is calling?**" This is a polite way of asking the identity of someone we don't know. It can be used in person or over the telephone. The expression "Whom am I speaking to?" means the same thing, but it is only used in telephone conversation.

Activities

Here are some activities to help you check your understanding of this program.

THE LIFE OF RILEY

We call a life of ease where everything is done for us "the life of Riley." Sam Wolf is talking to Grandpa over the phone. Grandpa wants to invite Sam to Riverdale for a picnic, but Sam is so busy enjoying himself at the retirement community he doesn't have a free day. Look at Sam's schedule and fill in the blanks.

Grandpa: How about Sunday afternoon, Sam?
Sam: I'd like to, Malcolm, but I'm playing golf with the boys on Sunday.

1. Grandpa: How about Monday then?
   Sam: I'd love to, Malcolm, but I'm _____

2. Grandpa: How about Tuesday then?
   Sam: I'd love to Malcolm, but I'm _____

4. Grandpa: How about Wednesday then?
   Sam: I'd love to Malcolm, but I'm _____

5. Grandpa: How about Thursday then?
   Sam: I'd love to Malcolm, but I'm _____

SUN	golf with the boys
MON	tennis lesson
TUE	choir practice
WED	group discussion
THUR	trip to upstate New York

REPORTED SPEECH

Now Grandpa is off the phone with Sam. He's remembering what Sam said and telling Ellen.

Sam: I can't come Sunday.   Grandpa: He said he couldn't come Sunday.

Now you take Grandpa's part. Report what Sam said.

1. Sam: I love Cedar Hills.   Grandpa: _____
2. Sam: I'm learning to play tennis.   Grandpa: _____
3. Sam: Life is wonderful here.   Grandpa: _____

TELEPHONE LANGUAGE AND "IN-PERSON" LANGUAGE

The expressions we use when talking over the telephone are often different from the expressions we use when speaking to someone in person. Look at this list of expressions. Tell whether they are telephone expressions or "in-person" expressions.

1. Can I speak to Ms. Roberts, please? _____
2. Can you tell me where to find Ms. Roberts? _____
3. I'm Bob Jones. _____
4. This is Bob Jones. _____
5. Who are you? _____
6. Whom am I speaking to? _____

PROGRAM 48

"Lost and Found"

ACT I

ACT II

In this program, you will study...

VOCABULARY

Do you know the meaning of these words from Program 48?

check
dollar amount
paycheck

GRAMMAR AND EXPRESSIONS

Do you know what these phrases or expressions mean?

Oh, no!
get used to
It's easy for you to say.

PRONUNCIATION

Do you know how to pronounce this four-syllable word?

independent

U.S. LIFE

What kind of account allows you to make purchases without depositing money first?

☞ YOUR TURN

Do you prefer paying with cash or by personal check or by credit card?

"Lost and Found" ▶ 127

Here is the complete script with study material for Program 48. Use these materials before *or* after you listen.

INTRODUCTION TO ACT I

Today on TUNING IN THE U.S.A., Robbie is in his bedroom, searching for some **missing**[1] money. It was the money he made by working as a bicycle messenger. Robbie is upset. When he got home from work, he put the money in his dresser drawer. At least, he thinks that's what he did! Robbie tells Marilyn about his problem. And she helps him find his money—in an unexpected place.

ACT I

Robbie: *[He speaks to himself as he looks through the drawers of his dresser.]* **Oh, no!**[2] My money is gone! Where is it? I know I put it in one of these dresser drawers. Not in this **one.**[3] Maybe it's in the next one. Forty-five dollars and eight-five cents. *[He calls.]* Mom! *[He goes to find her.]* Where are you? Mom?

10 Marilyn: *[She calls back.]* Robbie? It's just me. Your mother's not here. I'm **doing the laundry.**[4] **What's up?**[5]

Robbie: Marilyn, my money's gone. I put it in my dresser. It was in my top drawer, and now I can't find it.

Marilyn: Wait a minute. **Start at the beginning.**[6]

Robbie: Yesterday I got my **paycheck**[7] from Speedy Messenger Service. Forty-five dollars and eighty-five cents! They
20 **cashed**[8] the check for me, and when I got home, I put the money in my top drawer.

Marilyn: You're sure it's gone?

Robbie: I'm **positive!**[9] All that work for nothing! I must have bicycled a hundred miles. **And what do I get from it?**[10] I lose my money!

Marilyn: Robbie, it still has to be in the house. Calm down.

30 Robbie: **That's easy for you to say.**[11] "Calm down!"

Marilyn: You know what it sounds like to me?

Robbie: What?

---

[1] **missing:** lost
[2] **Oh, no!**
We say "Oh, no" when something bad happens unexpectedly.
Oh, no! I locked my keys inside the car!
Oh, no! It's going to rain.
[3] **one:** drawer
[4] **doing the laundry:** washing the clothes
[5] **What's up?** = What's happening?
[6] **Start at the beginning.** = Tell me everything that happened in order.
[7] **paycheck:** payment an employee receives from his or her employer: weekly or monthly *paycheck*

TOTAL HOURS	YOU EARNED		TOTAL	PERIOD ENDING
	REGULAR	OVERTIME		
10	40.	—	40.	6/11/90

[8] **cashed:** gave cash in exchange for the check
[9] **positive** [pä´zə tiv]: absolutely sure
[10] **And what do I get from it?** = What reward do I get?
[11] **That's easy for you to say.** = It's easy for you to be calm (because nothing bad happened to you).

	Marilyn:	It sounds like you need a **checking account.**[12]
	Robbie:	A checking account?
	Marilyn:	Yes. When you pay for things with checks, your money stays safely in the bank. Not in your top drawer.
40	Robbie:	I've never had a checking account.
	Marilyn:	It's easy to use. The bank gives you a book of checks with your name printed on each one. You write in the **dollar amount**[13] for whatever amount you want.
	Robbie:	Will you just help me look for my money.
	Marilyn:	First, I need to put the clean laundry in the clothes dryer. It'll only take a second.
50		
		[They put the clothes in the dryer.]
		Okay. Now, **shall we**[14] go back upstairs and search your room?
	Robbie:	We can try. But I don't think you're going to find anything!
	Marilyn:	Wait a minute. I think I know what happened. Do you hear something?
	Robbie:	The clothes dryer is so noisy. I can't hear anything.
	Marilyn:	But that's it! Look! *[She opens the door to the clothes dryer.]* There are coins inside the clothes dryer. Oooo, here are some wet dollar **bills!**[15]
60		
	Robbie:	Hey! That's my money! And those are the pants I wore to work yesterday. Marilyn, I never took the money out of my pants pocket!

END OF ACT I

[12] **checking account:** a bank account where the holder can draw money out in the form of personal checks See **U.S. Life.**

[13] **dollar amount:** a numerical figure in dollars

[14] **Shall we . . . ?** = Do you want to . . . ?

[15] **bills:** paper money

U.S. LIFE

Cash is a good way to make small purchases, but carrying large amounts of cash is dangerous. It can be lost or stolen. Cash should never be sent in the mail. The most convenient method of payment is by personal check. We *open* a checking account at a bank by *depositing* money. The bank provides a *checkbook* of personal checks with our name and address on them. The person we write a check to takes the check to his own bank and deposits it into his own account, or receives the cash amount (*cashes* the check). When we *make out* (write) a check to someone, we must remember to *deduct* that amount from our *balance* (the part of the original deposit remaining in the account) after we make a purchase. If we write a check for more money than we have in the bank, the bank will refuse to pay the check. (The check *bounces*.)

☞ YOUR TURN

- Do you have a personal checking account?
- Do you always record every check you write in the checkbook ledger?

Focus In

In Act I, Marilyn asks Robbie, **"What's up?"**
The phrase "What's up?" is an informal way of asking someone what's happening or what he's thinking about.

You look worried. What's up?

INTRODUCTION TO ACT II

This time on TUNING IN THE U.S.A., *Robbie is at the Riverdale Bank with his father. It's time for Robbie to open a checking account. Before long, he'll be going to college, and he'll be living in a more* **independent**[1] *way. Robbie needs to keep his money in a safe place. The checking account will also allow him to write checks for the things he wants to buy: It's all part of* **growing up.**[2]

ACT II

Philip: Ms. Thomas, are there any special problems **opening**[3] a checking account for my son?

Ms. Thomas: Oh, no, Mr. Stewart. There shouldn't be any problem. *[She speaks to Robbie.]* How old are you, Robbie?

Robbie: I'll be eighteen in a few more months.

Ms. Thomas: No, it's fine for a young man to have a checking account. As long as you're
10 **ready**[4] for it.

Robbie: I think I'm ready.

Philip: We talked it over, Ms. Thomas, and Robbie and I both think it would be good for him to **get used to**[5] managing his own money.

Ms. Thomas: Well, fine. There's no problem. But when any **minor**[6] opens an account, we always ask for a letter from a parent giving us permission to do so.

20 Philip: I'll write one up right now.

Ms. Thomas: Fine. Here, you can use this pen and paper.

Philip: Thanks. *[He writes the letter.]*

[Outside the bank, a little later]

Philip: Well, that was easy.

Robbie: Yeah, that was the easy part. Now the **hard part**[7] begins. Now when I buy something, I have to know exactly how much money I have in
30 my account.

Philip: That's the idea. Hey. How about letting *me* buy *you* something?

Robbie: Sure, Dad.

Philip: How about some lunch?

[They enter a restaurant and sit at a table.]

Robbie: When the lady at the bank . . .

Philip: Ms. Thomas . . .

Robbie: Yeah, when Ms. Thomas asked me if I was ready to have an account, I
40 was a little bit angry.

[1] **independent** [in də pen′ dənt]: responsible
[2] **growing up:** becoming an adult
[3] **opening:** starting; establishing
[4] **ready:** mature enough
[5] **get used to:** become accustomed to
[6] **minor** [mī′ nər]: person under the age of 18 years
[7] **hard part:** the difficult part

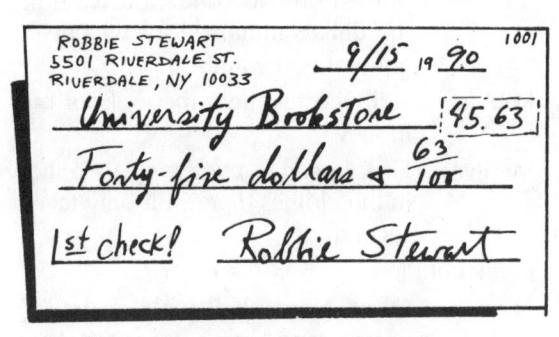

Robbie's first check

"Lost and Found" ▶ 131

	Philip:	Oh?
	Robbie:	Well, I'm ready to **manage**[8] my money. I hope I am. I mean, I'd better be. I'll be going away to college next year. I'll have to buy all my own books and supplies and other stuff.
	Philip:	I'm sure you're ready, Robbie. I've been **watching**[9] you this year.
	Robbie:	And what have you seen?
50	Philip:	Well . . . for one, you know where money comes from.
	Robbie:	Yeah, from work. Look at you, Dad. You work hard.
	Philip:	But so do you. When you decided you wanted to buy a car, you started to look for a job right away.
	Robbie:	And I got one!
	Philip:	Your mom and I were proud of you for doing that. So, that's the first part of **dealing**[10] with money, knowing what it takes to earn it.
60		
	Robbie:	And what's the next part?
	Philip:	Knowing how to use it. Not spending too much or spending **unwisely.**[11]
	Waiter:	Excuse me. Would either of you **care for**[12] dessert?
	Philip:	Robbie?
	Robbie:	The **double chocolate cake**[13] sure looks good. Do you think it's too expensive, Dad?
70	Philip:	*[He is amused.]* Uh, I think we can **manage**[14] it. How about two **slices**[15] of double chocolate cake.
	Waiter:	Certainly, sir.

END OF ACT II

[8] **manage** [mə′nij]: be responsible for
[9] **watching:** observing (your behavior)
[10] **dealing:** handling; managing
[11] **unwisely** [ən wīz′lē]: in a foolish or irresponsible way
[12] **care for:** want
[13] **double chocolate cake:** an extremely rich chocolate cake (double = twice the normal amount)
[14] **manage:** be capable (of doing something)
[15] **slices:** sections

Focus In

In Act II, the waiter asks, "**Excuse me. Would either of you care for dessert?**" The indefinite pronouns *either, neither,* and *each* are singular:

***Neither** of the students **knows** the answers.*
not: *Neither of the students know the answer.*

The indefinite pronouns *both, all,* and *many* are plural:

***Both** of the students **are** here.*

The indefinite pronouns *some, none,* and *a lot* may be singular or plural:

***Some** of the money **is** gone.*
***Some** of the students **are** gone.*

U.S. LIFE

There is another way to make payments that has become very popular in the United States in the last 20 years—by *credit card.* As with a checking account, credit card purchases are not made with cash. The amount of the purchase is *charged* to our personal account. The difference is that we are not required to deposit money into this account. The money is a *loan* by the credit card company. A *statement* of our account is mailed to our home each month, telling how much of our *available credit* (amount the company will lend us) we have used. If we pay the entire balance each month, there is usually no *interest* charge. (Interest is a fee we pay for borrowing money.) If, however, we choose not to pay the entire balance, an interest charge is added to our account. This interest is usually very high, sometimes almost 2% **per month.** Credit cards are a very convenient way to make purchases—provided we pay the balance on time.

☞ YOUR TURN

Have you ever lost or had stolen a large amount of cash? Did you get it back?

Activities

Here are some activities to help you check your understanding of this program.

USED TO

The phrase *used to* can occur in two entirely different constructions. *Used to* + past participle expresses an action that happened repeatedly in the past. *Get used to* + gerund expresses an action in the present that we are becoming accustomed to. Robbie is telling Marilyn about his new checking account. Make sentences with *used to* or *get used to* + gerund.

1. Robbie: "In the past, I never _____ (*manage*) my money very well."
2. Robbie: "I'm _____ (*manage*) my money slowly but surely."
3. Robbie: "Before, I _____ (*lose*) money very often."
4. Robbie: "It's hard to _____ (*balance*) a checkbook."

HOPE FOR/WISH FOR

We *wish for* something that is not realistic for us to expect to get. We *hope for* something that we have a good chance of getting. Use *hopes for* or *wishes for* in the following sentences.

1. I _____ good weather for our picnic.
2. She _____ a handsome millionaire to get married to.
3. Everybody _____ a successful fund-raising dinner.
4. Johnny _____ an A on his history exam. (Johnny studied hard.)

NOW YOU TELL THE STORY

Here are some of the events of this episode. See if you can put them in the correct order. Remember to "start at the beginning."

____ Marilyn found Robbie's money in the clothes dryer.
____ Robbie and Phil went to the bank to set up a checking account for Robbie.
____ Robbie and Phil got a double chocolate cake dessert.
____ Robbie got his paycheck cashed.
____ Robbie couldn't find his money in the dresser.

PROGRAM 49

"A Dark and Stormy Night"

In this program, you will study...

ACT I

VOCABULARY

Do you know the meaning of these words from Program 49?

stormy
thunder
power failure

GRAMMAR AND EXPRESSIONS

Do you know what these phrases or expressions mean?

I should say so.
You know what that means.

PRONUNCIATION

Do you know how to pronounce these words?

imagine
emergency

Hint: The "g" in each is pronounced softly, like the letter "j."

ACT II

U.S. LIFE

What telephone number do we call in an emergency in the United States?

☞ YOUR TURN

How do people get help in an emergency in your country?

"A Dark and Stormy Night"

INTRODUCTION TO ACT I

Today on TUNING IN THE U.S.A., *Philip, Ellen, and Robbie are at home on a* **stormy**[1] *night. It's raining. There is* **thunder**[2] *and* **lightning.**[3] *Just as the family is about to sit down to dinner, the storm causes a* **power failure.**[4] *All the electricity in the neighborhood goes out. Philip lights some candles, and the family begins to feel comfortable without electricity—until Ellen remembers an elderly neighbor who lives alone. The Stewarts decide to invite her to share a candlelight dinner with them.*

ACT I

Ellen: Okay, I guess I'll call Robbie for dinner.

[The sound of thunder]

Philip: Ellen, **come stand**[5] by the back door. Look at that rain.

Ellen: *[She is concerned.]* This is quite a storm!

Philip: Remember the last time we had thunder and lightning like this? It was two or three years ago. We lost our electrical power.

Ellen: Luckily, it was in the **middle of the day.**[6] Losing your electricity at night is a lot different from losing it during the day.

Philip: We must have talked about that because I remember going out the next day to buy a box of candles—**just in case of**[7] a power failure.

Ellen: Well, let's hope *that* doesn't happen tonight. Shall I call Robbie to come to dinner now?

Philip: **Uh-oh.**[8] Ellen, don't call him yet. I forgot to finish **mashing**[9] the potatoes. Would you hand me the electric mixer, please? Thanks. *[He uses the mixer.]*

Ellen: *[She is frightened.]* Philip?

Philip: Ellen? There go the lights. It has happened again. We've lost our electricity.

Robbie: *[He calls from the other room.]* Mom? Dad?

---

[1] **stormy:** having a storm or very bad weather

[2] **thunder:** the booming sound that accompanies a flash of lightning

[3] **lightning** [līt´ning]: the flash of light in the sky caused by the discharge of electricity between clouds or between the ground and a cloud during an electrical storm

[4] **power failure:** interruption of electrical service to an individual home or an entire area due to some damage to electrical generating equipment or the electrical distribution system

The hurricane destroyed power lines in the Carolinas and caused a *power failure.*

[5] **come stand:** come (here and) stand . . .
Come +verb is a common elliptical expression (where some words are left out).

[6] **middle of the day:** late morning to early afternoon

[7] **just in case of . . .** = in the event of; if

[8] **Uh-oh.** = Oh, no.
This is a vocative, that is, not a word, but a sound that expresses meaning. (See Episode 44, Act I.)

[9] **mashing:** making a puree of boiled potatoes by crushing with a kitchen utensil or an electric mixer

	Ellen:	We're here, in the kitchen, Robbie.
	Robbie:	*[He enters the kitchen.]* **I can't see a thing.**[10] What happened?
	Philip:	A power failure, I **imagine**.[11]
	Robbie:	Well, what'll we do?
40	Philip:	*[He opens a drawer.]* I have a box of candles in this drawer, just for an **emergency**[12] like this. Robbie, why don't you go call the power company? Tell them we have a problem on Linden Street.
	Robbie:	OK, Dad. *[He leaves.]*
	Ellen:	What can I do to help, Philip?
	Philip:	Well, **we do need**[13] some matches.
	Ellen:	I know just where to find those. *[She knocks over a chair by accident.]*
	Philip:	Ellen? Are you all right?
50	Ellen:	Ooh. I just **knocked over**[14] a chair. But I'm all right. Here—a book of matches.
	Philip:	*[He strikes a match.]* There—that's better. Now, look around you. Doesn't the kitchen look great in candlelight?
	Robbie:	*[He enters.]* I called the power company. They already knew about the electrical problem. A tree fell onto a power line on the next street. They don't know how long the lights will be out.
60		
	Ellen:	Philip . . . Robbie . . . I just thought about Mrs. Romero. She's quite old, and she lives all alone in that big house. Wouldn't she be more **comfortable**[15] spending the evening with us?
	Philip:	Ellen, **set another place**[16] for dinner. I'll go invite her over right now.

END OF ACT I

[10] **I can't see a thing.** = I can't see anything.
The use of *a thing* gives more emphasis to the expression.

[11] **imagine** [i maj´ən]: think

[12] **emergency** [i mər´jən sē]: any unexpected event that we must respond to if we want to avoid danger or bad consequences

Call 911 if there is an *emergency*.

[13] **We do need . . .** = We need . . .
The auxiliaries *do/does* or *did* are only used in affirmative sentences for increased emphasis:

Motorist: Officer, I didn't go through a red light, did I?
Police Officer: Yes, you *did* go through a red light!

[14] **knocked over:** bumped into and overturned

[15] **comfortable** [kəm´fərt ə bəl]: at ease
Comfortable in this sense means "free from worry."

[16] **set another place:** add a chair, dinner plate and cutlery to the dinner table for another person to sit and eat

U.S. LIFE

A loss of electrical power can be just an inconvenience or it can have life-threatening consequences. To commuters trapped in a subway tunnel, office employees stuck in the elevator of a tall building, or a patient in the middle of a heart operation, a power failure is nothing to laugh about. Fortunately, most hospitals operate on their own electrical power in such emergencies. To a family in the suburbs, a power failure in the evening can be a welcome change from the routine of television and homework. The glow of candlelight gives everyone a glimpse (small look) at what life before electricity was like.

☞ YOUR TURN

Have you ever been in a power failure? Can you remember what you were doing when the lights went out?

Focus In

In Act I Philip says, "**We must have talked about that.**"
The past modal *must have* + past participle expresses probability in the past.

I must have bicycled 100 miles. = I probably bicycled 100 miles.

INTRODUCTION TO ACT II

This time on TUNING IN THE U.S.A., *the lights are out in Riverdale. There is a big rainstorm this evening, and there is no electricity. Robbie and Ellen are waiting for Philip to bring an* **elderly**[1] *neighbor, Mrs. Romero, to their house. They are inviting her to spend this dark evening with them. And she proves to be a welcome guest because she's a good* **storyteller.**[2]

ACT II

[The sound of thunder]

Robbie: Mom, do you think Mrs. Romero will want to spend the evening with us?

Ellen: I don't know, Robbie. Your dad is going to invite her.

Robbie: Hey, Mom, this is going to be an interesting night, isn't it?

Ellen: **I should say so!**[3] No electric lights. That doesn't happen every night.

10 Robbie: **And you know what that means...**[4]

Ellen: Tell me.

Robbie: No homework!

Ellen: And no TV, either.

Robbie: Maybe we can make a fire in the fireplace. Then we can all **sit around**[5] and tell stories.

Ellen: Mrs. Romero would probably love to hear a good story. Look! **Here they are now.**[6] [calling] Hello! We're
20 glad you could join us.

Mrs. Romero: And I'm **ever so**[7] glad to be here.

Philip: Careful on the steps, Mrs. Romero. Robbie, will you hold the candle so we can see better?

Ellen: I'll hold the candle. Robbie was just going out to the garage to get some **logs**[8] for the fireplace.

[Later, after dinner. There is a fire in the fireplace.]

[1] **elderly:** old
We use *elderly* to refer to persons in the later years of their life. It is more respectful than *old*.

She is an *elderly* widow.

[2] **storyteller:** person who tells a story

[3] **I should say so!** = I strongly agree with what you said!

[4] **And you know what that means.** = I think you understand what that means.

[5] **sit around:** gather together

[6] **Here they are now.** = They are arriving right now.

[7] **ever so:** very
Ever so is an old-fashioned expression used mostly by the older generation.

[8] **logs:** lengths of tree trunk or thick branches for building a fire

Mrs. Romero:	Ellen, your dinner was just **delicious**![9] And you were so kind to invite me tonight.
Ellen:	Well, we were **concerned**[10] about you—all alone in that big house with no electricity.
Robbie:	Yeah, we thought you might get frightened.
Mrs. Romero:	Oh, no, I wasn't frightened. Being a **widow**[11] can get lonely at times. But frightened by the dark? No, not I.
Robbie:	I thought it was kind of scary.
Mrs. Romero:	Robbie, I'm eighty-four years old. When I was a young girl growing up in Oklahoma, there was no electricity.
Ellen:	There wasn't?
Mrs. Romero:	Well, in the cities and larger towns they had electrical power, but where I lived we were twenty miles from the nearest town. A trip to town on horseback took a full day.
Robbie:	On horseback?
Mrs. Romero:	Of course. It was my grandfather who bought the first car **for miles around**.[12] He traveled a lot in his work.
Ellen:	What was his work, Mrs. Romero?
Mrs. Romero:	Why, he was one of the first doctors in the Oklahoma **territory**.[13] Someday, maybe Dr. Stewart would like to hear an interesting story.
Philip:	Well what about right now?
Robbie:	Yes, I want to hear your interesting story.
Mrs. Romero:	Robbie, it's not exactly a short story.
Robbie:	Mrs. Romero, the longer the better.
Mrs. Romero:	Well, let's see. It was **back in 1892**.[14] My grandfather had just become a doctor. His first wife . . .

END OF ACT II

[9] **delicious** [di lish′əs]: (with reference to food or drink) having an excellent taste

[10] **concerned:** worried

[11] **widow:** woman whose husband has died

[12] **for miles around:** an area large enough to be measured in miles

[13] **territory**
Large areas of the United States were called *territories* before they were divided into states.

The Kansas Territory
The Oregon Territory

[14] **back in 1892 . . .**
To emphasize the remoteness of a time in history we use the expression *back in* . . .

Gold was discovered in California *back in* 1849.

U.S. LIFE

Storms and other natural catastrophes such as earthquakes, fires, and floods can cause prolonged disruptions in essential services. A family may not only be without electricity. Water, gas, and telephone service may also be lost. Smart people have supplies stored up in case of such emergencies. Here is a partial checklist of essential emergency supplies:

- flashlight with spare batteries
- first aid kit and instructional handbook
- portable radios with spare batteries
- fire extinguishers
- airtight containers of drinking water
- canned or dehydrated foods, powdered milk, and juices
- a camp stove
- gloves
- matches
- a wrench for turning off gas or water mains

Well-prepared families also have a plan of action prepared for emergencies, which gives each member a specific duty and a place to be.

Focus In

Mrs. Romero:	**Robbie, it's not exactly a short story.**
Robbie:	**Mrs. Romero, the longer the better.**

Robbie is encouraging Mrs. Romero to tell her story, no matter how long it is.

☞ YOUR TURN

- Have you ever been without essential services for a long time?
- Do you have a plan of action ready for any emergency?

Activities

Here are some activities to help you check your understanding of this program.

THE BIG BLACKOUT

When one action interrupts another in the past, we often use two different tenses to show this—the past and the past continuous:

I was *taking* a shower when the telephone *rang*.

Look at these sentences. They are from a news story about the New York City blackout of 1965, when a power failure left the city in total darkness. Make sentences with the past continuous, the past, and *when*. Look at the example.

Cab driver: "I drove along Broadway. Then the lights went out."
"I *was driving along Broadway* when *the lights went out.*"

1. Night watchman: I rode the elevator. It suddenly stopped in between floors.
   "_____."

2. Policeman: We responded to a call in the Village. Everything went dark.
   "_____."

3. Subway rider: I took the subway to Queens. It quit halfway there.
   "_____."

4. Doctor: I delivered a baby. Somebody turned out the lights.
   "_____."

5. Restaurant customer: I asked my girlfriend to marry me. Her face disappeared into the dark.
   "_____."
   The waiter lit a candle and she said "yes."

WHO SAID IT?

Here are some lines of dialogue from this episode.
Do you remember who said them?

_____: I just thought about Mrs. Romero. Wouldn't she be more comfortable spending the evening with us?

_____: No homework!

_____: A trip to town on horseback took a full day.

_____: Careful on the steps, Mrs. Romero.

PROGRAM 50

"The Wooden Whistle"

ACT I

ACT II

In this program, you will study...

VOCABULARY

Do you know the meaning of these words from Program 50?

profit
market
expert

GRAMMAR AND EXPRESSIONS

Do you know what these phrases or expressions mean?

Once upon a time...
Not that I care.
nothing in sight

PRONUNCIATION

Can you find the accents in these three-, four-, and five-syllable words?

demonstrate
manufacture
imagination

U.S. LIFE

Do know the meaning of the word "entrepreneur" [än- trə prə nər´]?

☞ YOUR TURN

Have you ever invented anything?

"The Wooden Whistle" ▶ 139

Here is the complete script with study material for Program 50. Use these materials before *or* after you listen.

INTRODUCTION TO ACT I

Today on TUNING IN THE U.S.A., *Grandpa is in the basement of the Stewart home. He is making a wooden toy—a whistle that sounds just like a train whistle. When his granddaughter Susan comes downstairs to see what he is doing, she is immediately interested in what he is making. Perhaps the toy company she works for might want to* **manufacture**[1] *and sell Grandpa's toy. Grandpa agrees to let Susan* **give it a try.**[2]

ACT I

[There are knocking and scraping noises.]

Susan: Hello! **Is anybody home?**[3]

Grandpa: Susan? Is that you?

Susan: Grandpa? Grandpa, what are you doing down in the basement?

Grandpa: I'm making something. Come have a look.

[Susan goes downstairs to the basement.]

Grandpa: How's my favorite granddaughter?

Susan: You mean, how's your only granddaughter. I'm fine. Grandpa, 10 this looks beautiful! But what is it?

Grandpa: It's a wooden toy.

Susan: But what does it do?

Grandpa: Well, it . . . no, I won't tell you what it does. I'll **demonstrate.**[4] Now close your eyes.

Susan: Okay. They're **shut tight.**[5]

Grandpa: Now, pretend you're standing on a hillside, looking across a field—a field of wheat. There's **nothing in** 20 **sight,**[6] and then suddenly you hear this. *[He blows on a whistle.]*

Susan: There's a train coming! A real train!

Grandpa: That's it!

Susan: Can I open my eyes now?

Grandpa: Oh, sure.

Susan: This little whistle made that train sound? How **unbelievable!**[7] May I try it?

Grandpa: Of course.

[She blows on the whistle.]

30 Susan: *That* is a great toy, Grandpa!

Grandpa: You think so? It's pretty **simple.**[8]

---

[1] **manufacture** [man yə fak´chər]: produce (something for sale) on a mass scale

[2] **give it a try:** try

[3] **Is anybody home?**
This is the usual greeting we call out when we enter someone's house and they may not be expecting us.

[4] **demonstrate** [de´mən strāt]: show (how something works)

The salesman *demonstrated* how to use the vacuum sweeper.

[5] **shut tight:** close completely and securely

[6] **nothing in sight:** nothing can be seen for a great distance
This expression says in a literal or figurative way that nothing or nobody is near.

My car broke down and I started walking. There wasn't a service station or a farm house *in sight.*

[7] **unbelievable** [ən bə lē´və bəl]: (literally) impossible to believe
We often use this expression to exaggerate the qualities of something:

This pizza is *unbelievably* good.

[8] **simple:** not complicated; easy to understand

	Susan:	That's exactly what makes it great. It **leaves room**[9] for the child's **imagination.**[10]
	Grandpa:	Hmm. You're right. I know your father loved his.
	Susan:	Dad had a whistle like this?
	Grandpa:	**Once upon a time,**[11] he had one exactly like this.
40	Susan:	Grandpa, did you ever **think of**[12] selling these whistles?
	Grandpa:	Well, no. In my life I've **given away**[13] quite a number of them, but I've never sold one.
	Susan:	If you'll let me borrow this whistle, I'll show it at work. Maybe—just maybe—my company will want to do something with it.
50	Grandpa:	There's only one thing you *can* do with a toy whistle. And that's blow it. *[He laughs.]* **As I said,**[14] Susan, it's a simple toy.
	Susan:	Grandpa, what if Universe Toy Company wanted to manufacture the whistle and sell it?
	Grandpa:	Ah. **Do you really think they'd be interested?**[15]
	Susan:	They might be. Say yes, Grandpa.
60	Grandpa:	Well, it seems **funny**[16] to me, Susan, but you're the **expert.**[17]
	Susan:	So you'll **leave the matter in my hands?**[18]
	Grandpa:	All right. *And* I'll leave the whistle in your hands, too.
	Susan:	*[She laughs.]* Thanks, Grandpa. Let me try that again. *[She blows on the whistle.]*

END OF ACT I

[9] **leaves room:** allows to enter or take part
This movie script is just an outline. It leaves a lot of *room* for the actors to improvise.

[10] **imagination** [i maj ə nā´shən]: the ability of the mind to see the world in new or unusual ways:
That child has a lot of *imagination*.

[11] **Once upon a time . . .**
This is the standard opening to a fairytale (children's story):
Once upon a time there was a beautiful princess who lived in a castle . . .

[12] **think of:** consider

[13] **given away:** given as a gift, at no cost

[14] **As I said . . .**
This is a common opening to repeat something we already said.

[15] **Do you really think they'd be interested?** = Do you think they would want to buy it (the whistle)?

[16] **funny:** unusual
The word *funny* often applies to situations where humor is not involved:

He's been acting kind of *funny* lately. Is he having problems at home?

[17] **expert** [ek´spərt]: someone who is trained in a subject or area and knows it very well.
She's an *expert* in television repair.

[18] **Leave the matter in my hands.** = Let me handle the matter.

A Play on Words

Susan asks Grandpa to "leave the matter in my hands." Grandpa says, "*And* I'll leave the whistle in your hands, too." Which of these two expressions is the literal one?

U.S. LIFE

One part of the American character tends to see things in terms of their potential for making money. This is the "entrepreneurial" spirit. Another part of the American attitude is to do something "just for the fun of it." Which person in Act I represents the entrepreneur, Susan or Grandpa?

☞ YOUR TURN

Have you ever made money from an invention of your own?

Focus In

Susan says, "**This little whistle made that train sound? How unbelievable!**"
Susan is very surprised by the sound of the whistle. She could have said:

How wonderful!
How amazing!

The word *how* used this way makes the adjective stronger.

INTRODUCTION TO ACT II

This time on TUNING IN THE U.S.A, *Ellen and Grandpa Stewart are waiting for Susan to arrive for dinner. Today is the day that Susan showed Grandpa's toy train whistle to her toy company. Will they want to buy Grandpa's idea? He and Ellen are anxious to know how Susan's meeting* **turned out.**[1] *When she brings* **bad news,**[2] *Grandpa isn't really upset. He wasn't making the whistle to sell,* **anyway.**[3]

ACT II

[*Grandpa climbs up the stairs to the kitchen.*]

Ellen: Oh, hi, Grandpa. I almost forgot you were down in the basement.

Grandpa: I've been working—perfecting my wooden train whistle.

Ellen: I thought it was already perfect. Susan gave me a demonstration.

Grandpa: And what'd you think?

Ellen: [*She laughs.*] I thought perhaps a train had **jumped the track**[4] and was headed straight for our house.

Grandpa: Good! [*He laughs.*]

Ellen: It's a great toy.

Grandpa: Dinner smells delicious.

Ellen: **Meatloaf**[5] and **baked potatoes.**[6] It's all ready. We're just waiting for Susan. She should be here any minute.

Grandpa: You know, today was the day she presented my whistle to the toy company.

Ellen: Yes, she told me. I wonder if they'll buy your idea?

Grandpa: I said something to Susan about a train whistle being just a simple toy. But she said, "That's what makes it great. It leaves room for the child's imagination."

Ellen: Hmm. "Leaves room for the child's imagination." She had a good thought.

Grandpa: She had a great thought! I tell you, that girl is **smart.**[7] **There's a reason**[8] she's so successful in the toy business.

Ellen: **Mmm-hmm.**[9]

Grandpa: **She knows a good idea when she sees one.**[10]

---

[1] **turned out:** resulted
The football game *turned out* badly for the home team. They lost 54-0.

[2] **bad news:** disappointing information
The weatherman had *bad news*. Another storm was coming. (opposite: good news)

[3] **anyway:** in any case; in the first place
We use *anyway* in many contexts. Like the word "but," *anyway* conveys the idea of opposition.

The dance was canceled. It was okay with me. I didn't want to go *anyway*.

[4] **jumped the track:** (the train) came off the track; derailed

[5] **meatloaf:** a casserole meat dish made with ground beef and an assortment of vegetables and spices

[6] **baked potatoes:** potatoes baked in their skins in the oven

[7] **smart:** intelligent

[8] **There's a reason . . .** = That is the reason (why she is successful).

[9] **Mmm-hmm.**
Another vocative expression. (See Episode 44, Act I.) Like "uh-huh," this one means "yes."

[10] **She knows a good idea when she sees one.**
This is a popular expression to say that someone has common sense.

Susan is a smart shopper. She knows a good bargain when she sees one.

	Ellen:	Like your whistle?
	Grandpa:	**Not that I care**[11] what happened in the meeting today, but . . .
	Ellen:	Grandpa, it sounds as if you care.
40	Grandpa:	Well, it would be nice if they wanted it. But if they don't that's okay. I just enjoy making them.
	Ellen:	That must be Susan right now.
	Susan:	*[She enters.]* Hi, Grandpa. Hi, Mom.
	Ellen:	Hello, dear.
	Susan:	Grandpa, I'm sorry.
	Grandpa:	**Now what's there to be sorry about?**[12]
	Susan:	They didn't want your wooden toy.
	Grandpa:	Well, that's okay.
50	Susan:	I really tried!
	Grandpa:	I'm sure you did. But I never really made those whistles **for profit.**[13] I just made them **for the fun of it.**[14]
	Susan:	Of course, everyone liked the whistle, but they didn't think it was **right**[15] for this year's **toy market.**[16]
	Grandpa:	That's all right. You did the best you could.
	Susan:	I did.
60	Grandpa:	Let's go eat. Aren't you hungry?
	Susan:	**I sure am!**[17] Where's Dad?
	Ellen:	He's upstairs—resting. He was **up all night**[18] at the hospital. He's just tired. But dinner's ready. Why don't you call him?
	Grandpa:	I'll call him—just the way I did when he was young. *[He blows on the train whistle.]* Come to dinner, Son! *[He blows on the whistle.]*
70	Philip:	*[approaching]* Hey! Is that what I think it is? Is that my old train whistle? It makes me feel as if I'm seven years old again!
	Grandpa:	*[He laughs.]* Maybe this whistle is **useful**[19] after all!

END OF ACT II

[11] **Not that I care . . .** = I don't care . . .
Not that + clause is simply a way to make a sentence negative. It is usually followed by a second clause that subtly contradicts the first:
Not that I'm going to buy you a present, but when is your birthday?

[12] **Now what's there to be sorry about?** = You have no reason to be sorry.

[13] **for profit:** to make money

[14] **for the fun of it:** not for profit, but for enjoyment

[15] **right:** suited to

[16] **toy market:** collection of toys to be sold
A *market* is the potential for sale that an item has: There is a big *market* for laptop computers this year. = A lot of people want to buy laptop computers.

[17] **I sure am!** = Yes!
This expression makes a very strong affirmative answer.

[18] **up all night:** out of bed
Philip worked all night and didn't get to bed.

[19] **useful:** have a purpose

U.S. LIFE

A great deal of time and planning goes into marketing a new product for sale. There is a saying in the business world that "time is money." A company that markets new products must spend a great deal of money before it sells any of them. There is no guarantee the public will buy a new product. For every successful product, there are many that fail. Deciding which product to develop is what gives entrepreneurs "gray hair."

☞ YOUR TURN

- Would you make a good entrepreneur?
- What qualities are necessary for the job?

Focus In

Ellen says, **"We're just waiting for Susan. She should be here any minute."**
Ellen uses *any minute* to mean "very soon."
If we want to talk about a shorter time, we can say "any second" or "any moment."

Activities

Here are some activities to help you check your understanding of this program.

UNIVERSE TOY COMPANY—THE ANNUAL REPORT

Companies make reports to their stockholders (people who have invested money in them) once a year in an "Annual Report." Make sentences for the report using the verb in parentheses. Use the present perfect progressive form if the information is about *how long*. Use the present perfect if the information is about *how much* or *how many*. Look at the examples.

(produce) 25,000 teddy bears
Universe has produced 25,000 teddy bears.

(produce) teddy bears since January, 1988
Universe has been producing teddy bears since January, 1988.

1. (make) wind-up Brenda dolls for three years
   _____

2. (spend) $30,000 to develop "Super Susie"
   _____

3. (sell) "Super Susie" since March 30, 1990
   _____

4. (sell) 45,000 "Super Susies"
   _____

5. (develop) three new product lines
   _____

MRS. ROMERO'S MEATLOAF RECIPE

Here is Mrs. Romero's world famous meatloaf recipe. Answer the questions below. Are you getting hungry?

2 lbs ground beef	1 clove garlic	Bake in 350°oven about 1 1/2 hours. Cut
2 eggs	1 tbsp parsley	four 3-inch slices of mozarella cheese
1/2 cp cornflakes	2 tsp salt	and arrange on the meatloaf. Melt cheese
1/2 cp chopped onion	1 tsp basil	in oven a few minutes and garnish with
1/2 cp tomato juice	1/4 tsp pepper	cherry tomatoes.

1. What does lbs stand for? _____
2. What does cp stand for? _____
3. How long does the meatloaf have to bake? _____
4. What does tsp stand for? _____
5. What does tbsp stand for? _____

PROGRAM 51

"And Justice for All"

ACT I

In this program, you will study...

VOCABULARY

Do you know the meaning of these words from Program 51?

jury
trial
defendant

GRAMMAR AND EXPRESSIONS

Do you know what these phrases or expressions mean?

feel sorry for
beyond any doubt

PRONUNCIATION

Do you know how to pronounce these words?

official
evidence

ACT II

U.S. LIFE

Do you know the name of the highest court in the United States? What American document is the highest law of the land?

☞ YOUR TURN

Have you or any member of your family ever worked in the legal system of your country? In what job?

"And Justice for All" ▶ 145

Here is the complete script with study material for Program 51. Use these materials before *or* after you listen.

INTRODUCTION TO ACT I

Today on TUNING IN THE U.S.A., *Robbie is handing out the family's mail. Marilyn receives a notice to appear for* **jury duty**[1] *at the* **county courthouse.**[2] *She is expected to serve as a member of a jury at a* **trial.**[3] *Marilyn has never done this before, and she wonders what it will be like. When she talks to Philip, he helps to answer some of her questions.*

ACT I

[*Music from the radio*]

Radio Announcer: And it's ten-twenty on a beautiful sunny Saturday morning.

Robbie: [*calling*] The mail is here! Hey, Dad, you got two letters and some **bills.**[4]

Philip: Thanks.

Robbie: Look at this envelope. It's addressed to Marilyn. And it's from the county courthouse.

Philip: Let me see it. Hmm. **County Clerk.**[5]
10   I think I know what it is. Is Marilyn in her room? I'll take this up to her. [*He knocks on Marilyn and Richard's door.*] Marilyn? It's Philip.

Marilyn: [*She opens the door.*] Good morning. I was just trying to finish writing a letter before the **mailman**[6] came. Did I miss him?

Philip: The mailman **has come and gone.**[7] He left this for you.

20 Marilyn: **Oh dear.**[8] It looks so **official.**[9] What is it? [*She opens the envelope.*]

Philip: It looks to me like a **notice**[10] for jury duty.

Marilyn: Philip, you're right. They want me to **appear**[11] next week at the county courthouse.

Philip: Ahhh. Well, I think you'll find it very interesting.

Marilyn: Really?

30 Philip: Sure. Jury duty is a very different way to spend your days. Very different from going to your **everyday**[12] job!

Marilyn: [*She thinks.*] Yeah ... I guess so. Philip?

Philip: Mmm-hmm.

Marilyn: I don't know if I can do it.

Philip: Why not?

---

[1] **jury [jə´rē] duty:** the obligation to serve on a jury
A jury is a 12-member group of citizens called to a courtroom to listen to facts presented at a trial.

[2] **county courthouse:** the county government building where trials take place

[3] **trial [trī´əl]:** a legal proceeding to settle an argument between two parties

[4] **bills:** requests for payment

[5] **County Clerk:** county official whose responsibilities include notifying citizens to appear for jury duty

[6] **mailman:** U.S. postal employee who delivers mail to residents

[7] **has come and gone:** has already visited and left

[8] **Oh, dear.**
This is an expression of worry or concern spoken at getting news of a serious nature.

[9] **official [ə fish´əl]:** coming from a branch of government; public

[10] **notice:** a paper with some official information
The FBI posted official *notices* about the criminals they are searching for.

[11] **appear [ə pēr´]:** come (when referring to a court of law)

[12] **everyday:** usual; common

The Supreme Court building in Washington, D.C.

40	Marilyn:	How can I ask Rita Mae for more time off from work? I already took my vacation.
	Philip:	Marilyn, Rita Mae **can't object.**[13] All employers know about jury duty. You're being called to **serve**[14] because it's your duty—your responsibility as a U.S. citizen.
	Marilyn:	Well, what about my job?
	Philip:	Nothing can happen to your job while you're on jury duty. It's **protected**[15] by law. No boss can
50		**fire**[16] a worker just because he or she has to spend a few days in a courtroom.
	Marilyn:	How do you know so much about this?
	Philip:	I was on a jury once.
	Marilyn:	Oh?
	Philip:	It was during a summer vacation when I was a medical student. **I'll never forget it.**[17]
60	Marilyn:	Tell me. What was the case about?
	Philip:	They said the man had stolen money. And they were right. So, the jury found him guilty. It was a pretty clear case.
	Marilyn:	Was it interesting for you?
	Philip:	It was facinating! I had never really seen the **legal system**[18] **at work.**[19] *[He laughs.]* For a few days, I even thought about **switching**[20] from
70		medicine to law.
	Marilyn:	I'm glad you didn't. You became a wonderful doctor.
	Philip:	Well, for a week, I was a pretty wonderful juror. At least, I thought so!
	Marilyn:	*[She laughs.]* I'm sure you were. Philip, thanks for telling me about *your* jury duty. I'm not worried about it anymore. In fact, I think jury duty will be interesting.

END OF ACT I

[13] **can't object:** can't refuse
[14] **serve:** spend time working in government service
He *served* in the Army for 5 years.
[15] **protected:** saved from harm; shielded
[16] **fire:** to take a person's job away
[17] **I'll never forget it.** = It made a lasting impression on my memory.
[18] **legal system:** the workings of the courts
[19] **at work:** in operation
[20] **switching:** changing

U.S. LIFE

The U.S. Constitution, which is the highest law in the land, says that any person accused of a crime has certain rights. He cannot be held in jail without being *charged* (formally accused of a specific crime). He has the right against *self-incrimination* (against being forced to confess guilt). He has the right to *legal counsel* (the advice of a lawyer), even if he cannot afford to pay the lawyer's fee. He has the right to hear the charges against him in a courtroom trial in front of a jury of his *peers* (other citizens like himself). Jury members are selected at random from the population. They then go through a *screening process* before being admitted to the jury, where they are asked questions to determine if they are biased (they have already decided in their mind about the guilt or innocence of the accused). If the judge and the defense and prosecution lawyers are satisfied that they are not biased, they are admitted to the jury.

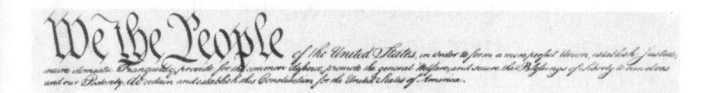

YOUR TURN

Have you ever been to a criminal trial in the United States? What decision did the jury reach, guilty or innocent?

Focus In

Philip says, "**You're being called to serve because it's your duty—your responsibility as a U.S. citizen.**" The verb *being called* is in the present continuous **tense (-ing)** and the **passive voice.** Passive voice constructions use the verb *to be* as an auxiliary. They make the subject the receiver of the action of the verb.

INTRODUCTION TO ACT II

This time on TUNING IN THE U.S.A., *we begin at a trial at the county courthouse. Marilyn is a juror at this trial. It is one of her duties as an American citizen. She is helping the law to work. Later, at home, the Stewarts have dinner together, and Marilyn tells her family all about her experience in the courtroom as a member of the jury.*

ACT II

Judge: [She bangs on her desk.] **Members of the jury, have you reached a decision?**[1]

Marilyn: We have, Judge.

Judge: How do you find the **defendant**?[2]

Marilyn: We, the jury, find the defendant, James Barker, **not guilty**.[3]

Judge: Thank you, members of the jury. James Barker, you're free to go.

[Inside the Stewarts' home, later that day]

10 Grandpa: Robbie, would you please pass me another one of those fine dinner rolls?

Ellen: Robbie!

Robbie: Yeah, Mom?

Ellen: Your grandfather is talking to you. Would you please pass Grandpa the dinner rolls? It's the second time he's asked for them.

Robbie: Oh, I'm sorry, Grandpa. I was just thinking about Marilyn in the
20 courtroom.

Grandpa: [joking] It's okay, **my boy**.[4] I prefer my dinner rolls hot, that's all.

Robbie: **Here you go,**[5] Grandpa.

Grandpa: Thank you.

Robbie: Hey, Marilyn, could you explain why you let **that Barker guy**[6] go free?

Marilyn: Because he wasn't guilty. He was innocent.

Robbie: But I thought someone saw him steal
30 the car.

---

[1] **Members of the jury, have you reached a decision?** This is the formula the judge uses to request a decision by the jury.

[2] **defendant** [dē fen´dənt]: person accused of an illegal act

[3] **not guilty** A person is *not guilty* when he or she has been determined in a court of law not to have committed the illegal act he or she was accused of.

[4] **my boy:** young man This expression is used mostly by the older generation.

[5] **Here you go.** = (informal) Here you are.

[6] **that Barker guy . . .** = (informal) Mr. Barker. This way of referring to someone we don't know shows a lack of respect for the person.

Marilyn:	*One* person thought he saw him do it. But that wasn't enough **evidence**⁷ to send the man to jail.
Ellen:	You mean you doubted that he was guilty?
Marilyn:	I did. And the judge had told us that we had to be **certain**⁸ of his guilt—**beyond any doubt.**⁹ **Otherwise,**¹⁰ the jury had to let him go free.
Ellen:	Was it a hard decision to make?
Marilyn:	Not really. His boss said he was at work at the time the car was stolen.
Grandpa:	So, all the jurors agreed that the man was innocent, right?
Marilyn:	Only in the end. Finally all twelve of us agreed. At first, three jurors thought he was guilty. But we talked and talked about it—for three hours—and finally we all agreed.
Ellen:	How did it feel being a juror? You had a lot of **power**¹¹ over the man's life.
Marilyn:	I know. It was a big responsibility, Ellen. It made me listen very carefully to everything that was said in court.
Robbie:	**I feel sorry for the man**¹² whose car was stolen.
Marilyn:	I felt sorry for him, too. His car is still missing.
Robbie:	I wonder if the guy will ever get it back? Mom, would you pass the basket of dinner rolls back this way?
Ellen:	Mmm-hmm.
Robbie:	Hey, the basket is empty. Who ate the last roll?
Grandpa:	I confess. I'm the guilty one. No need for a judge and jury. I ate it. I've always loved Ellen's dinner rolls.

[Everyone laughs.]

END OF ACT II

Focus In

Robbie:	Hey, Marilyn, could you explain why you let that Barker guy go free?
Marilyn:	Because he wasn't guilty. He was innocent.

Grandpa confesses that he is *guilty* of eating the rolls. We can be certain that he is not *innocent.*

⁷ **evidence** [ev´ə dəns]: the facts presented in a trial which are used to prove the guilt or innocence of the defendant
⁸ **certain** [sər´tən]: sure
⁹ **beyond any doubt:** without doubt
¹⁰ **otherwise . . .** [əth´ər wīz] = if not . . .
¹¹ **power:** the authority and means to impose one's will on others
The government has the *power* to raise an army and to levy taxes on the citizens.
¹² **I feel sorry for the man . . .** = I sympathize with the man . . .
We all *felt sorry* for the victims of the earthquake.

U.S. LIFE

In the United States, a person accused of a crime is *presumed innocent.* This means that it is the responsibility of the prosecution to prove he is guilty by showing evidence in court. Many *suspects* (people the police believe committed a crime) are not arrested because, although the police may feel sure that a certain person has committed a crime, they do not have *sufficient evidence* (facts) to establish a case against him. Getting evidence is therefore a very important part of the job of prosecuting criminals. Getting evidence must be done within the law. The Supreme Court of the United States (the highest court in the land) has decided that the police, in order to get evidence against a person, may not violate that person's rights. They may not, for example, break into a suspect's house to get evidence. They must obtain a *search warrant* (a legal permit issued by a judge) to enter a home or car to search it. Unless evidence is gotten legally, it may not be presented in court. Many people feel that the legal system protects criminals and makes the job of the police too difficult. Others are very happy with the way the system works, especially when they are accused of something they didn't do.

☞ YOUR TURN

- Do you feel the legal system protects criminals too much?
- Have you ever been accused of something you didn't do? Do you remember how you felt?

Activities

Here are some activities to help you check your understanding of this program.

VOCABULARY OF THE LEGAL SYSTEM

See if you can match these words with their definitions. Write the letter of the definition next to the word at the left.

_____ 1. jury
_____ 2. innocent
_____ 3. guilty
_____ 4. defendant
_____ 5. legal system
_____ 6. notice
_____ 7. trial
_____ 8. evidence
_____ 9. biased
_____ 10. charged
_____ 11. search warrant
_____ 12. suspect

a. the workings of the courts
b. accused person at a trial
c. the people who listen to evidence at a trial and decide if the defendant is guilty or innocent
d. court proceeding
e. a paper with some official information
f. person police think committed a crime
g. facts that prove guilt or innocence
h. paper issued by a judge permitting police to enter a home
i. mentally decided for or against something
j. formally accused of a crime
k. proven to have committed a crime
l. proven not to have committed a crime

JOURNALISM—THE PASSIVE VOICE

Newspaper stories use the passive voice a lot because, in the news of the world, events happen *to* people. Since we usually consider people, and not things, to be the most important part of a sentence, we want to make them the subject. This requires using the passive voice. Look at this example from a news story about an earthquake flood.

"The earthquake destroyed the home of John Beaumont." (active voice)

It would be better to make *John Beaumont* the subject:

John Beaumont's home was destroyed by the earthquake. (passive voice)

Change these news story sentences from active to passive voice. Use *was/were* + past participle.

1. "The war ruined many buildings."
"_____"

2. "The flood killed 123 people."
"_____"

3. "The fire destroyed most of San Francisco."
"_____"

4. "The news shocked many people."
"_____"

5. "The robber stole all our valuables."
"_____"

PROGRAM 52

"Home, Sweet Home"

ACT I

In this program, you will study . . .

VOCABULARY

Do you know the meaning of these words from Program 52?

hurrah!
welcome home

GRAMMAR AND EXPRESSIONS

Do you know what these phrases or expressions mean?

You are a sight for sore eyes!
Hear! Hear!
all the comforts of home
Here's to you.

PRONUNCIATION

ACT II

Do you know how to pronounce these words?

champagne
fascinating

Hint: Each has one silent letter.

U.S. LIFE

Do you know how to propose a toast in English?

☞ YOUR TURN

What's the best part of taking a long trip away from home, leaving or returning home?

INTRODUCTION TO ACT I

Today on TUNING IN THE U.S.A., *Richard arrives home from his trip around the United States. He has been taking pictures for his book of photographs,* FAMILY ALBUM U.S.A. *His mother and father are at home. So is his wife Marilyn and his brother Robbie. They all sit together with Richard in the kitchen. They drink tea and talk about his travels. Grandpa and Susan are not home. But they will be there later to help celebrate Richard's return.*

ACT I

Richard: *[He plays the harmonica and sings.]* "When Richard comes driving home again. **Hurrah, hurrah!**[1] Hello, Riverdale! *[He turns the car into the driveway.]* There it is—the old house. It's never looked as good to me as it does today. **Home, sweet home.**[2] *[He enters the house.]*

Marilyn: *[calling]* Richard? Is that you?

10 Richard: It's me, **all right**.[3]

Marilyn: Hi, honey.

Richard: *[embracing]* Hi, Marilyn.

Ellen: *[approaching]* **Oh, you are a sight for sore eyes!**[4]

Richard: Hi, Mom!

Ellen: *[She calls.]* Robbie, your brother is home!

Philip: *[approaching]* **Welcome home,**[5] Son.

Richard: It's good to see you, Dad . . .

20 Robbie: *[approaching]* Hey, look who's here!

Richard: The **wandering**[6] photographer. How are **ya doin'**,[7] Robbie?

Robbie: *[They shake hands.]* Good.

Ellen: You must be tired from your trip. Would you like some tea?

Richard: I'd love some, Mom, as soon as I **unpack**[8] the car.

Ellen: Come on into the kitchen when you're done. I want to hear all about your trip.

30 *[Later, in the kitchen]*

Ellen: More tea, Richard?

Richard: Yes, please, Mom.

Philip: So where did you **start out from**[9] this morning?

[1] **hurrah** [hər rä´]: cry of joy at some good news

[2] **Home, sweet home.**
This is a traditional saying to express love for one's home.

[3] **. . . all right:** for sure
This tag on ending can be used to add emphasis to any affirmative statement.

[4] **Oh, you are a sight for sore eyes!** = It's a relief to see you again after such a long time!

[5] **Welcome home.**
This is the standard polite way to receive a returning family member back into the home.

[6] **wandering:** traveling freely from place to place

[7] **. . . ya doin'** = spoken form only for: "you doing"

[8] **unpack:** remove one's things from

[9] **start out from:** begin (the day's travel)

	Richard:	I was up at **Niagara Falls,**[10] near Buffalo, New York. What spectacular views! That waterfall is amazing!
	Ellen:	It must be getting a little cold up there **this time of year.**[11]
40	Richard:	Yeah, it was **chilly**[12] last night. No **camping out**[13] for me. I decided to **treat myself**[14] to a motel room with a good bed, a color TV, and plenty of heat!
	Robbie:	**All the comforts of home.**[15]
	Richard:	Not quite . . .
	Marilyn:	Mmm-hmm.
	Philip:	Did it get a little **lonesome**[16] out there, Son?
50	Richard:	It did—except when Marilyn came out to travel with me last month.
	Marilyn:	We had such a good time together.
	Richard:	Until you had to leave. And then, well, I got a lot of work done. **That's for sure.**[17]
	Ellen:	You know, Richard, you're very lucky to have work that you love to do. Look how far it's taken you this year. All over the country.
60	Richard:	It's true. But you know what makes me feel lucky today is having you all to come back to. I missed all of you. Mom, Dad, Marilyn, even you, Robbie!
	Richard:	*[They all laugh.]* Susan and Grandpa. Hey, where are they, **anyway?**[18]
	Philip:	Grandpa is picking up Susan at the train. She's coming out for the dinner party tonight.
70	Richard:	The dinner party?
	Philip:	Yes. It's a **homecoming party.**[19] And you're the **guest of honor.**[20] They can't wait to see you!
	Richard:	And I can't wait to see them! This should be a great evening. What a homecoming!

END OF ACT I

Focus In

Here are some ways to say "Welcome home."

Hi, honey. (Richard's wife)
Oh, you are a sight for sore eyes. (Richard's mother)
Hey, look who's here. (Richard's brother)

☞ YOUR TURN

- Have you ever returned home to a celebration after a long trip away? Where had you gone?
- Do you enjoy long trips?

[10] **Niagara Falls:** famous waterfalls in upstate New York on the Niagara River

[11] **this time of year:** this season (summer, autumn, winter, spring) of the year
[12] **chilly:** moderately cold (weather)
[13] **camping out:** sleeping outdoors at night
[14] **treat myself:** give myself something; indulge myself
[15] **All the comforts of home.**
This saying refers to the conveniences of a modern home: running water, heat, electricity, and so on.
[16] **lonesome:** lonely; suffering from solitude
[17] **That's for sure.**
This expression emphasizes our agreement with something that someone says.
[18] **anyway:** in fact
[19] **homecoming party:** party given in honor of a family member's return home after a long absence
[20] **guest of honor:** the person who is the reason for a party or celebration

U.S. LIFE

Americans are no different from people anywhere when it comes to homecomings. The joy at returning home after a long absence is a universal human feeling. But where homecoming celebrations are concerned, probably no city on earth tops New York. You have missed something spectacular if you haven't seen a New York City "ticker tape" parade (a parade in which ticker tape from the Wall Street stock markets is thrown from the windows along the parade route). When Charles Lindbergh flew nonstop across the Atlantic Ocean in 1927, he was greeted by a joyous crowd on his return to New York. Perhaps the greatest ticker tape parade of all time was held in 1969 when the three American astronauts Buzz Aldrin, Neil Armstrong, and Michael Collins paraded down Broadway after they returned from the first mission to put men on the moon.

INTRODUCTION TO ACT II

This time on TUNING IN THE U.S.A., the Stewart family has gathered together to give Richard a welcome-home party. They listen as Richard tells them about his experiences **on the road.**[1] *But the last few months have been busy for all the Stewarts. And so they begin to share their stories with Richard. The family is together again.*

ACT II

All: *[singing]* **"For he's a jolly good fellow, for he's a jolly good fellow, for he's a jolly good fellow . . . which nobody can deny!**[2]

Grandpa: **Hip, hip . . .**

All: **Hooray!**[3]

[Grandpa laughs.]

Philip: *[He opens a bottle of champagne.]* **Champagne**[4] **for everyone!** *[He holds up his glass and taps it.]* **I'd like to propose a toast.**[5] To Richard . . . and his camera. Welcome home!

All: To Richard. The **roving**[6] photographer. Welcome home. **Home to stay!**[7]

Grandpa: Richard, was your trip around the country everything you expected?

Richard: It was much more than I expected, Grandpa.

Grandpa: I believe it.

Richard: And, Grandpa, I got pretty good at this. *[He plays the harmonica that Grandpa gave him for his thirtieth birthday.]*

[Grandpa laughs.]

Robbie: Grandpa's harmonica!

Grandpa: Sounds pretty nice.

Susan: Richard, did you get all the photographs you needed for your project?

Richard: I may need a few more, Susan. But I'm sure I can get them **right around here.**[8]

Philip: It sounds to me as if you don't want to go traveling again for a while.

Marilyn: Not unless I go with him. *[She laughs.]*

Richard: That's right!

---

[1] **on the road:** traveling

[2] **"For he's a jolly good fellow . . . which nobody can deny!**
Words to a song honoring a guest of honor

[3] **Hip, hip . . . Hooray!**
The cheer that ends the above song, usually said three times.
Three cheers for Freddie!
Hip, hip . . . Hooray!
Hip, hip . . . Hooray!
Hip, hip . . . Hooray!

[4] **champagne [sham pān´]:** a fizzy alcoholic drink made from fermented white grapes
Champagne is the usual drink served for celebrations.

[5] **I'd like to propose a toast.**
This is the formula for introducing a toast. A *toast* is a short remark praising a guest of honor. Following the remark, all guests raise their glasses and take a drink.

[6] **roving:** wandering

[7] **home to stay**
Home to stay or *here to stay* expresses the speaker's wish never to leave home or this place (here) again.

[8] **right around here:** in this area

A New York ticker tape parade

	Marilyn:	I'll never forget being at Glacier National Park. Ever since I was a little girl, I've wanted to go there!
40	Robbie:	And you did! You even had a chance to **sleep under the stars.**⁹ To eat by a campfire!
	Ellen:	A week ago, you could have done that right here, Richard. Did you hear that Riverdale had a power failure while you were away? We all sat around the fire right in the living room.
	Richard:	Really? I want to hear all about it.
	Grandpa:	And did you know I went back to school?
50	Richard:	Grandpa, I didn't know that, **either.**¹⁰ Hey, what have I missed by being away?
	Philip:	You missed seeing me run my first race. Next year, Ellen may be right **by my side.**¹¹ Robbie might be there, too!
	Robbie:	Dad, I'm going to be at college!
60	Ellen:	[She laughs.] That's right, Philip! And I told you I'd *try* running, but I didn't make any promises to run a race.
	Grandpa:	**Next thing you know,**¹² he'll have me running too.
	[Everyone laughs.]	
70	Richard:	[He holds up his glass and taps it.] Umm... I'd like to propose a toast now. I guess this is a toast to all of you. In the last few months I've seen a lot of our country. It's beautiful and **fascinating**¹³ out there. But the best part of the whole trip is coming home again. **So here's to all of you**¹⁴—all of us—the family!
	All:	[toasting] Ahh. **Hear! Hear!**¹⁵ To the Stewarts—to us—the family!

END OF ACT II

⁹ **sleep under the stars:** sleep outside without the cover of a tent or shelter
¹⁰ **either:** also (used with negative sentences)
¹¹ **by my side:** with me; next to me
¹² **Next thing you know...** = Soon after that...
This common expression links events in a story.
¹³ **fascinating** [fas´ə nā ting]: extremely interesting
¹⁴ **So here's to all of you.** = Here is a toast in your honor.
¹⁵ **Hear! Hear!**
This is a cry of approval after a toast or a speech.

U.S. LIFE

The songs, sayings, and rituals used in celebrations are handed down in a culture from generation to generation. They are an important way of continuing our cultural heritage. Each culture has its own way of celebrating. In diplomatic ceremonies, when people from different cultures meet, both sides must be careful to respect each other's *protocols* (established practices). Some historians believe that the success that ex-President Richard Nixon had in his meetings with the leaders of the People's Republic of China was because the Chinese liked him personally. He was an effective *toastmaster* at the state dinners. The same has been said of ex-President Reagan. Celebrating can be, at times, a very serious business.

Focus In

Philip says, **"I'd like to propose a toast."** But first he gets everyone's attention by tapping his glass. This means he wants to say something for everyone to hear. He raises his glass and says something nice about Richard.

YOUR TURN

- Do you enjoy large formal dinners with many toasts and speechmaking?
- Have you ever been a *toastmaster*?

Activities

Here are some activities to help you check your understanding of this program.

RICHARD'S TRIP

Marilyn was putting Richard's clothes into the washer when she found a bunch of postcards addressed to her from Richard when he was in Arizona and New Mexico. Richard had forgotten to mail them! Read the postcards and answer the comprehension questions below.

> Dear Marilyn,
> Taos, New Mexico is one of the most charming places I've ever been. Life seems so much slower than New York. The mission is older than most buildings back East! Can't wait to see you.
> —Richard
>
> Marilyn Stewart
> 41 Riverdale Dr.
> Riverdale, N.Y. 11758

> Dear Marilyn, Sept. 16
> Today I visited the Hopi Indian Reservation and I learned about some of their fascinating customs. They finally agreed to let me take some shots. My love to everyone, and especially you.
> Richard
>
> Marilyn Stewart
> 411 Riverdale Dr.
> Riverdale, N.Y. 11758

True or False

1. Richard took a walking tour of the Grand Canyon. ____
2. Richard took photos of the Grand Canyon. ____
3. Taos, New Mexico is a busy town. ____
4. Taos, New Mexico has a long tradition. ____

NOW IT'S YOUR TURN

On a separate piece of paper write a postcard to someone in your family or a close friend. Use some of the expressions you see above.

ANSWER KEY

Program 27: "Moving In"

Act II Focus In
Eva: I think he's been playing all afternoon.

Activities

FOLLOW THE MAP
1. next door to
2. across from
3. around the corner from
4. in front of

POLITE EXPRESSIONS
1. Richard
2. Michael
3. Richard
4. Eva
5. Marilyn
6. Eva
7. Eva

PREPOSITION DECISIONS
1. since
2. for
3. since
4. for
5. for

Program 28: "Just the Two of Us"

U.S. Life
Americans can drive at 16 years of age.
There is no legal age for dating. It's up to parents.
Americans are eligible to vote at age 18.
The age requirement for getting married in the United States varies from state to state.

Activities

WHICH CAME FIRST?
2. Susan noticed Richard and Marilyn at the concert.
5. Richard and Marilyn left the party.
4. Richard met Robert, the photography editor at the magazine.
1. Richard and Marilyn were talking about their first dates together.
3. Susan invited them to a party after the concert.
6. Richard and Marilyn rode the bus home to Riverdale.

IN-LAWS
1. mother-in-law
2. daughter-in-law
3. father-in-law
4. son-in-law
5. brother-in-law

TAG QUESTIONS
1. did they?
2. didn't she?
3. does he?
4. is it?
5. have we?

Program 29: "I Didn't Mean To"

Act I Focus In
Enjoy the movie.

Act II Focus In
equally as

Activities

MAKE A MATCH
1. e
2. d
3. f
4. a
5. b
6. c

TWO USES OF *SHOULD*
1. P
2. O
3. P
4. P
5. O
6. O
7. O
8. P

AM I GETTING THROUGH TO YOU?
1. hurtful
2. helpful
3. hurtful
4. helpful
5. helpful
6. helpful
7. hurtful
8. hurtful

Program 30: "A Song From Long Ago"

U.S. Life
Bob Dylan

Act I Focus In
learning

Act II Focus In
don't you?

Activities

USED TO
1. used to walk
2. didn't use to be
3. used to buy
4. used to open

157

5. use to have
6. used to work
7. used to sell
8. used to earn
9. use to have
10. used to sing

TOO AND EITHER
1. Max was, too.
2. Max didn't either.
3. Max could, too.
4. Max wouldn't either.
5. Max did, too.
6. Max is, too.
7. Max does, too.
8. Max can, too.

Program 31: "Recycling"

U.S. Life
A place where used glass, aluminum, and paper are collected to be processed and used again.

Activities

PHRASAL VERBS
woke up
took out
figure out
line up
came along with
melt it down
taking up
run out of
filled up

SO MUCH / SO MANY
so many
so much
so many
so much
so many
so much

APOLOGIES
Answers may vary.
1. How clumsy of me. I'm sorry for spilling soda on your carpet.
2. I'm sorry. Is this your seat?
3. Excuse me.

Program 32: "A Getaway Vacation"

U.S. Life
A national park is a large area owned and maintained by the federal government in its natural state for the recreational use of the public.

Activities

USE OF THE ARTICLE THE
___ Glacier National Park
___ Seattle
the Cascade Mountain Range
___ Mount Rainier
the Columbia River
___ Canada
the Canadian Royal Mounted Police
the Rocky Mountains
___ Montana
___ Flathead Lake
the Riverdale Mall

Program 33: "It's a Deal"

U.S. Life
Walt Disney

Activities

WHO WOULD SAY IT?
1. Davillo
2. Susan
3. Davillo
4. Susan
5. Susan
6. Davillo

MOVIE TRIVIA QUIZ
1. Robert Redford
2. Jean Cocteau
3. Steamboat Willie
4. Steven Spielberg
5. Luis Buñuel

RETELL THE EPISODE
6. Susan and Mr. Davillo agreed on how to do the project.
1. Mr. Davillo came to Susan's office in New York.
3. Mr. Davillo told Susan he was Maxy Manners' voice.
4. Susan came out to California to visit the studio.
2. Mr. Davillo explained that he wanted the movie to be in theaters at the same time the Maxy Manners toy was in the stores.
5. Susan watched the filming of a scene at Mr. Davillo's studio.

Program 34: "The Great Northwest"

U.S. Life
Environmentalists, who want to preserve the forests as nature preserves, and the lumber industry, which wants to use the forests as an economic resource.

Activities

THE TOWN MEETING
order
logger
cut down
environmentalist
our children

ANSWER KEY ▶ 159

ASKING PERMISSION
1. Would you mind if I closed the window?
2. Would you mind if I sat down here?
3. Would you mind if I took a picture?
4. Would you mind if I used the telephone?
5. Would you mind if I used the restroom?

OBJECTING
1. What are we going to do for transportation?
2. What are we going to do for recreation?
3. What are we going to do for education?
4. What are we going to do for electricity?
5. What are we going to do for wood?

Program 35: "Ethnic Food"

U.S. Life
New York, San Francisco, Los Angeles, and Chicago all have excellent ethnic foods because there are people of so many nationalities in those cities.

Activities

A HEALTHY DIET
better
easier
more fattening
more worried

MATCH UP
1. j
2. a
3. g
4. f
5. h
6. i
7. b
8. d
9. c
10. e

IDENTIFY THE FOOD
1. a
2. d
3. c
4. f
5. i
6. e
7. j
8. h
9. g
10. b

Program 36: "Riverdale Day"

U.S. Life
A community project is a job done by a group of volunteers from a neighborhood.

Activities

I'VE ALREADY . . .
I've already done the outside walls.
I've already cut the grass on the ball field.
I've already taken the trash to the dump.
I've already brought it over to the football field.

RETELL THE STORY
4. Philip arrived at the ball field to work.
2. Philip made scrambled eggs for breakfast.
1. Robbie got up early and made peanut butter and jelly sandwiches.
6. Jimmy and Robbie were painting the bathroom stalls when Philip arrived.
3. Philip helped Robbie out the door with his painting tools.
5. Mr. Hopper asked Philip if he was looking for Robbie.

IDIOM REVIEW
how's it going
just wait till
talk about
hardly
take your time
we made it
seems like yesterday
headed
changing for the better
more or less
by the way
give you her best

Program 37: "On the Nature Trail"

U.S. Life
recreational vehicle

Activities

WHAT DOES IT STAND FOR?
RV stands for **recreational vehicle.**
BA stands for **Bachelor of Arts degree.**
TV stands for **television.**
NYC stands for **New York City.**
LA stands for **Los Angeles.**
PD stands for **police department.**

QUESTION TAG REVIEW
1. are you?
2. don't you?
3. didn't you?
4. haven't you?
5. have you?

YOUR HOME ON WHEELS
there is
there is
there is
there are
there is
there is
there are
there is

Program 38: "The Windy City"

U.S. Life
Chicago

Activities

MAKING SUGGESTIONS
Answers may vary.

SPEAKING OF . . .
1. d
2. e
3. c
4. b
5. a

MIND IF . . . ?
1. Mind if I turn down the TV?
2. Mind if I take your picture?
3. Mind if I sit there? or Is that seat free?

Program 39: "Such a Good Teacher"

U.S. Life
They are video games.

Activities

WHO SAID IT?
1. Robbie   Mr. Pollard
2. Mr. Pollard   Robbie
3. Robbie   Mr. Pollard
4. Robbie   Mr. Pollard
5. Mr. Pollard   Robbie
6. Robbie   Mr. Pollard
7. Mr. Pollard   Robbie

CHECK YOUR SPELLING
terrific friends disgusting beautiful

Program 40: "The Motor City"

U.S. Life
Ohio, Indiana, Illinois, Michigan, Wisconsin

Activities

PERFORMANCE EVALUATION
1. Pete works faster than Joe.
2. Medved works more efficiently than Jalil.
3. Robert works harder than Jack.
4. Paul works more carelessly than Ed.
5. Maury works more diligently than Sal.

PRONUNCIATION ROUNDUP
1. late   weight
2. bite   sight
3. buy   high
4. make   lake
5. fried   died

Program 41: "College Bound"

U.S. Life
SAT (Scholastic Aptitude Test)

Activities

REGRETS
1. I could have gotten an A in American History.
2. I could have made an effort in math.
3. I could have taken good notes in English class.
4. I could have gotten up earlier.
5. I could have used my time better in school.

WHO SAID IT?
1. Alexandra
2. Robbie
3. Susan
4. Ms. Lubecki
5. Robbie

PERSONALITY QUIZ
1. Sure. The longer the better.
2. Sure. The more difficult the better.
3. Sure. The more challenging the better.
4. Sure. The harder the better.
5. Sure. The earlier the better.

Program 42: "The Health Run"

U.S. Life
marathon

Activities

WHO IS IT?
1. Philip
2. Philip
3. Ellen
4. Ellen

THINGS IN COMMON
1. They both are watching what they eat.
2. They both are exercising more.
3. They both are planning to run in a race next Saturday.

THE HANDICAPPED TRIATHLON
1. true
2. false
3. false
4. false

Program 43: "Continuing Education"

U.S. Life
A community college is a two-year college.

Activities

THE OLD DAYS
1. knew architecture
2. knew big machines
3. put in long hours
4. was as careful

ANSWER KEY ▶ 161

THE CLASS SCHEDULE
1. Construction Methods
2. Modern Marketing
3. Construction Methods
4. 13 hours

Program 44: "They're Playing Our Song"

U.S. Life
Jazz and Cajun music come from New Orleans. Folk music comes from the Appalachian Mountain region. Country music comes from the plains states.

Activities

AN AMERICAN FOLK SONG
I'm half crazy,
All for the love of you!
I can't afford a carriage,
On the seat.

DO YOU KNOW WHAT THE QUESTION WAS?
1. I don't know what "jamboree" means.
2. I don't know where Bob Dylan lives now.
3. I don't know how many songs he wrote.
4. I don't know why I can't sing in tune.
5. I don't know when the concert begins.

THE AMERICAN MUSICOLOGIST
1. a
2. b
3. b
4. c

Program 45: "Campus Life"

U.S. Life
College students stay in a dormitory.

Act I Focus In
roommate

Activities

ROBBIE'S WISHING WELL
1. I wish I could decide which college to attend.
2. I wish I had more self-confidence.
3. I wish there weren't so many colleges to choose from.
4. I wish I had used my time better in school.

SOCIAL REGISTER
Greetings
3. Hi.
2. How are you today?
1. Hello.
Surprise
1. My Goodness!
3. Wow!
2. That's amazing!

Apologies
3. Oops.
2. Sorry.
1. I'm so sorry.
Introductions
1. I'd like you to meet Mary.
2. This is Mary.
3. Meet Mary.
Salutations
2. Nice meeting you.
1. It was a pleasure meeting you.
3. So long.
Requests
3. Please turn the music down.
2. Would you please turn down the music.
1. Would you mind turning down the music.

Program 46: "The Volunteers"

U.S. Life
Tennessee

Activities
Answers may vary.

Program 47: "The Life of Riley"

U.S. Life
A retirement community is a community that is populated mostly or entirely by elderly retired people.

Activities

THE LIFE OF RILEY
1. having a tennis lesson on Monday.
2. having choir practice on Tuesday.
3. participating in group discussion on Wednesday.
4. taking a trip to upstate New York on Thursday.

REPORTED SPEECH
1. He said he loved Cedar Hills.
2. He said he was learning to play tennis.
3. He said life was wonderful there.

TELEPHONE LANGUAGE AND "IN PERSON" LANGUAGE
1. telephone
2. in person
3. in person
4. telephone
5. in person
6. telephone

Program 48: "Lost and Found"

U.S. Life
a credit card account

162 ◀ ANSWER KEY

Activities

USED TO
1. used to manage
2. getting used to managing
3. used to lose
4. get used to balancing

HOPE FOR/WISH FOR
1. hoping for
2. wishing
3. hoping for
4. hoping

NOW YOU TELL THE STORY
3. Marilyn found Robbie's money in the clothes dryer.
4. Robbie and Phil went to the bank to set up a checking account for Robbie.
5. Robbie and Phil got a double chocolate cake dessert.
1. Robbie got his paycheck cashed.
2. Robbie couldn't find his money in the dresser.

Program 49: "A Dark and Stormy Night"

U.S. Life
911

Activities

THE BIG BLACKOUT
1. I was riding the elevator when it stopped between floors.
2. We were responding to a call in the Village when everything went dark.
3. I was taking the subway to Queens when it quit halfway there.
4. I was delivering a baby when somebody turned out the lights.
5. I was asking my girlfried to marry me when her face disappeared into the dark. The waiter lit a candle, and she said "yes."

WHO SAID IT?
Ellen
Robbie
Mrs. Romero
Philip

Program 50: "The Wooden Whistle"

U.S. Life
An entrepreneur is a person who creates and runs his own business.

Activities

UNIVERSE TOY COMPANY: THE ANNUAL REPORT
1. Universe Toy Company has been making wind-up Brenda dolls for three years.
2. Universe Toy Company has spent $30,000 to develop "Super Susie."
3. Universe Toy Company has been selling "Super Susie" since March 30, 1990.
4. Universe Toy Company has sold 45,000 "Super Susies."
5. Universe Toy Company has developed three new product lines.

MRS. ROMERO'S MEATLOAF RECIPE
1. pounds
2. cup
3. one and a half hours
4. teaspoon
5. tablespoon

Program 51: "And Justice for All"

U.S. Life
The United States Supreme Court is the highest court in the United States. The United States Constitution is the highest law of the land.

Activities

VOCABULARY OF THE LEGAL SYSTEM
1. c
2. l
3. k
4. b
5. a
6. e
7. d
8. g
9. i
10. j
11. h
12. f

JOURNALISM—THE PASSIVE VOICE
1. Many buildings were ruined by the war.
2. 123 people were killed by the earthquake.
3. Most of San Francisco was destroyed by the fire.
4. Many people were shocked by the news.
5. All our valuables were stolen by the robber.

Program 52: "Home, Sweet Home"

U.S. Life
A toast can be proposed with the words "Here's to (name)" or "I'd like to propose a toast to (name)."

Activities

RICHARD'S TRIP
Answers may vary.

USEFUL VOCABULARY AND EXPRESSIONS

The number after each word indicates the episode in which the word or expression first appears.
adj = adjective; adv = adverb; n = noun; v = verb

A
a great deal [a lot of] (43)
a sight for sore eyes (52)
about to (32)
accepted [adj] (41)
aching (42)
active (47)
activity room (47)
add in (35)
adios (44)
admire (37)
advisor (41)
African-American (45)
After you (28)
alarm [n] (46)
all kinds (38)
all over (27)
all over [everywhere] (43)
all right [for sure] (52)
all right! (42)
all the comforts of home (37)
all the time (28)
an awful lot (43)
an easy drive (47)
animated movie (33)
another (45)
antique (30)
any minute (46)
any minute now (39)
anyway [in any case] (50)
anyway [in fact] (52)
apologize (31)
appear [arrive] (31)
appear [in court] (51)
apply to (41)
appreciate (32)
arcade (39)
arrange (32)
as long as (28)
assign (39)
astronomy (45)
at [the price of] (46)
at work (51)

B
background (45)
bad news (50)
baked potato (50)
ball field (36)
bandage (29)
barbecue grill (27)
basement (29)
bean sprouts (35)
best friend (45)
beyond any doubt (51)
bill [n] (48)
black bear (37)
bleeding (29)
Bless you. (41)
blues (38)
border (32)
boring (40)
Boy! (42)
Boy Scout (44)
break [v] (40)

brew (47)
bright [color] (40)
bring in (40)
Brooklyn Bridge (27)
brother (38)
bucket (35)
buddy (34)
builder (36)
bulldozer (36)
butcher (27)
button (30)
by trade (34)

C
cabin (33)
calf/calves (37)
camp out [v] (37)
campground (37)
campsite (37)
care for [want] (48)
cared for [maintained] (47)
carry on (41)
cart (35)
cartoon (33)
cash [v] (48)
cat and mouse (39)
catalogue (41)
catch my breath (27)
catch on fire (46)
catch up to (35)
cattle auction (29)
Central Park (28)
certain [sure] (51)
chainsaw (34)
champagne (52)
change one's mind (45)
character (33)
charcoal (27)
check [n] (40)
check [v] (30)
checking account (48)
cheer (42)
chilly (52)
chop [v] (29)
cider (41)
clean up after oneself (45)
clear off (45)
close call (39)
close up (46)
coffee break (42)
Columbia University (41)
come down with [an illness] (41)
come out (29)
come up with (34)
coming right up (40)
comments (34)
community college (43)
concerned (34)
conservationist (34)
construction (43)
container (31)
continuing education (43)
convenient (45)
core (45)
County Clerk (51)

county courthouse (51)
cross fingers [for good luck] (32)
cute (33)

D
damaged (29)
darkroom (29)
dates (28)
deal [n] (35)
deal [v] (48)
defendant (51)
definitely (40)
delicious (49)
delighted (38)
demonstrate (50)
design [n] (33)
design [v] (45)
detective (42)
developing bath (29)
developing solution (29)
diet (35)
digging (36)
diner (40)
dinner party (35)
disgusting (39)
display [n] (27)
disturb (31)
do business with (33)
do my best (30)
doc [slang for doctor] (42)
doesn't hurt (41)
dollar amount (48)
donation (46)
donuts (35)
doorway (47)
dormitory (45)
double chocolate cake (48)
Douglas fir (34)
drag [v] (31)
drawer (32)
drawing (43)
driveway (31)

E
eagle (37)
earaches (36)
eggplant (35)
either (30)
elderly (49)
elk (37)
emergency (49)
energy (36)
engineering (33)
environmental (31)
escaped (28)
ever since (32)
every so [very] (49)
everyday [usual] (51)
evidence (51)
exactly (28)
exchange student (45)
exercise program (42)
exhausted (42)
exhibit (28)
expert (50)

exposure (29)
extra (46)

F
fall [n] [autumn] (41)
fancy-looking (37)
fascinating (52)
feel [think] (46)
feel free to (40)
feelings (38)
fella' [slang] (34)
fellow (42)
fiddle [n] (44)
fight a fire (46)
figure out (31)
film producer (33)
find (37)
finish line (42)
fir (34)
fire [dismiss from a job] [v] (51)
fire chief (46)
fire drill (46)
fireworks (27)
fit someone's needs (41)
folks (37)
for a while (30)
for every (45)
for miles around (49)
for one thing (38)
for profit (50)
for the fun of it (50)
Forest Service (34)
forever (45)
Fourth of July (27)
free [at no charge] (30)
free [not occupied] (34)
fresh (35)
fresh (47)
fried egg (40)
from now on (29)
fun (28)
funny [unusual] (50)
furniture (27)

G
garbage (31)
garden (30)
general store (46)
genius (41)
George Washington Bridge (28)
get a chance (38)
get going (31)
get hurt (27)
get lost (31)
get off (28)
get off work (40)
get together [v] (36)
get used to (48)
give a hand (36)
give away (50)
give it a try (50)
give me a break (39)
glacier (32)

163

Glacier National Park (32)
go up (43)
going on (35)
good [intelligent] (45)
good heavens (45)
good shape (42)
good-looking (30)
gospel (38)
grab (31)
grade (41)
great (27)
Greenwich Village (44)
grow up (48)
guess [v] (30)
guess what? (32)
guest of honor (52)
guide (40)
guilty (51)
guy (40)

H
half over (41)
handful (35)
handle [n] (31)
handle [v] (35)
hang on (34)
happy ending (46)
hard part (48)
hardly (28)
hardly ever (45)
Have a seat (41)
Health Run (42)
hear, hear! (52)
heating (43)
height (30)
help yourself (41)
himself (33)
hip, hip, hooray! (52)
home, sweet home (52)
homecoming (52)
honest (29)
honey [term of endearment] (32)
horseback (37)
How do you do? (28)
hunt (34)
Hurray! (32)

I
imagination (50)
imagine [believe] (37)
imagine [think] (49)
improvement (36)
in fact (30)
in spite of (28)
independent (48)
ingredient (35)
involved (36)
item (35)
It's a small world. (42)

J
jerk [n] (29)
jump the track (50)
jury (51)
just [equally] (29)
just [exactly] (38)

just in case (36)
just in case of (49)
just that (41)

K
keep it up! (42)
keys [of a piano] (30)
kingdom (33)
kitten (46)
kitty (39)
knit (32)
knock over (49)

L
lab [laboratory] (45)
latest (43)
laundry (37)
lead the way (31)
leading (33)
learning experience (43)
leave room (50)
legal system (51)
lemonade (37)
lick your lips (39)
lid (30)
lifeguard (36)
lifetime (43)
lightning (49)
like (37)
lined up (31)
little bit (38)
lobby (28)
local sights (38)
logging company (34)
logs (49)
lonesome (52)
long (37)
long ago (30)
look in on (33)
lose your temper (29)
loud (31)

M
machine (42)
mailman (51)
major field of study (41)
major subject (45)
make [add up to] (46)
make a living (34)
make it plain (38)
make out (46)
making out (29)
manage [be capable of] (48)
manufacture (50)
mark (34)
mash (49)
materials (43)
meanie [slang] (33)
meatloaf (50)
melt down (31)
member (43)
merely (39)
mess up (29)
metal (31)
methods (43)
midmorning (42)

minor (48)
miss [v] (32)
missing (48)
mix and match (45)
mm-hmm [yes] (50)
monthly (31)
moose (37)
mostly (36)
Motor City (40)
motor home (37)
move aside (30)
mushrooms (35)
music box (32)
music hall (28)

N
need [v] (39)
neighborly (31)
Niagara Falls (52)
nightclub (38)
no way [slang] (39)
no wonder (31)
Not at all. [You're welcome.] (41)
nothing in sight (50)
notice [n] (51)
notice [v] (30)
nowadays (43)

O
off [away from work] (32)
official (51)
oh, dear (51)
oh, no! (48)
old [former] (30)
old growth (34)
on our way (38)
on the road (52)
once upon a time (50)
open [to start] (48)
operation [company] (34)
orchid (37)
other (45)
otherwise (51)
ouch! (29)
out (37)
outside (37)

P
Pacific Northwest (32)
paint brush (36)
paper piano roll (30)
part [musical] (30)
pass through (40)
pay a visit (37)
paycheck (48)
pediatrics (42)
perhaps (43)
photojournalism (31)
piano bench (30)
pick (37)
picture (33)
pile (31)
pitcher (37)
pizza place (39)
place (38)

player (39)
player piano (30)
pleased (39)
point (40)
positive (48)
power (51)
power failure (49)
presentation (33)
pretend (44)
pretty much (40)
print a picture (29)
prizewinner (29)
products (34)
protect (51)
public (34)
pumper (46)

Q
quartet (28)

R
rake [v] (41)
rather (27)
reach (47)
ready (27)
real [adv] (41)
realize (43)
recognize (33)
recycling center (31)
regular (37)
regular spot (44)
relish [n] (27)
rescue team (33)
retired [adj] (37)
retirement community (47)
retrain (40)
right [correct] (30)
right [suited to] (50)
right around here (52)
right on time (38)
rights (34)
ring up (46)
robot (40)
roller (36)
rough ground (36)
rove (52)
rude (28)
ruins [v] (29)
rule [v] (33)
run out [of something] (31)
running shoes (42)

S
saddle up (37)
scrambled eggs (36)
scraper (36)
sea bass (35)
search [n] (41)
serve [v] (51)
set [adj] (33)
set a place [at the dinner table] (49)
sheets of music (30)
shift (40)
shopping center (39)

Useful Vocabulary and Expressions

short notice (32)
show someone around (47)
shrimp (35)
shut tight (50)
sides (34)
sidewalk (31)
signal (46)
simple (50)
since [because] (38)
siren (46)
sit around (49)
site (43)
sitting room (45)
sleep under the stars (52)
slice (48)
smart (50)
smooth (36)
snack-food (42)
Snow Belt (41)
So long. [good-bye] (34)
soda (39)
sort of (28)
soul music (38)
sounds [v] like (30)
space program (45)
speaking of (38)
special [n] (40)
spray-paint (40)
stall [n] (36)
stand for (37)
step [v] (43)
stiff (29)
stop [n] (38)
stormy (49)
story [argument] (34)
storyteller (49)
strange (31)
stream (37)

strength (38)
string [of a musical instrument] (38)
string quartet (44)
stroll (44)
studio (33)
stuffed [adj] (31)
stupid (29)
suite (45)
Sun Belt (41)
supper (46)
Sure thing. [Ok.] (35)
swallow whole (39)
sweetheart (32)
switch (51)
system (43)

T
tag (30)
tah-dah! [exclamation of success] (44)
take [film production term] (33)
take a look (47)
take it slowly (27)
take my place (32)
take part (42)
take your time (27)
talk about (35)
tea kettle (35)
territory (49)
thankful (46)
Thanks to you. (39)
That's for sure. (52)
the real thing (37)
the right word (28)
There you go! (44)
thin strips (35)
think of (50)

this size (46)
thunder (49)
Timber! (34)
tissue (41)
toast (52)
too much for someone [too difficult] (42)
tough (39)
tour [n] (37)
town meeting (34)
toy market (50)
tractor (36)
trained [in a job] (45)
training (42)
trash can (31)
treat (52)
trial (51)
trunk (31)
truth (29)
tune in (44)
turn [n] [in a game] (39)
turn out (50)

U
Uh-huh. [Yes.] (44)
Uh-oh. [Oh, no.] (49)
unbelievable (50)
union (40)
University of Michigan (41)
unpack (52)
unwisely (48)
up [awake] all night (50)
up [completely] (38)
up until now (39)
upstairs (29)
use [need] (31)
useful (50)

V
video game (39)
vitamins (42)
volleyball (27)
volunteer (46)

W
wander (52)
watch (48)
watch one's diet (42)
way (33)
We made it. (27)
Welcome home. (52)
What's up? (48)
wheat toast (40)
whenever (33)
whenever (44)
why [well] (30)
widow (49)
wild (35)
wildflower (37)
wildlife (37)
William Shakespeare (39)
willing (41)
within [a certain time] (43)
wonder [v] (34)
working trip (32)
workplace (40)
written work (39)
wrong (30)

Y
yoo-hoo (38)
you all (27)
You and who else? (39)